*Assassins against the Old Order*

# Assassins against the Old Order

## Italian Anarchist Violence in Fin de Siècle Europe

NUNZIO PERNICONE
AND FRASER M. OTTANELLI

UNIVERSITY OF
ILLINOIS PRESS
Urbana, Chicago, and Springfield

Library of Congress Cataloging-in-Publication Data
Names: Pernicone, Nunzio, 1940–2013, author. | Ottanelli, Fraser M.,
    author.
Title: Assassins against the old order : Italian anarchist violence in fin
    de siècle Europe / Nunzio Pernicone and Fraser M. Ottanelli.
Description: [Champaign, Illinois] : University of Illinois Press, [2018]
    | Includes bibliographical references and index.
Identifiers: LCCN 2017057350| ISBN 9780252041877 (hardcover : alk.
    paper) | ISBN 9780252083532 (pbk. : alk. paper)
Subjects: LCSH: Anarchism—Italy—History—19th century. |
    Anarchism—Italy—History—20th century. | Political violence—
    Italy—History—19th century. | Political violence—Italy—
    History—20th century. | Anarchists—Italy. | Italy—Politics and
    government—1870–1914.
Classification: LCC HX902 .P467 2018 | DDC 363.3250945/09034—dc23
LC record available at https://lccn.loc.gov/2017057350

E-book ISBN 978-0-252-05056-5

# Contents

# Preface

This book is the product of an unlikely friendship. Within the broad confines of the radical left, Nunzio Pernicone and I came from very different political backgrounds. The child of Italian immigrant parents, Salvatore and Rose, Nunzio was raised in New York's Greenwich Village. From an early age he was exposed to his father's anarchist views and stories "about the days when he directed and acted in an amateur theatrical group (what Italians call a *filodrammatica*) that performed plays to help raise funds for Tresca's *Il Martello* and other Italian radical newspapers."[1] Nunzio's adolescent reverence for anarchists carried over into his subsequent academic career. His first book on the topic, *Italian Anarchism, 1864–1892*, was published in 1993. He then switched his focus to Italian American anarchists, writing many articles on their bitter internal factional struggles and antifascist activities and the Sacco and Vanzetti case. This work culminated in his definitive biography of Carlo Tresca, one of the most significant and colorful Italian American radical leaders, published in 2005. In contrast to Nunzio, I was born and raised in Florence, Italy, the child of an Anglo-American mother and an Italian father; moreover, my formative political experiences took place in the context of the innovative analysis and policies championed by the Italian Communist Party (PCI) in the 1970s. Just like Nunzio, however, my political experiences and ethnic background shaped the topics I chose to pursue as a historian. While Nunzio's first book focused on nineteenth-century radicals in Italy, I "traveled" in the opposite direction, researching and writing a book on the Communist party of the United States from the Depression to World War II, published in 1991. Also, after this first book, the focus of my research shifted to the study of Italian American radicals, in my case the interaction between migration, labor, politics, and the development of ethnic identity from the onset of mass migration through the end of the 1930s.

Although we were aware of each other's work for years, Nunzio and I met for the first time in February 2001. The occasion was a conference organized by Philip V. Cannistraro titled "Fascism, Anti-Fascism, and the Italian American Community" presented by the John D. Calandra Italian American Institute of Queens College/CUNY and the Graduate Center of the City University of New York. Papers dealt with a range of topics on diverse reactions of the Italian American community and its leaders, both on the left and on the right, to Mussolini and Fascism. Nunzio's presentation focused on anarchists and drew on his research on Tresca; mine was a collective biography of the prevalently Communist and pro-Communist Italian American antifascists who volunteered to fight against fascism during the Spanish Civil War. The conference was attended by a combination of academics and (mostly) Italian American labor and community representatives.

At the conclusion of the conference, presenters, friends, and some attendees reconvened for dinner at John's Restaurant, a century-old establishment that had once been a favorite meeting place for Italian American "sovversivi." There Nunzio and I sat across from each other. My first impression was that he was distant and guarded. I had been warned by another presenter that, like Tresca and the other anarchists he wrote about, Nunzio had a strong dislike for Communists and, by extension, was wary of anyone who associated with and wrote about them. Proximity forced us to talk, however, and by the time he left to catch the train back home, we had found common ground on several issues and promised to keep in touch.

At first we exchanged sporadic e-mails, primarily requesting specific material about topics we were separately researching. Eventually the contacts became more frequent and the topics broadened. We swapped information on the latest book we had read, recounted stories and shared insights we had gleaned, mainly from archives in Italy, regaled each other with anecdotes (not always flattering) about the people we were writing about, and carped about the vagaries of academic life. Of course, we also shared our views about contemporary politics. Since we often were on the same side of issues, we joked that we had established the Popular Front alliance that had eluded our respective anarchist and Communist forbears in the 1930s.

Eventually, Nunzio asked me to read and comment on his ongoing research on Italian anarchist violence at the end of the nineteenth century. As I went through and we talked about successive drafts of the book, I appreciated his meticulous attention to detail, distinctive skills as a storyteller, and extensive archival research on both sides of the Atlantic. Mostly, however, I witnessed his determination to provide an intimate account of the lives, values, and actions of individual anarchists within the context of general considerations of broad economic, social, and political conditions.

In March 2013, Nunzio called to tell me that he had been diagnosed with terminal cancer. He also noted that, unless I agreed to finish his book, ten years of research "would end up gathering dust in a file cabinet." Throughout the next month he sent me more than seven hundred typed pages of drafts for eighteen chapters, along with various notes and assorted documents. In May I traveled to see him one last time at his home in Newtown, Pennsylvania. Although he was clearly in pain, his trademark energy, enthusiasm for the topic, and quick wit remained evident; the taped record of our conversation has provided an important guide for the subsequent organization of this book. My contribution to the work is to have edited it "down" to seven chapters, along with writing the introduction and conclusion and updating the bibliography. I think Nunzio would be happy with the final product.

As I worked on finishing the book, I depended on the assistance of a number of colleagues and friends who generously shared their time and expertise. In particular, I thank Marcella Bencivenni, Spencer Di Scala, Andrew Lee, Luigi Tomassini, Mary Anne Trasciatti, and Kenyon Zimmer, all of whom provided essential criticism and suggestions. Finally, I wish to express my gratitude to Christine Zervos, Nunzio's widow, for her support and hospitality.

# Introduction

"No matter where one hears of the life of some ruler or royal personage being attempted, one may always be certain to find that the assassin bears an Italian name."[1] So commented the *New York Evening Journal* after Gaetano Bresci assassinated King Umberto of Italy on July 29, 1900. To reinforce its implicit message of the Italian anarchist as bloodthirsty menace, this Hearst newspaper featured on its editorial page a drawing of a swarthy, unshaven "Italian" with a malevolent grin on his face, his chest exhibiting a banner bearing the word "Anarchy"; his right hand held a smoking revolver while his left hand grasped the right of a slant-eyed, buck-toothed Chinese Boxer, whose left hand brandished a sword dripping blood. The caption read: "Fellow Barbarians: In the Same Business."[2] Among Anglo-Saxons, then and later, Italian violence was frequently attributed to "innate" tendencies, a stereotype to which not only the Victorian bourgeoisie but even London's anarchist paper *Freedom* subscribed when it wrote "An Englishman is averse to blood. . . . But for the Italian it has for centuries been as natural to strike as for the Englishman to deliberate. Their character and their temperament cannot be gauged on the same plane."[3]

Italian anarchists did indeed compile a formidable record of political assassinations during the 1890s: President Sadi Carnot of France was killed by Sante Caserio in 1894; Prime Minister Antonio Cánovas del Castillo of Spain by Michele Angiolillo in 1897; Empress Elizabeth of Austria by Luigi Lucheni in 1898; and King Umberto of Italy by Gaetano Bresci in 1900. No less important were the unsuccessful assassination attempts committed during the same decade: Paolo Lega against Italian prime minister Francesco Crispi in 1894; and Pietro Acciarito against King Umberto in 1897.

None of the Italian assassins bore even the slightest resemblance to the grotesque portrait depicted in the *New York Evening Journal*, yet such renderings were commonly encountered in U.S. and European newspapers throughout the 1890s. But gross representations of anarchists in the press merely conformed to the ubiquitous tendency of government officials and a credulous bourgeoisie to regard anarchists as a demonic menace to society, a practice dating from the inception of the anarchist movement in the days of the First International. So pervasive was the acceptance of the belief that the anarchists constituted a dangerous species distinct from normal human beings that the propensity to portray them in bizarre and ludicrous terms infected even some of the great novelists of the nineteenth century—thus the *Princess Casamassima* of Henry James and Joseph Conrad's *Secret Agent*. This image of the anarchist as a demented and murderous creature still dominates contemporary popular culture and mind while the term *anarchy* has become synonymous with "violence" and "chaos." This book, through a specific focus on attempted and successful acts of political assassination carried out in the 1890s, aspires to dispel this myth by providing a full-length study of historical, social, cultural, and political conditions along with the transnational experiences that led to Italian anarchist violence at the end of the nineteenth century.

Paradoxically, this understanding of Italian anarchist violence as rooted in a blend of specific racial and psychological characteristics was not restricted to Anglo-Saxons, as it also dominated the thinking of social scientists and politicians in nineteenth-century Italy. Although never so blatantly racist as Anglo-Saxon observers, Italian social scientists frequently reinforced the stereotypical image of the Italians as innately violent with ill-considered generalizations of their own. Francesco Saverio Nitti, a professor of political economy at the University of Naples, suggested that the "Southern imagination" was a contributory factor to the Italian assassin's motivation.[4] Of major influence in determining prevailing attitudes toward anarchists were the pseudo-scientific theories propounded by Cesare Lombroso and collaborators like Scipio Sighele and Enrico Ferri of the Italian positivist school of criminal anthropology. Lombroso, Italy's most famous criminologist, spoke of "the exaggerated individualism which characterizes the Latin races" as a factor contributing to violence.[5] Lombroso and his theories of biologically determined psychopathology dominated Italian thinking about anarchists and criminality throughout the last quarter of the nineteenth century and beyond. In his famous book *Gli Anarchici* (1894) and in numerous articles written before and after, Lombroso asserted that anarchist ideology was "atavistic" and "repressive"; its ideas harkened back to prehistoric society before the rise of institutions of authority. Anarchists possessed characteristics inherently different from those of "normal" people. Lombroso classified them—especially perpetrators of violence—into four types of psychopathology: the moral criminal; the born criminal; the passionate criminal; and the occasional or spontaneous criminal.[6] These characteristics derived from predisposing factors, chiefly heredity. In a synoptic article, Lombroso wrote that anarchists "are always epileptics, moral madmen, half-educated or not educated at all; in their earlier years of life usually mild-mannered, but presently bloodthirsty, and believing that they are fulfilling a duty in committing a crime; never dreaming that under pretext of politics they are all working out the old grudges of their debased poverty."[7] Not all disciples of the positivist school of criminology subscribed to Lombroso's biologically determinist view of criminality and anarchism. The noted criminologist, attorney, and socialist leader Enrico Ferri attributed the causes of anarchist criminality to social and economic factors, as well as hereditary tendencies. A political rival of the anarchists, who voiced no protest when Prime Minister Crispi suppressed them with "exceptional laws," Ferri distinguished between legitimate, idealistic revolutionaries—by which he meant the heroes of the Risorgimento—and the "regressive," "sick," and "degenerate" rebels like the anarchists.[8]

Although Lombroso's theories and methodology (based on phrenology) were eventually discredited as pseudoscience even in his own time, especially by French criminologists, the popular conception of anarchists as "madmen" and "born criminals" (while ignoring his very poignant insights about Italy's wretched poverty and oppression as contributory factors to anarchist violence) had become gospel among the bourgeoisie and political ruling classes throughout Europe and the Americas. Thus, in the wake of Gaetano Bresci's assassination of King Umberto of Italy, the *New York Times* wrote, "A perversion of faculty, a criminal instinct or tendency to evil, unbalanced by a moral sense, a cerebral state of mind that amounts to disease, or something not far short of it, are the antecedent conditions of an assassination."[9]

Considering the almost universal tendency to associate anarchists with murderous mayhem and with terrorism in the modern sense of the word, "propaganda of the deed"—defined as individual acts of various forms of violence intended to bring about revolutionary change—has been treated superficially or not at all by authors of many major studies of anarchism, especially those in English. Inadequate research and analysis is particularly acute as "propaganda of the deed" relates to Italian anarchist perpetrators, a deficiency that has not deterred sensationalist treatment whenever their *attentats* (assassinations and bombings) have been addressed. Only the insurrections of the 1870s led by Italian anarchists have received extensive treatment in English, notably by Richard Hostetter, by T. R. Ravindranathan, and by one of the authors of this book.[10] Common historical interpretations generally presume the existence of a direct causal relationship between anarchist theory and anarchist violence. The most widely read studies of anarchism by James Joll and Barbara Tuchman give great prominence to the deeds of Caserio, Angiolillo, and Bresci, but the authors fail to probe beneath the surface of the phenomenon and, in the case of Tuchman, provide what can only be described as absurd characterizations and explanations. In her book *The Proud Tower*, Tuchman's anarchist assassins and bomb throwers are depicted as wretched individuals from the lower depths of society who responded like Pavlovian automatons to the calls for violence issued by anarchist intellectuals above. Tuchman maintains that anarchist theorists and thinkers "poured out tirades of hate and invective upon the ruling class and its despised ally, the bourgeoisie." These words, she claims, then found resonance among "the little men whom misfortune or despair or the anger, degradation and hopelessness of poverty made susceptible to the Idea until they became possessed by it and were driven to act. These became the assassins."[11] Personal adversity was undeniably an important factor that drove some anarchists to turn bombers and assassins, but Tuchman's fanciful account portrays the anarchist intellectuals issuing "trumpet calls for action, for a 'propaganda of the deed,' to accomplish the enemy's overthrow. . . . Unknown to them, down in the lower depths of society, lonely men were listening. . . . Suddenly one of them, with sense of injury or a sense of mission, would rise up, go and kill."[12]

Regrettably, several authors of the most insightful and comprehensive studies of anarchism—George Woodcock, Daniel Guérin, and Peter Marshall—have surprisingly little or nothing to say about individual acts of revolutionary violence committed specifically by Italian anarchists. While the literature includes several articles that deal very intelligently with "propaganda by the deed" in a broad European or national (Spain and Germany) context—studies by D. Novak, Walther L. Bernecker, Andrew R. Carlson, and Ulrich Linse—Italian perpetrators receive minimal attention.[13] Only Carl Levy, an outstanding authority on Italian anarchism, has delved insightfully into the subject of Italian anarchist assassins, albeit in a short, synoptic article.[14]

Italian scholars, many of them anarchists, have produced a very sizable and sympathetic literature devoted to preeminent Italian anarchists and to their movement: Pier Carlo Masini, Gino Cerrito, Maurizio Antonioli, Adriana Dadà, Giampietro Berti, Davide Turcato, and several others.[15] The old studies of Ettore Sernicoli (1894) and Ettore Zoccoli (1907), the former a police inspector, remain important contributions and provide valuable information.[16]

Biographies of individual assassins have been produced by Giuseppe Galzerano, Arrigo Petacco, Massimo Ortalli, and Roberto Gremmo.[17] Only the
recently published (2011) book by Erika Diemoz provides a study of Italian
anarchist violence spanning the mid-1890s to the 1930s.[18] A number of Marx-
ist historians, notably Aldo Romano, Franco Della Peruta, Enzo Santarelli,
and Gastone Manacorda, to name some of the best, also have contributed to
the literature on Italian anarchism, albeit from a more critical and sometimes
overtly hostile perspective.[19] Other Italian historians who have provided excellent contributions to the history of Italian anarchism include Nello Rosselli, Leo Valiani, and Elio Conti.[20] However, none of the Italian historians
mentioned above, regardless of political sympathies, has produced a book
on "propaganda of the deed" that is comprehensive in scope and based on
original research.

As this book puts Italian anarchist violence during the late nineteenth
and early twentieth centuries into perspective, several crucial points must
be stated emphatically. First, although political violence is the focus of this
study, assassinations and bombings were not the defining feature of the Italian anarchist movement. Political violence was but one dimension of Italian
anarchism. Second, unlike the majority of studies that simplistically charac-
terize the *attentats* perpetrated by Italian, French, and Spanish anarchists in
the 1890s as individual manifestations of a collective phenomenon, namely,
anarchist "terrorism," this book underscores the critical fact that "propaganda
of the deed" as conceived and carried out by Italian anarchists possessed
unique and distinctive characteristics that derived exclusively from their
multilayered experiences. Therefore, to shed light on the singularity of Italian
anarchist political violence in the nineteenth century, the book concentrates
on the following subthemes: the intricate connection between the revolutionary tradition of the Risorgimento with Italian anarchist violence in the
1890s; the role of the Russian anarchist revolutionary Mikhail Bakunin; the
anarchist insurrections in southern Italy of the 1870s; the suppression of the
First International in Italy and the resulting transformation in the ideology
and structure of the movement; the changing and diverse attitudes toward
political violence that resulted from this transformation as expressed by the
movement's principal theorists and intellectuals; the role of government
repression in Italy, France, and Spain as the major generator of retaliatory
political violence; a comparative discussion of violence as perpetrated by
Spanish, French, and Italian anarchists; and the experiences of Italian migrant
laborers at home and abroad. Finally, while treating each assassination within
its historical context, this book also provides biographical portraits and analysis of the major Italian perpetrators of political *attentats* in fin-de-siècle Italy,

France, and Spain. In conclusion, then, the book provides a full-length study of the historical, economic, social, cultural, and political conditions, the social conflicts and left-wing politics along with the transnational experiences in Italy, France, Spain, Switzerland, and the United States that led to Italian anarchist violence at the end of the nineteenth century.

# 1 The Risorgimento and the Origins of Anarchist Violence

Pace pace ai tuguri del povero
guerra guerra ai palagi e alle chiese
non sia scampo all'odiato Borghese
che alla fame agli stracci insultò

Ma nel dì della vendetta
che vicina il cuore m'addita
come belva inferocita
da ogni lato ruggirà

Peace peace to the hovels of the poor
war war to the palaces and the churches
no escape for the hated bourgeois
who insulted hunger and rags

But on the day of vengeance
that my heart tells me is approaching
like a ferocious beast
from everywhere will roar

—Stanislao Alberici Giannini, *Inno dell'Internazionale*, 1874–75

In October 1876, two months after the death of the Russian revolutionary Mikhail Bakunin, his disciple Errico Malatesta delivered an impassioned encomium to his deceased mentor at the Bern Congress of the Anti-Authoritarian International: "Bakunin is one of those who devoted himself heart and soul to the cause of socialism in Italy. It is to him, more than any other, that we owe the formation and first congresses of the International in Italy. It is to him that we owe our initial revolutionary education. We have always loved him . . . and his memory will always remain in our hearts."[1]

The "initial revolutionary education" that Malatesta ascribed to the teachings of Bakunin was education in theories and values of anarchism. He would later explain that the commonplace assumption that Italian anarchists derived their ideas about violence from the great Russian revolutionary was seriously mistaken:

The idea of violence, even in the sense of the individual *attentat,* which many today believe characteristic of anarchism, was inherited by us from democracy. . . . Even if we had not become anarchists of the First International, it would have equally sufficed for us to be democrats to adopt revolt, even armed, against oppression. . . . Before accepting the teachings of Bakunin, the Italian anarchists—Fanelli, Friscia, Gambuzzi—had admired and exalted Agesilao Milano, Felice Orsini, and the *coups de main* typical of Mazzini. When they passed over to the International, they were not taught anything in this camp that they had not already learned from Mazzini and Garibaldi.[2]

Coming from the man who was Italy's preeminent anarchist thinker and activist for more than fifty years, Malatesta's contention concerning the Risorgimento origins of anarchist violence is noteworthy. Acknowledgment of this connection was not something the dominant political and social classes of post-Risorgimento Italy would readily provide. One highly respected scholar who broke silence on this sensitive issue was the future prime minister, Francesco Saverio Nitti. In 1898, while a professor of political economy at the University of Naples and in the midst of the anarchist campaign of assassinations, Nitti insisted that the "readiness of the anarchist spirit" to express itself in *attentats* directed against monarchs and prime ministers represented a "historic tradition which . . . has never been broken. . . . Caserio, Angiolillo, Lucheni follow without intending to do so, perhaps without knowing that they do so, the tradition of Agesilao Milano, Orsini, and the numberless [democratic republican] conspirators and regicides whom the middle classes in Italy have glorified."[3]

That political violence was an integral feature of the Italian Risorgimento is an incontestable fact, and without the "*spinta*" (push or thrust) provided by the violent actions of revolutionary democrats—as historian Luigi Salvatorelli has argued—Italian independence and unification might never have been achieved.[4] If anarchists are understood to be the inheritors of the Risorgimento's tradition of political violence, it is hardly surprising that they should have adopted the same methods of struggle—insurrections, bombings, and assassinations—employed by revolutionary democrats. Subsequent exposure to the theories of violence imported from foreign revolutionaries such as Bakunin and Kropotkin served primarily as reinforcement of ideas and tendencies previously acquired.

Italian anarchism in its early formative years may be considered an amalgam of two revolutionary ideologies and traditions: the revolutionary democracy of Carlo Pisacane, Giuseppe Mazzini, and Giuseppe Garibaldi along with lesser-known republicans in whom libertarian tendencies were innate, and the anarchist socialism introduced into Italy by Mikhail Bakunin.

The legacy of political violence, in theory and practice, inherited by Italian anarchists dates as far back as the period preceding the French revolution and the Napoleonic imperium. Vittorio Alfieri, Italy's greatest eighteenth-century poet and dramatist, wrote an eloquent justification for tyrannicide in his famous work *Della Tirannide* in 1777. Offshoots of the Freemasons, early societies such as the Adelfia, Filadelfia, Sublimi Maestri Perfetti, Apo-fasimeni, and the Carboneria advocated and employed violence in the cause of national liberation. Insurrections, bombings, and assassinations were all deemed legitimate tactics. Filippo Buonarroti, the early communist and master conspirator, who founded the Sublimi Maestri Perfetti in 1818, urged the working classes in his *Conspiration des égaux* (Conspiracy of Equals) of 1828 to organize militarily, asserting that "no means are criminal which are employed to obtain a sacred end."[5] Buonarroti's more famous *Conspiration pour l'Égalité* (History of Babeuf's Conspiracy) of 1828 "remained the bible of two generations of young revolutionaries all over Europe," containing justification for violence and revolutionary dictatorship.[6]

The Carboneria, Italy's most famous secret society, played a key role in the failed military uprisings of 1820 and 1821 against the Bourbons in the Kingdom of Naples and the Savoyards in Savoy and Piedmont. The Savoy expedition included the participation of Italy's most original theorist of guerrilla warfare, Carlo Bianco di St. Jorioz. Described by Mazzini as "a terrorist: a terrorist by method, not [a terrorist] in his heart,"[7] Bianco began his career as an officer in the Piedmontese army, but his role in the 1821 uprising earned him a death sentence. Escaping to Spain, Bianco fought in support of Major Rafael del Riego's antiabsolutist *pronunciamiento* of 1820 to restore the liberal Constitution of 1812. That experience resulted in Bianco's publication of his *Della guerra nazionale d'insurrezione per bande applicata all'Italia* in 1830. Briefly the chief organizer for Buonarotti's Apofasimeni, Bianco shifted his allegiance to the secret society Mazzini founded in 1831, Giovane Italia (Young Italy), in whose cause he refined his instructions for guerrilla warfare in the *Manuale practico del rivoluzionario italiano* (1833). In this treatise, Bianco declared that "all the rules of warfare cease to apply the moment that insurrection breaks out. All means are sacrosanct when their sole aim is the annihilation of the country's enemies. To obtain the liberation of Italy is the only law." Warfare by guerrilla bands should not allow a respite, Bianco insisted. "We are resolved to fight an unending war if necessary. . . . If we are defeated, reverses will only provoke us the more. If we are defeated, our daring will be redoubled."[8]

Bianco's theories about military tactics greatly impressed Mazzini, and the two revolutionaries became close associates.[9] His influence was readily discernible in Mazzini's instructions to the affiliates of Giovane Italia: "The insurrection presents in its characteristics the germ of the program for the future Italian Nationality. . . . Young Italy distinguished the insurrectionary phase of the revolution. The revolution will begin when the insurrection triumphs. . . . The war of insurrection by bands is the war by which all Nations emancipate themselves from foreign conquest. It takes the place . . . of a regular army. . . . Young Italy therefore prepares the elements of a war by bands, and will provoke it as soon as the insurrection breaks out."[10] Mazzini was confident that the Italian people were capable of emancipating themselves without foreign assistance, wearing down the enemy by repeated insurrections.[11] Failure was not a deterrent. Echoing Bianco, Mazzini declared, "If one [insurrection] fails, the third or fourth will be successful. If failure is repeated what matter? The people must be taught not resignation but steadfastness. They must learn how to rise and be defeated and rise again a thousand times, without being discouraged."[12] Bakunin and Malatesta would advance the same argument, believing that even in failure, insurrection constituted an exercise in revolutionary preparedness.

As Young Italy acquired a measure of influence in Piedmont, Liguria, Lombardy, and, to a lesser degree, in Tuscany, the Papal States, and the Bourbon realm, Mazzini hatched numerous conspiracies to generate uprisings in the early 1830s, but all of them, like a proposed army insurrection in Piedmont in 1833, ended in dismal failure. After the axis of political rebellion shifted back to the Carboneria, which mounted revolts in the duchies of Modena and Parma and the Papal States, with equally disastrous results, Mazzini and Young Italy resumed the initiative with a plan for military incursion into Savoy (still part of the Savoyard domain) in 1834. Approximately two hundred Italian, Polish, French, Swiss, and German volunteers assembled in Switzerland under the command of Gerolamo Ramorino, a former captain in Napoleon's army and a member of the Carboneria. But Ramorino proved totally inept and corrupt, and the volunteers too few, untrained, and poorly armed. The disintegration of the expedition began with Ramorino's defection. Mazzini offered the command to Bianco, but the theorist of guerilla warfare recognized the hopelessness of the enterprise and declined. Savoyard authorities, informed of the plot by spies, easily suppressed the revolutionaries during the few encounters that ensued, but most of the volunteers never left Switzerland. The debacle, Mazzini later wrote, "ended the first period of Young Italy."[13]

Undeterred by previous failures, Mazzini was the inspiring force behind the two most important insurrectionary attempts conducted by revolutionary democrats, endeavors similar in many respects to the anarchist uprisings of 1874 and 1877, albeit with far more tragic consequences. Mazzini in 1843 had entered into a conspiracy hatched by the brothers Attilio and Emilio Bandiera, two naval officers in the Austrian navy (the Habsburg navy was manned by Italians from Venice and Dalmatia), who hoped to advance the cause of Italian independence by launching an insurrection in the Kingdom of Naples and the Papal States. Once again, spies (and possibly the British government as well) revealed the revolutionaries' plans to the Austrian and the Papal authorities, and so when the Bandiera brothers and nineteen volunteers landed on the coast of Calabria not far from Cosenza in July 1844, they were easily captured by Neapolitan soldiers and subsequently executed along with several of their comrades.

The Bandiera brothers were soon followed into the pantheon of Risorgimento martyrs by Carlo Pisacane. Born of noble parentage in Naples, Pisacane was an officer in the Bourbon army but abandoned his military career for the path of revolution. By 1848–49, Pisacane had already become an important associate of Mazzini and played a major role in the Roman Republic of 1849, serving as chief of staff to the republic's army of patriotic volunteers. Under the influence of the French anarchist Pierre-Joseph Proudhon and the Italian republican federalists Carlo Cattaneo and Giuseppe Ferrari, Pisacane's thinking evolved beyond Mazzianism to the point of becoming Italy's first revolutionary socialist or proto-anarchist. He insisted that national and social questions were inextricably connected, to be resolved by means of simultaneous social and political revolution. Not only the Austrians and Bourbons but the rich and propertied classes had to be overthrown, and private property, religion, and the state abolished. The twin goals of national liberation and social transformation could be accomplished only by a mass rising of the Italian peasants spurred to action by a socialist vanguard.

As a leading figure in Mazzini's Partito d'Azione formed three years earlier, Pisacane in 1857 decided to put theory into practice by leading an insurrectionary band that would capitalize on widespread discontent within the Kingdom of Naples and spur the peasants to rebel. Mazzini promised to assist Pisacane's conspiracy by fomenting an uprising of workers in Genoa and Livorno that he hoped would extend the rebellion to other regions. But the enterprise began to unravel at the very start, when Mazzini called off the rising in Genoa after learning that authorities were privy to the conspirators' plan. The attempted rising in Livorno was suppressed within a few hours. Pisacane, meanwhile, had departed for the Neapolitan kingdom on June 25, 1857, in a commandeered steamship together with twenty-two comrades. Landing first on the island of Ponza, a penal colony, the insurgents liberated some two hundred prisoners (most of them common criminals) before going ashore on June 28 near the town of Sapri in Calabria. Many of the liberated prisoners had promised to join Pisacane's campaign but defected as soon as they reached land. At the final encounter at Sanza on July 2, the local peasants in whom Pisacane had placed so much trust joined with Neapolitan troops in hunting down the invaders, many of whom were killed on the spot. Pisacane shot himself rather than be taken prisoner by the hated Bourbons.[14]

Pisacane's Sapri expedition would subsequently have great importance for the anarchists because its theoretical premise was the tactic known as "propaganda of the deed." Formulation of the theory of propaganda of the deed has frequently been attributed incorrectly to the anarchists Errico Malatesta and Carlo Cafiero in Italy or Paul Brousse in France. Instead, propaganda of the deed was first articulated by Pisacane in the *Testamento politico* he wrote on the eve of his fatal misadventure. He declared,

> Propaganda of the idea is a chimera, the education of the people is an absurdity. Ideas result from deeds, not the latter from the former, and the people will not be free when they are educated, but will be educated when they are free. The only work a citizen can do for the good of the country is that of cooperating with the material revolution; therefore, conspiracies, plots, attempts, etc., are that series of deeds through which Italy proceeds toward her goal. Milano's bayonet was more effective propaganda than the thousand volumes written by the theorists.[15]

Pisacane's allusion to Agesilao Milano reflected another element of continuity between the revolutionary democrats and the anarchists—assassination, or rather tyrannicide, as the act was invariably conceived by its perpetrators. All the early secret societies advocated or sanctioned the assassination of oppressors, and subsequently, as Alessandro Luzio has written, "the obsession with tyrannicide . . . spread through the Mazzinian ranks, with or without the master's consent."[16] Mazzini himself was torn over the legitimacy of assassination and sometimes assumed contradictory positions. Never in favor of unnecessary bloodshed, Mazzini in the Giovane Italia program of 1831 disapproved of "terror erected to a system"[17] and later, in 1856, he distinguished between "the theory of the dagger" and the "practical use of the dagger," stating that "the *theory* of the dagger has never existed in Italy; the "practical use of the dagger" will disappear when Italy will have its own life, recognized rights and justice. Today I disapprove, deplore [use of the dagger]."[18] Yet in the same letter Mazzini explicitly stated that in certain situations the use of the dagger was not only understandable but justified, declaring "long live the theory of the dagger."[19]

Mazzini's struggle against King Carlo Alberto of Piedmont revealed his willingness to overcome his inherent distaste for political murder. Mazzini acknowledged in his autobiographical notes that the Savoyard's death would not save Italy; nevertheless, "I considered Carlo Alberto worthy of death."[20] Mazzini therefore became involved in a plot to assassinate the king just prior to Ramorino's expedition in 1834. By his own admission, Mazzini provided the volunteer assassin, Antonio Gallenga, with money, a passport, and his favorite lapis-handled dagger to accomplish the deed. But Gallenga shrank from the task and the assassination conspiracy came to nothing.[21]

Mazzini's frequent associate in revolutionary enterprises, Giuseppe Garibaldi, was more forthright with his endorsement of political assassination. Writing in 1880, the great guerrilla fighter, referring to several prominent *attentatori* ("perpetrators") of the Risorgimento, maintained that "The political *attentat* is the secret to accomplishing the revolution. The Sovereigns call the friends of the people murderers. True republicans like Agesilao Milano, Pietri, Orsini, Pianori, Monti e Tognetti were called murderers; today instead they are martyrs and the object of widespread veneration."[22] Garibaldi drew a direct link between the actions of these men and more recent attempts to assassinate Kaiser William I, King Alfonso XII of Spain, Umberto I of Italy, and Czar Alexander II. According to Garibaldi, Heinrich Max Hödel and Karl Eduard Nobiling, Juan Oliva Moncasi and Francisco Otero González, Giovanni Passanante, and finally Alexander Soloviev and Leo Hartman "are the precursors of the future."[23]

With or without the involvement or inspiration of major figures like Mazzini and Garibaldi, numerous political assassinations and failed attempts occurred throughout the Risorgimento. Count Pellegrino Rossi, the chief minister serving Pius IX in Rome, was stabbed to death during an antipapal demonstration on November 15, 1848. Duke Charles III of Parma, a cruel and mentally unstable ruler hated by his subjects, also fell under the knife on March 26, 1854. Historically more important was Agesilao Milano's failed attempt to kill King Ferdinando II of Naples on December 8, 1856. A devoted Mazzinian, at age eighteen Milano had fought in the 1848 uprising in Calabria before his conscription into the Neapolitan army. Apparently, he had harbored the ambition to commit a "great act" for some time. The opportunity arose when Milano and his regiment were assembled for inspection by the Bourbon king. As the despised king rode by on horseback, Milano sprang from the ranks with bayonet in hand and dealt his target a slight wound to the chest. At his trial Milano claimed he had planned to assassinate Ferdinando II in order to bring happiness to the Neapolitans. Denied clemency by the king, Milano was executed a few days later, thereby assuring his status as a martyr of the Risorgimento.[24]

Although Milano and Pisacane had failed in their purpose, the next episode of democratic violence demonstrated that assassination attempts could produce positive results. Because the "Italian question" could be resolved only within the context of Great Power politics, Emperor Napoleon III and France were destined to play a decisive part, either for or against independence. His pivotal role inevitably turned the emperor into a potential target. To avenge the suppression of the Roman Republic by French troops in 1849, a shoemaker from the Romagna named Giovanni Pianori, with Mazzini's knowledge but not his involvement, attempted to assassinate Napoleon III on April 28, 1856, and was duly executed on May 14. The next attempt against the emperor was perpetrated by Felice Orsini, a deed representing one of the most important *attentats* of the nineteenth century. At one time a fervent associate of Mazzini, Orsini had served as a member of the Roman Constituent Assembly in 1848 and collaborated with Mazzini in failed attempts in 1853 and 1854 to ignite rebellion in the Lunigiana region of Tuscany, later to become a stronghold of anarchist marble quarrymen. By 1857, however, Orsini had severed relations with Mazzini because he considered the old prophet insufficiently revolutionary to achieve national independence and unity. While in exile in England, Orsini invented a new type of antipersonnel bomb that would subsequently bear his name. Loaded with fulminate of mercury, the Orsini bomb was a spherical device with extending spikes that detonated upon contact once thrown against a target. On January 14, 1858, Orsini and several accomplices hurled three such bombs at the carriage transporting Napoleon III and his wife Eugénie to the opera house—ironically—to see Gioachino Rossini's *William Tell* where, in a climactic finale, the main character shoots an arrow from his cross-bow into the heart of the tyrant Gessler. The emperor and his spouse emerged unscathed, but the poorly aimed bombs killed eight bystanders and wounded 142 others. Before his execution on March 18, Orsini wrote a letter to the emperor, expressing regret for his action but urging him to aid Italy's fight for national liberation:

> Remember that so long as Italy is not independent, the peace of Europe and your Majesty is but an empty dream. May Your Majesty not reject the words of a patriot on the steps of the scaffold! Set my country free, and the blessings of twenty-five million people will follow you everywhere and forever.[25]

In another letter, this one addressed to Italian youth, Orsini rejected assassination as a means of struggle, but his letter to Napoleon III implicitly warned that other attempts might be forthcoming unless he assisted the Italian cause. A year after Orsini's beheading, several factors—not least of which was his desire to play a dominant role in Italian affairs—prompted the emperor to join with Piedmont in a war against Austria. The prospect of being targeted for assassination by other Italian patriots almost certainly entered into his calculations.[26]

The subsequent machinations of Napoleon III, Prime Minister Camillo Benso di Cavour, and King Vittorio Emanuele II, which resulted in the partial unification of Italy in 1860, could not have succeeded without the conquest of Sicily and the Bourbon South achieved by the military campaign of *I mille* (the Thousand) led by Giuseppe Garibaldi. But when Garibaldi's expedition was prevented by Piedmontese troops from advancing north of the Kingdom of Naples to capture Rome, the revolutionary democrats who had spurred the drive for unification remained dissatisfied. Italy without Rome was not Italy. After receiving unofficial sanction from the new Italian government in Florence, Garibaldi led another military expedition of volunteers to capture Rome in August 1862, but he was double-crossed and stopped by Piedmontese troops at Aspromonte in the toe of Calabria. The irrepressible Garibaldi launched another expedition to seize Rome in 1867, this time opposed by Papal and French troops. His force of four thousand men was routed at the battle of Mentana, a village to the northeast of Rome, on November 3, 1867. The courage, tenacity, and indomitable spirit repeatedly demonstrated by Garibaldi were always respected by the anarchists. Nor did they forget that Garibaldi's final break with Mazzini in 1871 and his strong endorsement of the Paris Commune and the First International provided considerable impetus to the rise of socialism and anarchism in Italy. It was Garibaldi who famously heralded socialism as "the sun of the future."[27]

The seizure of Rome by Piedmontese forces on September 20, 1870, the penultimate phase of Italian unification, did not put an end to republican violence. A continuing source of nationalist agitation was "*Italia irredenta*" — the northern regions of Trentino and the port of Trieste still under Austrian control. The struggle for "*Italia irredenta*" attracted a native of Trieste, Guglielmo Oberdan, who had been an engineering student in Vienna before his conscription into the Austro-Hungarian army. But rather than participate with his regiment in Austria's occupation of Bosnia-Herzegovina in 1878, Oberdan deserted in 1878 and fled to Rome, where he continued his studies at the university and joined the irredentist circles led by the republican Matteo Renato Imbriani. Convinced that "the cause of Trieste had need of the blood of a Trieste martyr,"[28] Oberdan and his accomplice Donato Ragosa obtained Orsini bombs and plotted to assassinate Emperor Franz Joseph when he visited Trieste on the occasion of the five hundredth anniversary of the Habsburg dynasty. Betrayed to the police, Oberdan received no clemency from the emperor and was hanged on December 22, 1882, shouting "*Viva l'Italia*" and "*Viva Trieste Libera*" on the scaffold. The young man's martyrdom was immediately heralded by Italian patriots, who organized Oberdan societies throughout Italy, and Oberdan continued to be celebrated until the lost territories were "redeemed" after World War I.[29]

Veneration of the revolutionary democrats and other rebels who committed acts of political violence against the representatives and institutions of the *ancien regime*, foreign and domestic, was an attitude almost universally shared by young converts to the anarchist movement. Armando Borghi, Italy's foremost anarcho-syndicalist, explained that the generation of anarchists who came of age in the 1890s "had grown up adoring the heroes who sacrificed themselves on the altar of liberty."[30] Approbation for the militant revolutionaries and martyrs of the Risorgimento was only to be expected of the anarchists who succeeded radical democrats as the vanguard of revolution in Italy.

Ironically, the glorification of Risorgimento conspirators, insurrectionists, and regicides was elevated into an act of heroism in post-1861 unified Italy. Streets were named after regicides, statues erected in their honor, and towns took pride in having given birth to them. Admiration and apology for regicides was perpetuated by public education. Professor Francesco Saverio Nitti underscored how "In the schools, they speak, even now [1898], with a mysterious respect for Agesilao Milano. . . . He has been, nay is, considered a martyr." Most teachers made little distinction between martyrs and murderers. "An individual becomes thus an avenger and the deliverer of society." Nitti was astonished at how many tyrannicides, from Brutus to Milano, were justified in history textbooks: "There is praise for all."[31]

The historian Guglielmo Ferrero, also writing in the era of the *attentat*, lamented the same tendency: "Is not all our education the continuous glorification of violence of every sort?" Italian classical instruction was reduced to "a hymn to brutal force, beginning with the apotheosis of the assassinations committed by Kodro and Aristogeiton [in ancient Athens] to the regicide of Brutus. . . . And all the history of the Middle Ages, all of modern history, and even the history of our own Risorgimento, as taught today, is nothing more that the glorification . . . of brutal and violent acts."[32]

Mainstream admiration of political violence was encouraged, as previously noted, by Italian literature and also music. Throughout the later decades of the nineteenth century, middle-class audiences applauded and cheered wildly at Rossini's *William Tell* (1829), along with Giuseppe Verdi's *I Vespri Siciliani* (1855), which celebrated the Sicilian insurrection against Charles of Anjou and the French occupiers in 1282. Antonio Somma's libretto for Verdi's *Un Ballo in Maschera* (1857) depicted the assassination of King Gustav III of Sweden, although censors forced Verdi to substitute a fictitious governor of Massachusetts as the victim. During Giacomo Puccini's *La Tosca* (1900), Italian patrons then and later exulted when the heroine's dagger dispatches the tyrannical Baron Scarpia, fictitious police chief of Papal Rome in 1800.

But although the insurrections, bombings, and assassinations perpetrated by revolutionary democrats such as Milano, Orsini, and Oberdan were justified and worthy of veneration, the same acts, as we will see, committed by a new generation and class of revolutionaries in their pursuit of liberty and social justice were not.[33]

When it comes to the realities behind the *attentats* perpetrated by Italian anarchists in the 1890s, erroneous interpretations are attributable in large measure to ignorance of the Italian movement. Specifically, although seductive in their graphic imagery, descriptions of a mechanical relationship between anarchist theory and revolutionary practices place too much emphasis on the two titans of anarchism, Mikhail Bakunin and Peter Kropotkin, whose theories and ideas are most commonly associated with revolutionary violence and *attentats*. Bakunin is generally portrayed by Tuchman, Joll, and others not merely as a "trumpeter" but as an entire orchestra pounding out resounding calls for violence. The stereotype of Bakunin that emerges in most of the literature is that of a diabolical figure bent on mass destruction and bloodshed. Max Nomad describes him as "The Apostle of Pan-Destruction"; Fritz Brupbacher labels him "The Demon of Revolt"; Eugene Pyziur claims that Bakunin "elevated destruction itself to the rank of a program"; Joll asserts that Bakunin believed "in the virtues of violence for its own sake and a confidence in the technique of terrorism which was to influence many other revolutionaries besides anarchists."[34] Aileen Kelly, who interprets Bakunin in terms of his alleged psychopathology, writes that "the guiding inspiration of Bakunin's revolutionary ideology, in particular of the cult of spontaneous destruction . . ., was to be his distinctive contribution to the modern revolutionary tradition."[35] Among the best scholars who eschew demonizing Bakunin as the half-mad avatar of destruction and terrorism are Max Nettlau, Arthur Lehning, E. H. Carr, and Mark Leier.[36] The ideological influences of Bakunin and, as we will see, Kropotkin were highly significant in many ways, but rather than precipitants to assassinations and bombings, as they are so often portrayed in standard accounts, they actually served to moderate and even restrain the violence committed by Italian anarchists.

When he arrived in Italy in January 1864, Bakunin (1814–76) had already established his reputation as one of the most important and feared revolutionaries in Europe. The anarchist phase of his quixotic career was now commencing and would flourish for another decade. Disillusioned by the failure of the Polish uprising of 1863, Bakunin had abandoned his belief in Pan-Slavism and national liberation movements in favor of social revolution undertaken internationally that would sweep away all the institutional foundations of the old order. The social class in which Bakunin placed his revolutionary faith was not the bourgeoisie, which had revealed its counter-revolutionary nature during the revolutions of 1848–49, nor the proletariat of Europe's advanced industrialized nations, envisioned by Karl Marx as history's new revolutionary class. Skilled industrial workers represented for Bakunin the aristocracy of labor, which he believed had already become semi-bourgeoisie. He insisted that only the landless peasants of backward agrarian nations, like Russia, Spain, and Italy, constituted a genuine revolutionary class. Their allies in revolt would be city laborers and artisans, déclassé intellectuals and students, the unemployed, the riffraff of urban slums, even bandits—essentially all the oppressed and disaffected element in capitalist society. Leadership of this mass of popular insurgents was the responsibility of a revolutionary vanguard composed of prominent anarchists.[37]

Although Bakunin appealed to Mazzini to undertake an agrarian revolt in Italy, one that would precipitate the collapse of the Habsburg Empire and the Papal States, the ultimate objectives envisioned by both men were worlds apart. Mazzini conceived revolution essentially as a political phenomenon, a mass uprising of the "people" precipitated by urban revolts led by middle-class insurgents that would end in the creation of a unitary democratic republic. His conception of the people was largely an abstraction. While he desired a mass rebellion to expel the Austrians and topple indigenous dynasties like the Savoyards and Bourbons, Mazzini believed in class collaboration, not class struggle. He had no intention of stirring landless peasants to revolt against the bourgeoisie, destroy the state, and expropriate private property in order to build a collectivist or communist society. Mazzini sought a European federation of democratic republics; Bakunin instead wanted an international alliance of free peoples that would abolish the state in all its forms and suppress any institution that might evolve into a state, including the dictatorship of the proletariat envisioned by Buonarroti, August Blanqui, and Karl Marx. With such a gulf separating their political and social objectives, Bakunin could hardly rely on Mazzini as a revolutionary ally in Italy or anywhere else. In fact, Bakunin's primary objectives during his sojourn in Italy (1864–67) were the creation of secret societies that would subvert Marx's control of the First International, convert young Italian revolutionaries to his own cause by undermining their allegiance to Giuseppe Mazzini, and recruit the best of them for leadership roles in his secret societies. His writings and activities in Italy had nothing to do with propagating theories of violence.[38]

Anarchism appealed to Mazzinian democrats disillusioned with the outcome of the Risorgimento, who increasingly conceived of their struggle in terms of social revolution. Mazzini ultimately crystallized disenchantment and opposition within his own ranks when he heaped savage invective upon the Paris Commune in 1871, the event that inflamed the fighting spirit of young republicans like Andrea Costa, Carlo Cafiero, and Errico Malatesta.[39]

Through their transition away from Mazzini, Italian anarchists had nothing to learn about violence from their Russian mentor. Instead they established a direct linkage that was never broken between anarchism and the legacy of violence imbedded in the revolutionary traditions of the Risorgimento. At a fundamental level, Bakunin reaffirmed the conviction of radical democrats like Mazzini and Garibaldi (in contrast to other democrats like Carlo Cattaneo and Daniele Manin, who eschewed violence after 1848) that only by means of revolutionary violence could a new society be forged. The depth and strength of that conviction remained a pillar of anarchist ideology, ensuring that the movement's true believers would never accept nonviolent approaches to transforming society.

Although both Mazzini and Bakunin rejected terrorism and individual assassination in the abstract, they approved of such violence in special cases and circumstances.[40] Gerald Brenan, who studied Bakunin's influence on Spanish anarchism, wrote that "whilst there can be no doubt that Bakunin would not have approved of a *policy* of terrorism, it is also true that he did not boggle at isolated 'acts of justice.'"[41] When his good friend Alexander Herzen described the Polish revolutionary Berezovsky as a "fanatic" after the latter attempted to assassinate Czar Alexander II in 1867, Bakunin took issue with the pejorative label: "Berezovsky is an avenger, one of the most legitimate *justiciers* of all the crimes, of all the tortures and of all the humiliations which the Poles have suffered. Can't you understand? If such explosions of indignation did not take place in the world, one would despair of the human race."[42]

While moral ambivalence about terrorism did not dissuade Bakunin from his fervent belief that violence provided the only viable means of struggle in Italy, the Russian revolutionary did not approve of bloodletting on a mass scale, much less engaging in gratuitous violence for its own sake. Bakunin repeatedly insisted that institutions, not men, were the enemy.[43]

Bakunin's rejection of unnecessary or excessive violence represented perhaps his most important influence on Italian anarchists and their methods of revolutionary action. The principal conduit for Bakunin's restraining influence was undoubtedly Malatesta, his most enduring disciple. Malatesta's numerous articles about revolutionary violence are replete with echoes of Bakunin's admonitions against irrational hatred and unnecessary bloodshed. The following passage is just one example:

> We must be resolute and energetic, but we must constrain ourselves not to surpass the limits of necessity. We must do like the surgeon who cuts what is necessary to cut but avoids inflicting unnecessary suffering. In a word we must be inspired and guided by love for men, for all men. . . . There certainly will

be brutal rebellion, and it may even serve to deliver the final blow to demolish the existing system. But it does not find a counterweight in the revolutionaries who strike for an ideal, such a revolution will devour itself. Hate does not produce love, and with hate the world cannot be renewed. The revolution of hate, either will fail completely, or will produce a new oppression that could even call itself anarchical . . . but would not be any less oppressive for this fact, and it would not fail to produce the effects that every oppression produces.[44]

Many of the misconceptions concerning Bakunin and terrorism apply equally to the other "uncompromising apostle of the necessity of violence," Bakunin's alleged successor in this revolutionary métier, fellow Russian Peter Kropotkin.[45] While certainly a proponent of revolutionary violence, Kropotkin insisted that economic struggle against the bourgeoisie (expropriation) should become the anarchists' top priority. In his *Paroles d'un révolté*, Kropotkin wrote, "Expropriation—that is the guiding word of the coming revolution without which it will fail in its historical mission: the complete expropriation of all those who have the means of exploiting human beings."[46] For the Italian anarchists expropriation was, of course, an integral feature of the social revolution, and at the beginning of the 1890s Malatesta asserted that direct attacks against bourgeois and state property constituted a vital form of propaganda of the deed.[47] Increasingly throughout the decade, he and other *socialisti anarchici* expressed the pressing need for anarchists to participate in worker demonstrations and strikes, and developed greater enthusiasm for syndicalism, for the general strike as a precipitant for revolution and, finally, even for a united front of radicals to overthrow the Savoy Monarchy as a preliminary step toward social revolution.[48]

As a proponent of economic terrorism, Kropotkin largely rejected personal acts of indiscriminate violence, such as the bombing of cafés and other public places frequented by the bourgeoisie. Like Mazzini and Bakunin, however, Kropotkin was not averse to individual acts of violence if they genuinely promoted revolution action, and he understood how men could be driven to commit inadvisable deeds under desperate circumstances. As he grew older, Kropotkin became increasingly disturbed about terrorist bombings, arguing that institutions that had endured for centuries could not be destroyed with a few sticks of dynamite. This was a position more or less shared by Malatesta and those comrades of similar persuasion, but with their Risorgimento tradition of regicide to draw upon, it is doubtful that the majority of anarchist militants in Italy were dissuaded by Kropotkin from regarding kings, ministers, and other political representatives of the state as legitimate enemies.[49]

What the Italians derived from Kropotkin had nothing to do with violence but with his belief that the social revolution and anarchist society were predestined to come about in accordance with natural laws, regardless of the actions of men in the here and now. This theory of revolutionary fatalism proved to be an incredibly powerful disincentive to undertake violent action; it contributed greatly to the inability of serious revolutionaries like Malatesta to attract anarchist support for the insurrections he continually sought to organize.[50] A more consistent advocate of violence in all forms was French anarchist Élisée Reclus, but his influence on Italians appears to have been limited to individuals who had direct personal contact with him, such as Luigi Galleani. In the final analysis, whatever ideas about violence and revolutionary tactics the Italian anarchist might have absorbed from the great theoreticians of anarchism—Bakunin, Kropotkin, or Reclus—they would not have amounted to more than supplements to those previously inherited from the democratic revolutionaries of the Risorgimento.

The combination of the tradition of revolutionary democracy espoused by Mazzini with Bakunin's belief in the revolutionary instincts and spontaneity of the Italian masses found expression in a series of anarchist attempts at insurrection during the 1870s. In Malatesta's words,

> We rested our hopes on general discontent. Because the misery afflicting the masses was truly insupportable, we believed it enough to give an example, launching with arms in hand the cry of "down with the masters," in order for the working masses to fling themselves against the bourgeoisie and take possession of the land, the factories, and all that they produced with their toil and that had been stolen from them. For then, we had a mystical faith in the virtue of the people, in their capacity, in their egalitarian and libertarian instincts.[51]

"General discontent" among peasants and workers had become widespread and intense in a united Italy. The combination of poor harvests, economic downturns, onerous government taxation policies, which weighed most heavily on the poor, and inflationary policies that drove the price of bread to unaffordable heights, sparked a series of peasant revolts, wage strikes, cost-of-living demonstrations, and assaults on granaries and bakers throughout north central Italy and as far south as Rome and Naples. These spontaneous revolts were quelled by the army in a brutal demonstration of how unhesitatingly the new Italian liberal state would use violence against the working classes.[52] In this context of escalating social conflict, Italian anarchist followers of Bakunin felt conditions were ripe for insurrections. Andrea Costa recalled, moreover, that the internationalists believed it imperative to act in accordance with "the Garibaldian, Mazzinian revolutionary Italian traditions of the people." "More than anything," therefore, "violent action was considered a necessity. . . . We needed an affirmation—propaganda of the deed—to pose the problem."[53]

Plans to organize insurrectionary bands in various parts of Italy were initiated in Lugano, Switzerland, by Bakunin, Costa, Francesco Natta, and three ex-communards during spring 1874. The date for the insurrections was set for August 1874. But plans for insurrection went awry from the beginning. The police took preventive measures, arresting scores of internationalists and driving others underground in key areas—Tuscany, Romagna, the Marche, and Umbria.[54] The insurrection that was to set Italy ablaze proved to be an embarrassing fiasco for the International. But the authorities did not regard the failed attempt as an inconsequential episode. In its wake, all sections of the Italian Federation were ordered dissolved, hundreds of internationalists were placed under the formidable restrictions of *ammonizione* (see chapter 2), and hundreds more were arrested, jailed for lengthy periods under "preventive detention," and targeted for repeated home and workplace incursions intended to make their lives miserable. A series of mass trials were convened in 1875 and 1876. Many who escaped arrest went underground or into exile, thus inaugurating the diaspora of Italian anarchists that continued throughout the rest of the nineteenth century.[55]

On the defensive as a result of this failure and the repression that followed, the movement was shocked to learn that Bakunin had died in Bern, Switzerland, on July 1, 1876. Sixty-two years of age, his body had finally succumbed to the ravages caused by years of imprisonment in Habsburg and Romanov dungeons.[56]

In spite of these setbacks, the Italian Federation, meeting in congress under a torrential rain outside the small Umbrian town of Tosi on October 22, 1876, reaffirmed a belief that "revolutionary agitation" was "the only effective and uncorrupt means anarchist socialists possess to interest the masses and the living forces of humanity against privilege," and that therefore the Italian Federation would attempt another insurrection in the near future.[57]

Twenty-three-year-old Malatesta, fast emerging as the most dynamic anarchist revolutionary in Europe, called for "the complete abolition of the state in all its manifestations" by means of "continuous war against established organizations, that which we call permanent revolution."[58] To clarify the means by which Italian anarchists would engage in "permanent revolution," Malatesta and Cafiero issued a public statement, declaring that

> The Italian Federation believes that the *insurrectionary deed*, destined to affirm socialist principles by means of action, is the most effective means of propaganda and the only one which, without tricking and corrupting the masses, can penetrate to the deepest social strata and draw the living forces of humanity into the struggle sustained by the International.[59]

This declaration echoed Carlo Pisacane's *Testamento politico* of 1857. Italian anarchist Emilio Covelli discovered Pisacane's final testament in 1875 and shared its ideas with Malatesta and Cafiero, demonstrating once again that in matters of political violence the anarchists inherited ideas directly from the revolutionaries of the Risorgimento.[60] There is one paramount difference, however. Pisacane's belief that assassination of monarchs and high-ranking politicians constituted legitimate propaganda was not echoed in Malatesta and Cafiero's declaration. Their conception of propaganda of the deed meant small-scale guerrilla warfare.

Like Pisacane and Bakunin before them, the planners of the new insurrection still believed in the rebellious instincts of the peasantry; therefore, they chose for their target area the Matese mountain range (overlapping the provinces of Caserta, Benevento, and Campobasso), where the local population had fiercely resisted Piedmontese troops in the veritable civil war that followed unification, commonly disparaged as "brigandage." The intended guerrilla action had limited objectives, as Pietro Cesare Ceccarelli later explained:

> Partisans of propaganda of the deed, we wanted to carry out an act of propaganda. Persuaded that revolution must be provoked, we carried out an act of provocation. I do not say that in the depths of our hearts we did not harbor the hope of bigger things, . . . but the band had as its reason for being and its scope an objective outside such hopes. . . . We were a band of insurgents destined to provoke an insurrection . . . that can and must count only on the echo it may find in the population.[61]

The insurrectionists, Ceccarelli explained, planned to "rove about the countryside for as long as possible, preaching [class] warfare, inciting brigandage, occupying small towns and leaving them after having accomplished whatever revolutionary acts we could, and to proceed to that area where our presence would prove useful."[62]

Once again problems arose from the outset. A combination of defections along with government foreknowledge of the undertaking thanks to the reports from spies, spelled failure. Out of the hundreds expected to join the venture, only twenty-six materialized. On April 6, 1877, despite the certainty of failure and capture, the "Banda del Matese" set out on its revolutionary mission. Armed with a handful of antiquated weapons, sporting black and red cockades in their hats, and bearing a flag with the same anarchist colors, the insurrectionary band trekked about the mountains for several days, in snow up to their knees. Their main accomplishment was the burning of tax registers and property documents housed in two municipal archives. Having failed to spark social revolution, with no food left to sustain them and pursued by the *carabinieri* and twelve thousand troops dispatched by the government to hunt them down, the exhausted internationalists finally surrendered on April 11, 1877. They were transported in chains to the prison in Santa Maria Capua Vetere—Malatesta's birthplace—to await trial for daring to challenge the social order.[63]

Propaganda of the insurrectionary deed had failed to generate a flicker of response from the class it was intended to influence. The peasants in the Matese were fascinated by the audacious strangers and their symbolic gestures of resistance to the state. But once the internationalists departed, the savvy inhabitants returned to their normal routine, knowing that any sign of revolt would result in military suppression. Yet, notwithstanding their latest defeat, the internationalists refused to abandon this tactic, much less their commitment to revolutionary violence. Despite the failure of the "Banda del Matese" and the fact that as a result the movement was in a state of virtual paralysis, anarchists' view of reality dictated against a new undertaking. Anarchist leaders of the Italian Federation who had not yet fled into exile remained committed to the insurrectionary deed, if only to maintain the International's credibility in the eyes of the people. Plans for insurrections to be undertaken in February 1878 and spring 1879 were discussed, but the movement's internal weakness and government repression combined to render such endeavors illusionary. The authorities were fully aware that the International was incapable of undertaking another insurrection, but knowledge of its moribund state did not lessen the government's determination to destroy the organization once and for all. The pretext for delivering the coup de grâce came less than three months after the end of the trial of the members of the "Banda del Matese" in the form of a failed assassination attempt against King Umberto.

## 2  *Malfattori*: Government Repression and Anarchist Violence

| Perchè amiamo l'uguaglianza | Because we love equality |
|---|---|
| Ci han chiamati malfattori | We have been branded as malefactors |
| Ma noi siam lavoratori | But we are workers |
| Che padroni non vogliam. | Who reject bosses. |

—Pietro Gori, *Amore ribelle*, 1895

Umberto, the duke of Savoy and prince of Piedmont, inherited the Italian throne on January 8, 1878, after the death of his father, Vittorio Emanuele II. The late Savoyard ruler of Piedmont had been known as "*il Re Galantuomo*," (the honorable or gentlemanly king). His thirty-three-year-old successor would come to be known among the bourgeoisie as "*il Re Buono*" (the Good King), whereas workers would affix the title "*il Re Mitraglia*" (the Grapeshot King) to his name. All that Umberto shared with his dynamic father was a preoccupation with military affairs and mistresses, love of horses, near total ignorance of art and culture, and an incredibly long handlebar mustache. Losing his mother at age eleven and completely ignored by his father, Umberto was raised at the royal palace in Turin by high-ranking military men, priests, and courtiers, a combination that reinforced his intellectual deficiencies and guaranteed he would never rise above mediocrity, as a man and as a king.

At age twenty-four, Umberto wed seventeen-year-old Margherita of Savoy, his first cousin. Theirs was not a love match: he acquired a respectable wife; she married a throne. The strongest bond uniting Umberto and Margherita was their view of politics and monarchical power. As king, Umberto enjoyed considerable power in matters of foreign policy and war, prerogatives he believed befitting a true monarch. Saddled with a liberal constitution he ultimately would seek to circumvent, Umberto favored transforming Italy into an authoritarian state like Germany. Margherita was a reactionary down to her marrow. She would have been delighted if Italy's political system had been modeled on that of Czarist Russia, and after World War I she became a fervent supporter of Mussolini.[1] As one historian of the House of Savoy noted, Umberto and Margherita were from the outset in constant fear of being overthrown: "This forced the young sovereigns to continue to view their house . . . as an institution wholly apart from everything else Italian. Moreover, they believed their own dynastic interests to be above those of the nation. National development took on a lower priority than the security of the crown."[2]

Italian authorities also were preoccupied with Umberto's and Margherita's safety. A wave of *attentats* in Europe had generated belief that the International was conspiring to assassinate monarchists and high officials. The Russian populist Vera Zasulich had wounded General Feodor Trepov, the governor of St. Petersburg, in an assassination attempt in January 1878. A month later Prince Kropotkin, the governor of Kharkov, was gunned down by a masked assailant. Kaiser Wilhelm II escaped assassination attempts by Max Hödel and Karl Nobiling in May and June that same year. Once more in Russia, Sergei Kravchinsky, veteran of the Banda del Matese, assassinated General Mezentsov, head of the hated "Third Section," or secret police. In Spain, King Alfonso XII escaped an assassination attempt committed by the anarchist Juan Oliva y Moncasi that October.[3]

For officials inclined to believe in international conspiracies, the *attentats* committed outside Italy appeared even more ominous when on February 9, 1878, a worker named Emilio Cappellini threw a bomb into a funeral procession honoring the recently deceased King Vittorio Emanuele II as it passed the Uffizi Gallery in Florence, injuring several marchers. Ten days after the Florence bombing, police "discovered" forty-eight old and rusty Orsini bombs in the home of an internationalist in Livorno, claiming they were also to have been used against the city's funeral ceremony honoring the late king.[4]

Italian authorities knew that the *attentats* committed in Russia, Germany, and Spain had nothing to do with the International or an antimonarchist plot in Italy. But the fear generated by such misinformation was too useful to dispel. The government issued warnings that the internationalists were poised to unleash "criminal projects," a false claim enabling the implementation of preventive measures to safeguard Umberto and Margherita.[5]

But even the tightest security could not prevail against a determined assassin. On November 17, 1878, in Naples the royal carriage containing the king, his wife, son, and Prime Minister Benedetto Cairoli was proceeding along the Via Carriera Grande when a young man leaped onto the step of the vehicle shouting "*Viva Orsini*," "*Viva la Republica Universale!*" Wrapped within the folds of a red flag held in one hand was a sixteen-inch (forty-centimeter) knife. Immediately perceiving the assailant's purpose, Queen Margherita screamed "Cairoli, save the king!" The prime minister jumped between Umberto and the aspiring assassin, grabbing the man by the hair and deflecting the blow toward himself. The blade cut a deep wound in Cairoli's right thigh, where he had previously been hit by a Bourbon bullet. The king defended himself by hitting the young man on the head with his scabbard. Umberto had escaped the first assassination attempt on his life with only a scratch on his left arm.[6]

The would-be assassin was a twenty-nine-year-old cook named Giovanni Passanante. Born into a peasant family from Salvia, near Potenza in Lucania, Passanante's childhood was distinguished mainly by poverty. As a youth he worked as a goatherd and a domestic and later as a cook in Potenza. Discharged from this job because his employer discovered him reading—an activity many bourgeois considered dangerous if engaged in by members of the working classes, he eventually settled in Salerno, where he was employed intermittently again as a cook. After a failed attempt to operate a restaurant and another lost job as a cook, Passanante moved to Naples in June 1878 in search of employment. There Passanante led a lonely and unstable existence, changing jobs as a cook four times within five months.[7]

Like many subversives, Passanante, lacking formal education, was an autodidact. Little is known about his political persuasion, which appears to have been an inchoate mix of some Mazzini writings, republican newspapers, and ideas derived from discussions with other workers. Passanante's political activity prior to his *attentat* consisted of having distributed a seditious manifesto calling for the "Universal Republic" in Salerno in 1870. For this offense he served three months in jail. On the occasion of a republican congress held in Salerno in 1874, Passanante's domicile was searched by police but he was not arrested. No trace of subsequent activities was uncovered. At the time of his *attentat*, Passanante was neither an anarchist nor a socialist nor did he belong to the International or any other subversive organization.[8] He explained to his interrogators that he was "socialist republican," with allegiance to the "Universal Republic." Pier Carlo Masini aptly described Passanante's political orientation that of a "generic subversive."[9]

That Passanante had acted alone was a possibility the authorities refused to concede, particularly in light of the events that followed his assassination attempt. In Florence, on November 18, as a monarchist procession celebrating the king's escape marched along the Via Nazionale, a bomb was thrown into a crowd of spectators gathered in Via Guelfa, killing four and wounding ten others. In Pisa two days later, on the occasion of Queen Margherita's birthday, a bomb was thrown into another monarchist procession, this time with no

casualties. That the bomb throwers in Florence and Pisa were internationalists cannot be discounted. Nor can the possibility that the perpetrators were
agents provocateurs, working for the police to instill more fear in the bourgeoisie and garner greater support for the suppression of the International.[10]
Coming on the heels of Passanante's *attentat*, the Florence and Pisa bombings
precipitated a wave of arrests numbering in the hundreds that swept through
every city and town where the International enjoyed a following.[11]

Passanante's trial, conducted in the Court of Assizes of Naples on March
6–7, 1879, was a mere formality. Aside from the indisputable evidence against
him, reasons of state demanded a conviction and nothing could forestall
that outcome.[12] In his statements, prosecutor Francesco La Francesa linked
Passanante's *attentat* with the International and the other assassination attempts that had recently occurred.[13] Unable to plead insanity because court-
appointed psychiatrists had testified to the contrary, Passanante's defense
attorney, Leopoldo Tarantini, resorted to a grandiloquent plea for mercy. He
depicted Passanante as a "poor wretch," once a decent and religious man,
who had been led astray by ideas misunderstood by the uneducated masses,
dangerous ideas that "transformed him from an honest utopian into a ferocious regicide." True responsibility for the *attentat* of November 17, 1878,
Tarantini declared, was too much liberty, too much tolerance for radical
ideas. Not even the prosecutor had resorted to this reactionary argument.[14]

The jury required less than ten minutes to find Passanante guilty without
extenuating circumstances and he was sentenced to death.[15] Passanante's life
was spared by King Umberto, who commuted his assailant's sentence to life
imprisonment (*ergastolo*), explaining that "he is a poor deluded person."[16]
But execution would have been more merciful. Passanante was virtually
buried alive in a completely dark, damp, fetid dungeon situated beneath the
water line in the seaside Penitentiary of Portoferraio on the island of Elba.
Immobilized by heavy chains attached to a forty-pound metal ball to preclude
"escape," Passanante was denied visitors, reading material, or even a latrine.
Prison guards were forbidden to speak to him. After one year, Passanante
developed scurvy, lost all his body hair, and became discolored and bloated
like a corpse. If he had not been insane before his *attentat*, he certainly was
driven mad during his entombment, as evidenced by reports of his eating his
own feces.[17] In 1888, facing a major scandal should word of Passanante's horrible treatment leak out, the authorities transferred him to the Ambrogiana
asylum for the criminally insane at Montelupo Fiorentino, where he died in
1910.[18]

Passanante's *attentat* represented one the most important acts of revolt
committed since unification. After Umberto assumed the throne, supporters

of the House of Savoy expressed pride that Italy had not experienced *attentats* aimed at the monarchy. Passanante had demonstrated to the Italian people that the sacred person of the king was neither inviolate against the hand of man nor protected by the hand of God. Dangerous new forces were astir in Italy. Revolutionary elements that dared to dream of leading the working classes against the monarchy and the social order had to be eliminated.

Passanante's assassination attempt provided Italian authorities with the long-sought justification to destroy the International once and for all. The government sought to deliver a mortal blow to socialism and the International through the courts. However, prosecution and mass trials did not yield uniform results. Most of the internationalists arrested in the Marche, for example, were released in February 1875, and dozens of others awaiting trial in Rome, Florence, Bologna, Trani, and other cities went free when the courts quashed their indictments. In addition, when anarchists faced trial, the Italian judiciary exhibited a measure of independence and bourgeois jurors did not always render verdicts based on fear and prejudice. Consequently, identical cases that led to conviction in one city might result in acquittal in another. In Rome, ten internationalist leaders, accused of constituting a criminal association for the overthrow of the government, were found guilty and received sentences as high as ten years; in contrast, in Florence the mass trial of thirty-four internationalists ended with the jury acquitting all defendants save three. Similarly, in the Mezzogiorno, the jury in Trani absolved Malatesta and fourteen comrades of the charges of conspiracy and armed insurrection to the cheers of the local population and in Bologna the trial against Costa and seventy-eight other internationalists charged with conspiracy against the state also ended in a not-guilty verdict.[19] Finally, even the insurgents of the Banda del Matese, after spending sixteen months in prison, were acquitted of the most serious charges after a speedy deliberation by the jury of the Court of Assizes at Benevento near Naples at the end of August 14, 1878.[20]

Several factors accounted for the acquittals: shoddy police investigations and prosecutorial incompetence; the skill of defense attorneys; the testimony of renowned character witnesses for the defense, such as Aurelio Saffi, former triumvir of the Roman Republic of 1849 and Italy's foremost Mazzinian, Giuseppe Garibaldi, along with Italy's poet laureate Giosuè Carducci; the dignified behavior as well as the eloquence of the accused, and, finally, the consideration that many defendants had already spent many months in prison for what seemed a trivial outburst of youthful enthusiasm. Especially in the Mezzogiorno, popular discontent and disapproval of government policies was widespread even among the bourgeoisie, and so acquittals represented a form of political protest. The most significant factor accounting for acquittals, however, may have been bourgeois ignorance of the International's objectives and the threat it represented to middle-class interests and power.[21] Malatesta confirmed as much years later: "We were absolved despite the most explicit declarations of anarchism, collectivism, . . . and revolutionism, because the bourgeoisie, especially in the Mezzogiorno, did not yet feel endangered by socialism, and it was often enough to be enemies of the government to appear sympathetic to the jurors."[22] In the end, even the most serious charges were thwarted by an amnesty for political crimes the newly crowned King Umberto granted in January 1878, which expunged crimes against the state and nullified common crimes against state property by redesignating them as political.[23]

As government repression gained momentum, Cafiero and Malatesta realized that sooner or later the authorities would arrest them on one pretext or other. The two men now joined the exodus of Italian anarchist exiles. Cafiero left for Lugano and Malatesta sailed for Egypt, becoming the quintessential anarchist wanderer, experiencing expulsion from Switzerland, Rumania, Belgium, and France before ending up in London in 1881. Five years passed before Malatesta returned to Italy.

Government repression and persecution were among the most important precipitants of Italian anarchist violence. All too often, the post-Risorgimento period of Italy's history is viewed through the selective lens of Benedetto Croce and his myth of the Italian "liberal state." Liberalism—understood in the classic nineteenth-century sense of the term—was enjoyed only by the privileged classes, who possessed the requisite property and social status. In contrast, during the decades following unification, those who challenged economic and political power were subjected to pervasive violence, with or without the contribution of the anarchists. The suppression of "brigandage"— a virtual civil war between the Piedmontese army and recalcitrant peasants in southern Italy after 1860—left deep scars on the collective psyche in the Mezzogiorno and a permanent disinclination to trust the new government or have faith in its capacity to serve the interests of the people. Peasant agitation, strikes, and occasional rebellions were commonplace throughout the period in both the North and the South and were frequently suppressed by the guns of the *carabinieri* or the army. The same fate was often suffered by factory workers who struck on their own account or in affiliation with the nascent labor movement. The rate of common crime, a perpetual source of embarrassment to government officials, was also among the highest in Europe.

Whenever challenged by aggressive popular unrest, Italy's liberal state turned its guns on rebellious peasants and workers without the slightest compunction and arrested and incarcerated them and their supporters by the thousands. Nor was serious redress for the economic privation and suffering of the masses, the tragic reality that accounted for Italy's hemorrhage of emigration, ever forthcoming. Few among the propertied classes believed that the rights and liberties afforded by the Constitution extended to peasants, workers, and artisans. Working-class elements had been denied the right to vote when Italy was unified, and suffrage increased from 2 to 7 percent of the population only by 1882. With membership in the International overwhelmingly composed of artisans and workers, Italy's governments could safely disregard any notion that political subversives' constituent elements of the *canaglia* (rabble) should enjoy the same political and civil liberties as the upper bourgeoisie.

In light of these authoritarian practices, to regard violence as some sort of pathology unique to anarchists is therefore incorrect. Nineteenth-century Italy was a virtual police state for the anarchists. Although they never constituted a revolutionary threat, the anarcho-phobia of the governing class and the bourgeoisie was so pronounced that the state's arsenal of repressive measures remained perpetually poised to clamp down upon the anarchists and did so with calculated regularity and severity. That a handful of anarchists should have retaliated against police persecution and periodic government repression with bombs and assassination attempts is hardly surprising. What is remarkable is that they committed so few *attentats*. But whatever the tally, anarchist violence did not represent a new phenomenon in Italian history.

Within this context, Interior Minister Baron Giovanni Nicotera exploited the quixotic guerrilla action of the Banda del Matese and now Passanante's attempt on the life of the king to launch a major offensive against internationalists. Prefects dissolved sections of the International, their newspapers were suppressed; every important anarchist not already in police custody was arrested; and rank-and-file members throughout the country were harassed and many subjected to *ammonizione* (admonishment or cautioning). Additionally, as in the case of Cafiero and Malatesta, leaders who escaped imprisonment or evaded *ammonizione* fled the country; some were to spend many months or even several years in exile. Movement activities came to a standstill.[24]

Nicotera contrived to eliminate any measure of legal recognition and political legitimacy enjoyed by internationalists as evidenced by the early trials and the frequent acquittals. His principal tactic was to divest the International of political legitimacy by classifying it as an "association of malefactors" (*associazione di malfattori*) under the penal code and persecuting its adherents with the repressive instruments originally designed for use against common

criminals—*ammonizione* and *domicilio coatto* (internal police exile). The
threatening image of the internationalists as common *malfattori* was an easy
sell to Italy's ruling classes and major property owners, especially with the
fear of social revolution so deeply imbedded in their political consciousness.
All that was required to implement Nicotera's *malfattore* strategy nationally
was the full cooperation of the courts.

Previous reticence to condemn internationalists as constituting an "*associazione di malfattori*" largely evaporated after Passanante's *attentat* and
the bombings in Florence and Pisa.[25] The government initiated mass trials
to decapitate what remained of the International's leadership, deplete the
most important groups, and intimidate rank-and-file members into submission and passivity. Full cooperation from the courts was now forthcoming.
Judges and juries inflicted draconian sentences upon internationalists between March and June 1879.[26] The final and mortal blow to the International
was delivered by the highest level of the Italian judiciary, which by 1880 was
in lockstep with the government's contention that internationalists were
common criminals rather than political subversives. Thus the Court of Cassation in Rome ruled on February 16, 1880, that any group of five or more
internationalists constituted an "*associazione di malfattori*" under article 426
of the penal code.[27]

The decisions rendered by the Court of Cassation in Rome in February
1880 and its counterpart in Turin in July decisively nullified whatever status
as political subversives the Italian courts had grudgingly extended to the
anarchists in the early years of the International. Hereafter anarchist groups
were at the mercy of the state, subject to periodic persecution, as article 428
of the penal code (art. 248 under the Zanardelli Code of 1889) hung over
their heads like a cudgel ever ready to strike. As *malfattori*, the anarchists
were threatened not only with probable conviction in court; the designation
rendered them vulnerable to other repressive measures, such as unprovoked
searches of their homes, arbitrary arrests, preventive detention, suppression
of newspapers, and dissolution of groups. Worst of all, as *malfattori*, the
anarchists were constantly exposed to prosecution under the anticriminal
procedures known as *ammonizione* and *domicilio coatto*.[28]

*Ammonizione* and *domicilio coatto* had been designed in the wake of unification to quell social unrest in rebellious regions like Romagna and throughout the South. Specified in the public security regulations of March 20, 1865,
and modified by the law of July 6, 1871, *ammonizione* was intended specifically
for use against common criminals, not political subversives—those "discredited for crimes or misdemeanors against persons or property."[29] It subjected
individuals to extraordinary restrictions on their freedom of association and

movement, impediments that invariably caused social isolation and economic hardship.[30]

First promulgated on August 15, 1863, *domicilio coatto* had been initially designed for the suppression of criminal acts, such as brigandage. An individual guilty of violating any of the numerous restrictions imposed by *ammonizione* (the most common path) and "special vigilance" could be consigned to *domicilio coatto* for a period of one to five years, This meant confinement in a wretched prison, such as the Monte Filippo fortress above Porto Ercole, or in small, desolate islands off the coast of the Sicily and southern Italy, such as Favignana, Lampedusa, Lipari, Pantelleria, Tremiti, Ustica, Ventotene, and others. The anarchists, who became frequent occupants, referred to them as the "health islands."[31]

The effectiveness of these repressive measures derived from the fact that they were administrative rather than criminal procedures. There was no trial at which the accused was entitled to legal counsel. Imposing *ammonizione* was the function of a *pretore*, a junior magistrate; consignment to *domicilio coatto* was determined by a provincial commission composed of judicial and police officials over which the local prefect presided. Under the rules governing both procedures, the accused was not permitted legal counsel nor allowed defense; the individual was entirely at the mercy of the police who provided evidence and had no legal recourse to appeal a condemnation. This combination virtually assured conviction on demand. The decision to rely on *domicilio coatto* against radicals and dissenters transformed the institution—as one historian aptly put it—from "a savage weapon employed against brigands, vagrants, and *mafiosi* . . . [into] a concentration camp for anarchists and socialists."[32] *Ammonizione* and internal exile, often used in combination, served as the government's primary weapons against anarchists and socialists since the First International. But the state never realized that these repressive measures could function as a double edged sword. The suffering and privation to self and family invariably intensified the victim's militancy and hatred for the state and its rulers. It was no coincidence that several anarchists who attempted the lives of chiefs of state in the 1890s had been subjected to these punishments. Indeed, the measures employed to destroy the International would contribute decisively to the atmosphere of repression and retaliation that accounted—more than any other factor—to the bombings and assassinations perpetrated by Italian anarchists during the fin de siècle.

However, the suppression of the International, especially the tactics with which the authorities achieved this objective, decisively affected the ideological and organizational changes that significantly transformed Italian

anarchism by the end of the 1870s. Also instrumental in generating new
tendencies within the movement were the failed insurrections of 1874 and
1877, which cast doubts on the viability of insurrectionism and generated
disillusionment as the masses failed to respond to these revolutionary initiatives. The newly emergent tendencies gravitated in opposite directions:
on the one hand, toward more extreme forms of revolutionary ideology
and practices that rejected leaders and all forms of organization and exalted
terrorist violence instead of insurrectionism and, on the other, in the direction of acceptance of legalitarian tactics that would accelerate the rise and
predominance of parliamentary socialism.

Suspicion that all leaders, official or unofficial, were potentially authoritarian was pervasive from the very inception of the International in Italy,
a reflection of the Italians' rejection of Marx's authoritarian communism
and the London General Council by which Marx dominated the organization. Preoccupation with the threat of authoritarianism determined the
organizational structure of the Italian International or the lack thereof—its
only "official" bodies were a "correspondence commission" and "statistical
commission" that included only a handful of the movement's most trusted
figures.[33] Negative attitudes toward a formal, open organization began to
develop after the failed insurrection of 1874. The government repression that
followed was attributed to the perception that the International had been "a
vast conspiracy organized in open daylight: a definition that in and of itself
expressed the absurdity of the entire system," according to the new Italian
Committee for the Social Revolution.[34] The alleged absurdity derived from
the fact that as an open organization the International had been infiltrated
easily by "bourgeois troublemakers and spies," thereby enabling the government "to follow all its activities and strike it at the opportune moment."[35] This
conclusion marked the beginning of a ubiquitous tendency to believe that
not only the International but all forms of organization were an invitation
for government persecution. The combined effects of government repression
and ideological metamorphosis were most importantly manifest in the case
of the Italian Federation's prominent leader Andrea Costa, whose defection
from the anarchist movement began with his famous open letter "To My
Friends of the Romagna" in July 1879 and concluded with his final act of
apostasy—swearing allegiance to the king and constitution after his election
to Parliament as a socialist deputy in October 1882.[36]

Costa was perhaps the most popular anarchist leader in Italy—certainly in
his native Romagna. His initial defection in 1879 and his ultimate apostasy in
1882 caused a profound crisis whose debilitating consequences plagued the
movement for the rest of the nineteenth century. Malatesta traced the roots of

the crisis back to the early years of the International, when Marx and Engels sought to control the organization. The anarchists, led by Bakunin, rebelled against Marx's program and tactics, and established the Anti-Authoritarian (Anarchist) International in 1872. But even the Anarchist International retained authoritarian tendencies, albeit in less conspicuous form. Only a few prominent figures determined policy and molded opinion, while most rank-and-file militants were content to rely upon them for leadership and direction. Thus, when Costa defected, the rank-and-file of the Italian Federation divided and regrouped on the basis of personal allegiance rather than ideas. This tendency to follow leaders generated a counterreaction whereby leadership and organization itself came to be identified with authoritarianism. According to Malatesta,

> They began to preach and to practice disorganization; they wanted to elevate isolation, disdain for obligations, and lack of solidarity into a principle, as if these were a function of the anarchist program, while instead they are its complete negation. That is what happened to those who, in order to fight authority, attacked the principle of organization itself. They wanted to prevent betrayals and deception, permit free rein to individual initiative, ensure against spies and attacks from the government—and they brought isolation and impotence to the fore.[37]

In the 1880s, the failure of the insurrections in Italy, the assassination of Czar Alexander II on March 1, 1881, and the anarchist London Congress of July 14–20, 1881, which advocated the study of "chemistry," led many anarchists in Europe, the United States, and South America to transition from "propaganda of the insurrectionary deed" to "propaganda of the deed," labeled as individual acts of revolutionary violence.

In Italy, the preference for "propaganda of the deed," understood as an individual *attentat*, was embraced primarily by the *anti-organizzatori*—those anarchists who had become obsessively opposed to all forms of organization, rejecting them as harbingers of "authoritarianism" and unacceptable restraints on "free initiative." Hostility to organization was linked inextricably with fear of government persecution. The result was a fragmented movement of small, unconnected groups, which in the 1880s and 1890s became increasing isolated from the masses and their associations, especially labor unions. Self-marginalized, incapable of collective action, and surpassed in influence by legalitarian socialists, the *anti-organizzatori* (known as the *individualisti* by the 1890s) had no means by which to substantiate their existence as militant revolutionaries save by advocating individual violence, with delusional notions about its effectiveness. In contrast, the *organizzatori* (who by the late

1880s and 1890s progressively used the term *socialisti anarchici* to distinguish themselves from the *anti-organizzatori* and *individualisti*) remained advocates of collective action, principally in the form of the insurrectionary deed.

Although Italian anarchists of every persuasion still shared too much in common ideologically for the movement to experience a genuine schism, the emergence and rapid predominance of the *anti-organizzatori*—discernible in the orientation exhibited by the majority of anarchist newspapers published in the 1880s—spelled conflict with those comrades who still believed in the viability of an organized movement, whether a revived federation or comparable body. The identification of organization and collective activity with authoritarianism, in combination with legitimate fears of government persecution, ensured that many former internationalists and new recruits developed a state of mind that led to the decline and isolation of the anarchist movement in the 1880s and 1890s. The principal characteristics of the movement's downward spiral included atomization (*amorfismo*), steady loss of ground to legalitarian socialism, limited activity generally centering on the publication of newspapers, general absence from the nascent labor movement, and—most critical of all—progressive isolation from the masses the anarchists aspired to lead in revolution.

Although the incessant bickering between *organizzatori* and *anti-organizzatori* was in and of itself a source of debilitation and inactivity, the movement's various factions remained more united than divided in most matters of ideology, ethical values, customs, and life-style. Appreciable differences, although not always clearly defined, existed in regard to the issue of revolutionary violence, with the *organizzatori* still favoring collective action in the form of insurrectionism and the *anti-organizzatori* more inclined to espouse *attentats*, both assassinations and bombings. Advocacy of the individual deed of violence was not lacking a measure of logic once organization and collective action were rejected, for otherwise the *anti-organizzatori* arsenal of weapons would be empty. And more important for so many anarchists mired in isolation and immobility, advocacy of "propaganda of the deed"—as bombings and assassinations came to be known—enabled them to maintain the illusion that they still remained a viable force for revolution.

Theoretical support for the movement's new forms of ideological extremism embraced in the early 1880s was provided largely by two of the movement's revered activists and intellectuals—Carlo Cafiero and Emilio Covelli. For Cafiero the transition from insurrectionism to all forms of extreme violence was partly a reflection of his own emotional demons, but it remains true that he, more than anyone, provided the strongest ideological linkage between antiorganizationism and terrorism. While in Lugano, Cafiero discovered the

*Saggi storici, politici, militari sull'Italia* of Carlo Pisacane in the public library. Cafiero had long considered Pisacane the forerunner of Italian anarchism, and it was from Pisacane's treatises that he derived inspiration for his theory of action *à outrance*.[38] Pisacane's ideas were clearly discernible in Cafiero's famous (unsigned) article "L'action," published in *Le Révolté* (December 25, 1880), a clarion evocation of terrorism that many historians have attributed incorrectly to Kropotkin. Echoing the *Testamento politico* ("Ideas result from deeds, not the latter from the former"), Cafiero declared, "So it is action that we need, action and still more action. By engaging in action, we are working at the same time for the theory and practice of revolution, [because] it is action that generates ideas and action again that sees to their propagation throughout the world."[39] Rather than the parliamentary tactics now advocated by Costa, Cafiero insisted that "Our action must be permanent revolt by the word, by writing, by the dagger, the rifle, dynamite, sometimes even the ballot, when it comes to voting for [ineligibles like] Blanqui or Trinquet. We are consistent and will use any weapon when it comes to striking as rebels. Everything illegal is good for us. . . . How will we begin our action? Just look for the occasion; it will not delay in coming." Again channeling Pisacane, Cafiero urged that anarchists "must be present wherever one smells the odor of revolt and gun powder," because "every popular movement already bears within itself the seeds of revolutionary socialism; therefore, we must participate and give it direction." He warned, however, that "a clear and precise idea of the revolution is formulated only by a small minority, and if, to participate in the struggle, we wait until it presents itself as we have conceived it in our hearts, we will wait forever. Do not emulate the doctrinaires who ask for formulas before acting—the people carry the living revolution in their entrails, and we must fight and die for them."[40]

Cafiero's enthusiasm for violent action was reinforced by the assassination of Czar Alexander II. In his mind, the Russian bombers of the Narodnaya Volya (The People's Will) had substantiated Pisacane's dictum: "Conspire and plot without idols, without masters, without anyone claiming to command and anyone yielding to obey."[41] The czar's assassins, he believed, had demonstrated the tactical superiority of small, secret, and informal groups of revolutionaries over large-scale, public, and formally structured organizations such as the German Social Democratic Party and, by implication, the Anarchist International.[42]

Cafiero's approval of the means by which the czar had been dispatched was widely shared among Italian anarchists, and recommendations to emulate the Russians were now commonplace, especially among the *anti-organizzatori*. Luigi Felicò, coeditor of *Il grido del popolo* in Naples, the movement's most

important antiorganization newspaper, foresaw a major increase of revolutionary activity in Europe as a result of the czar's assassination and the martyrdom
("The Orgy of Blood") of Sophia Perovskaya and the other four perpetrators of
the deed: "The sound of that drum—I seem to hear it from a distance of a thousand leagues—is very mournful, and it says to the revolutionary socialists of all
the world: Death to the executioners of the People! Blood!, Blood!, Blood!"[43]
For Emilio Covelli, Cafiero's close comrade and childhood schoolmate, the assassination of Alexander II represented a "triumph of the revolutionary party."
He predicted that the czar's successor, Alexander III, would also suffer the
people's justice, with cries of "Down with the tyrant!" resounding throughout
the Russian empire.[44]

Cafiero, Covelli, Felicò, and other Italian advocates of terrorism actually
knew practically nothing about the Narodnaya Volya. Bearing no resemblance to the anarchist movement in Italy, the Narodnaya Volya was a highly
organized, hierarchical, and disciplined sect directed by a central executive
committee with undisputed leaders like Sophia Perovskaya and Andrei Iva-
novich Zhelyabov. Their populist program was incompatible with anarchist
ideals, and Russian anarchists opposed the Narodnaya Volya because of its
hierarchical organization and authoritarian tendencies. Coupled with un-
informed admiration for the Narodnaya Volya was the Italian anarchists'
unwillingness to acknowledge that the assassination of Czar Alexander II
accomplished little more than provide extra work for the hangman, or that
the slain czar's successor, Alexander III, annihilated the Narodnaya Volya
and became one of the most reactionary of all the Russian czars.[45] In their
ignorance, Cafiero, Covelli, Felicò, and other extremists had implicitly attributed to the Narodnaya Volya the characteristics and program of action
they now believed best suited to the Italian anarchist movement, concluding
incorrectly that the *attentat* was a means of struggle superior to insurrection
because it was spontaneous, unpredictable, conceived in secret, and almost
impossible for the authorities to prevent, and it preserved the sanctity of the
individual's "free initiative," the new mantra of the *anti-organizzatori*.[46]

Cafiero's advocacy of an atomized and clandestine movement had become
commonplace among the *anti-organizzatori*, now completely obsessed with
fear of authoritarianism and the threat of government repression. Luigi Felicò
typically inveighed against "leaders," "investitures," "loyalty oaths," and every
other manner of organization that threatens personal autonomy and "free
initiative," often a euphemism for individual acts of violence.[47] Local support
for this position enabled Felicò to oust Francesco Saverio Merlino as coeditor
of *Il grido del popolo*. Other well-known militants, such as Florido Matteucci,
a veteran of the Matese insurrection now exiled in Nice, voiced concern about

large-scale and permanent organizations such as the Italian Federation. He insisted that "before constituting even the smallest group, let us determine the purpose of this group, and let us gather together *only* those individuals *necessary* for *action* to realize that purpose," whether it be publishing a newspaper, distributing circulars, or committing violent acts against the authorities.[48] Matteucci, like Cafiero, was advocating a movement based on small, clandestine cells that would act independently and more or less spontaneously. A "reliable national organization," never mind a revived International, was precisely what most Italian anarchists had now come to oppose.

Italian *anti-organizzatori* were by no means alone in their rejection of organization and endorsement of terrorist deeds. The espousal of terrorism as the primary revolutionary tactic was also "officially" endorsed by the International Anarchist Congress convened in London from July 14–20, 1881.[49] Around the same time, several of Europe's most prominent anarchists, such as Johann Most and Élisée Reclus, provided their own imprimatur to the theory of "propaganda of the deed" in its new terrorist form, essentially consigning the insurrectionary deed to the scrap heap despite the contrary viewpoint of Malatesta, who would continue to believe that insurrectionism was the best revolutionary tactic to rouse the masses.

While the anarchists recognized that the designation of "*malfattori*" was a political and legal means employed by the authorities to facilitate repression of the movement, and while most reacted against this categorization with outrage, irony, and mock identification with the image, a few intellectuals—notably Emilio Covelli and Carlo Cafiero—went to the ideological extreme by including the "true" *malfattori* among the vanguard of class struggle and social revolution. Covelli was one of the movement's most tragic figures. Born into a rich, aristocratic family that afforded him a fine education, after graduating from the University of Naples with a degree in jurisprudence, Covelli continued his studies in Heidelberg and Berlin, where he attended the lectures of Eugen Dühring, acquired extensive knowledge of German communist theories, and became a critique of authoritarian socialism. Covelli in 1872 wrote the first discussion of Marx's *Das Kapital* by an Italian and two years later published an important treatise on socialism, *L'economia politica e la scienza*. His political career began when Cafiero convinced him to join the Naples section of the Italian Federation in 1875, distinguishing himself thereafter as one of the movement's foremost intellectuals and journalists. The same year he joined the International, Covelli discovered the writings of Carlo Pisacane, whose *Testamento politico* confirmed Covelli's advocacy of propaganda by the insurrectionary deed. Covelli was most likely one of the planners of the Matese insurrection, but when the adventure took place, he had already been arrested in Naples and incarcerated under "preventive detention" for several months. Upon release, he founded the newspaper *L'Anarchia* in Naples, a daring venture conducted in an atmosphere of repression that made him a constant target of local police. Eventually arrested and indicted on trumped-up charges, Covelli was acquitted at trial but placed under *ammonizione*. Rather than submit to this harsh punishment, Covelli joined the steadily growing diaspora of Italian anarchists, taking refuge in Paris, London, and Geneva.[50]

Disillusioned by the failure of the masses to respond to the anarchists' revolutionary undertakings, and victimized by persecution and economic hardship throughout his exile, Covelli became an outspoken apostle of violence against the state and the bourgeoisie. This conversion to ideological extremism was first signaled by his leaflet "Ai redattori della *Lotta!*" ("To the Editors of *la Lotta*," a socialist newspaper), written in London in November 1880, which declared that "the revolution is the continuous action of inciting and perpetrating every kind of crime against public order."[51] Precisely who would undertake "continuous action" by every illegal means Covelli revealed in *I Malfattori*, the newspaper he published in Geneva in 1881. The revolutionary struggle, he maintained, was divided into economic, political, and moral dimensions. The first was to be pursued by the working class, the second by the petite bourgeoisie, and the third—consciously or not—by the *spostati* (the *déplacés*). Together the three components constitute the army of the revolution. The *spostati* Covelli had in mind, however, were not the *auto-spostati*—anarchist leaders like Cafiero, Malatesta, and himself, who had voluntarily and permanently severed ties with their bourgeois or aristocratic origins. Covelli's *spostati* were "the *dangerous classes*, the *putrid precipitate* of the other social classes, the malefactors who for individual or social reasons fight and cannot but fight for the moral revolution, which is the final word of the social revolution, [and] the human liberty that develops according to the needs of their own nature, despite all the limits, ties, and compromises that make them unhappy."[52]

For confirmation of the theory of the *malfattori* as a vanguard element, Cafiero looked once again to Carlo Pisacane and the Sapri raid: "Where did he [Pisacane] go to seek combatants for his expedition? To prison, among the *malfattori*."[53] (Cafiero ignored the fact that the common criminals recruited from the penal island of Ponza abandoned Pisacane as soon as they reached the mainland.) A more recent affirmation Cafiero cited was a demonstration in Milan, in which neither anarchists nor socialists had participated: "All those arrested were unknown workers, many unemployed, a few in violation of the law, and some recidivists." Among this social element, whom he christened "*malfattori*"—were the new revolutionaries.[54]

Both Cafiero and Covelli had experienced disillusionment, economic adversity, police persecution, and emotional trauma—factors that exacerbated whatever psychological weaknesses that may have been innate. They advocated extremist ideologies because despondency drove their fertile minds to seek more radical alternatives to the intractable problems that appeared destined to reduce anarchists to insignificance as revolutionaries. Their ultimate acceptance of legalitarian positions had no detrimental impact on the anarchist movement other than the loss of its two most creative intellectuals. The legacy of Covelli and Cafiero, at this critical juncture, was their impassioned formulation of extremist yet challenging ideas that provided a theoretical foundation for the movement's new orientation toward antiorganizationalism and individual violence. The big question for the 1880s was whether their calls for violence *à outrance*, conducted by the *malfattori* or other social groups, would remain in the realm of abstraction or become a program for revolutionary action.

If, as many writers have presumed, a direct causal relationship existed between anarchist ideology and terrorist violence, then Italy in the 1880s should have experienced a significant wave of *attentats* in response to the exhortations of Cafiero, Covelli, Felicò, and others less known. But nothing of the sort transpired. Cafiero's call for permanent revolt by means of violence *à outrance* went unheeded, as did the London Congress's resolution to "study" chemistry. The biannual reports of prefects from every province do not indicate a single bombing attributable to the anarchists between 1882 and 1890.[55] Nor did the lauded assassination of Czar Alexander II provoke imitators among Italian anarchists at home or abroad. For Italian anarchists the 1880s were a period of relative nonviolence, although acts of violence were certainly contemplated, if not carried out.

While the *anti-organizzatori* exercised their vocal cords, demanding "Blood! Blood! Blood," the counterpoise to terrorism was represented chiefly by Malatesta, who more than anyone maintained an unflagging commitment to insurrectionism as the indispensable means of revolutionary action.[56] Malatesta returned to Italy in the spring of 1883, choosing Florence as his base of operations.[57] Once more arrested, this time with Merlino, he and Merlino took advantage of their "provisional liberty" to again flee into exile. Malatesta settled in Argentina and Merlino in London. Their departure constituted an incalculable loss for the movement in Italy, in particular the resurgence sparked by Malatesta's leadership in 1883–84 gradually faded after his departure.

What remained constant, however, was obsessive fear of authoritarianism and police persecution among the *anti-organizzatori*. Although their obstructionism helped preclude attempts at insurrections, the *anti-organizzatori* continued to entertain fantasies about the revolutionary potential of terrorist deeds. In Naples, a major stronghold of the *anti-organizzatori*, the publishers (including the intransigent Luigi Felicò) of *Humanitas* in 1887 remained fixated on the assassination of Czar Alexander II, as though oblivious to the repression that had followed in its wake. A principal contributor, Giovanni Bergamasco, expressed hope that dynamite would once again resound throughout the empire of Czar Alexander III: "That will be new progress in the life of revolutionary Russia."[58] In their irrepressible reverence for the Narodnaya Volya, the *Humanitas* group celebrated the sixth anniversary of the czar's assassination in 1881: "Every act of rebellion pleases and comforts us. Beyond being a healthy example to others, it is a sign and more proof that human nature aspires to independence, to anarchy.[59] When a new director of *Humanitas*, Emilio Zuccarini, committed the egregious sin of supporting Merlino's advocacy of an International Alliance, the *antiorganizzatori* broke away to publish *Il Demolitore* (the *Demolisher*) under the editorship of Bergamasco and Felicò. As the title indicated, terrorism was foremost on their agenda. Violent passages from the *Revolutionary Catechism* written by Sergey Nechaev and Mikhail Bakunin were published in the first issue. Such inflammatory writing prompted action from the police, who shut down *Il Demolitore* after two issues were published. But the advocates of "demolition" found no takers, for as had become customary by the 1880s, the *anti-organizzatori* were all talk and no action.[60]

Eighteen eighty-seven was nevertheless a good year for Italian anarchist extremists, primarily those living abroad. By this time an inchoate subcurrent of antiorganizationism had emerged among extremists who, as we have seen, called themselves *individualisti*, an ambiguous term easily misunderstood. The description became virtually synonymous with many of the *anti-organizzatori* who came into prominence in 1890s, anarchists like Paolo Schicchi, Luigi Galleani, Giuseppe Ciancabilla, Gigi Damiani, Giovanni Gavilli, Amilcare Pomati, and numerous others. Intransigent opponents of organization in every form, *anti-organizzatori/individualisti* were nevertheless staunch anarchist communists of Kropotkinist persuasion who advocated terrorism as a favored means of struggle. They were also defenders of "illegalism," the theory and practice of which was best represented by the fringe element of *individualisti* that revolved around Vittorio Pini and Luigi Parmeggiani. They, too, professed themselves to be anarchist communists but manifested tendencies typical of the egoistic individualism propagated by the German anarchist Max Stirner, whose writings did not become available to Italians in translation until the early twentieth century, when illegalism in Europe emerged as an actual lifestyle. As a purported method of revolutionary action, illegalism ostensibly encompassed any act of economic and physical violence (theft, counterfeiting, even murder) perpetrated against the state and the bourgeoisie. In practice, however, the stock and trade of the *illegalisti* was "expropriationism," their euphemism for theft.

In theory and practice, expropriationism or "propaganda by theft" in the late 1880s was predominantly a French phenomenon. All anarchists were familiar with Pierre-Joseph Proudhon's famous assertion that "Property Is Theft," and most believed quite literally that the bourgeoisie had acquired its property and wealth by such means. By 1875, the French anarchist and renowned geographer Élisée Reclus posited the theory that, because the basis of private property and capitalism was theft, it was acceptable for the individual to reclaim by means of robbery the value of the labor stolen from him by the capitalists.[61] Reclus's thinking thus laid the theoretical foundation for *la reprise individuelle* or individual expropriationism, in other words, theft. His theory was criticized by important contemporaries like Peter Kropotkin and Jean Grave, but Reclus's intellectual stature and prestige sufficed to establish propaganda by theft as a viable theory and practice. Subsequently, as the intellectual capital of the anarchist movement in France, Paris became the fountainhead for *la reprise individuelle* and the far more bizarre form of anarchist criminality called *estampage* or *vol entre camarades* (theft among comrades). Yet for the vast majority of anarchists in France, Italy, Spain, and elsewhere during the 1880s and 1890s *la reprise individuelle* remained an abstract theory—they were too honest and hardworking to engage in theft. Active expropriationists were few even in France save among extremists, and they were virtually nonexistent in Italy.[62]

The most famous practitioner of *la reprise individuelle* in France was Clément Duval. A wounded veteran who contracted small pox during the Franco-Prussian war, Duval spent four years recuperating in a hospital, after which he turned to crime out of sheer desperation. After serving a year in prison for a robbery that netted him a paltry 80 francs, Duval joined the anarchist group in Paris known as *La Panthère des Batignolles*. Two weeks after robbing jewels along with 15,000 francs and accidently burning down the mansion of a rich Parisian socialite in October 1886, Duval was apprehended while attempting to fence his loot. In the course of the encounter he stabbed a police officer several times. In prison awaiting trial, Duval published in *Le Révolte* what would become the expropriationists' standard justification for their activities: "I must declare from my point of view that I am not a thief. By creating man nature gave him the right to exist and the duty to exercise it. Therefore if society does not furnish him the means to subsist, the human being may legitimately take his necessities from where there is abundance."[63] Such arguments were hardly likely to sway bourgeois judges and jurors. On the contrary, Duval was condemned to death even though the wounded policeman survived; the sentence was commuted to life imprisonment, however, in the penal colony on Devil's Island in French Guyana, a tropical hell-hole known for its brutal treatment of prisoners. After some twenty failed attempts, Duval finally escaped in 1901 and spent his final years in New York, where he was greatly admired and supported by the followers of Luigi Galleani, who translated Duval's autobiography into Italian.[64]

Since the first years of the Italian Federation, Italian anarchists had believed that bourgeoisie property was based on theft and that in the course of the social revolution the institution of private property would be eliminated by means of expropriation. The vexing question that emerged in the late 1880s was the political and moral legitimacy of propaganda by theft, which, after all, meant expropriating the bourgeoisie one item at a time. In theory, at least, the issue posed no dilemma: he who stole from the bourgeoisie was not really a thief.[65]

The issue of propaganda by theft became more controversial for the Italian anarchists between 1887 and 1889, when several groups in exile had already imbibed heavily from the toxic brew of illegalism in Paris. These self-styled outlaws and expropriationists called themselves the *Gruppo Anarchico Intransigente, Gli Straccioni,* and *I Ribelli di St. Denis.*[66] The foremost Italian expropriationist living in France was Vittorio Pini.[67] What made Pini so dangerous, according to Italian police authorities, was the utter sincerity of his convictions. Born in 1860 into a poverty-stricken family in Reggio Emilia, Pini became politically active as an adolescent, first as a republican and then as an internationalist. Trained as a printer, he had to abandon the trade after his participation in a failed printers' strike in Milan, an experience that soured him on strikes as a method of struggle. To earn a living he became a fireman, and in the line of duty demonstrated indomitable courage and enormous physical strength. Once he left Italy in 1886, Pini went to Switzerland; he then went to France, where he worked initially as a stable boy, peddler, and shoemaker. Pini's conversion to anarchism resulted from contact with workers in Paris and his reading a translation of Kropotkin's *Parole d'un ribelle.* Although he had never engaged in criminal activities in Italy, Pini fell in with the Gruppo Intransigenti and specialized in robbing the houses of the rich bourgeoisie. Unlike some of his French and Belgian accomplices, for whom anarchism was merely a cover for their criminal activities, Pini utilized the proceeds of his robberies exclusively to support the movement. He himself lived an incredibly ascetic and abstemious life—he did not smoke, drink alcohol, cavort with women, or even possess his own domicile.[68]

These intransigents financed publications that relentlessly attacked Malatesta and Merlino, who envisioned a revolution that would emancipate all humanity, and instead advocated a genocidal bloodbath in which the masses will "cut the landlord's throat, burn their stinking hovels, take possession of the palaces that they themselves built, break open the strong boxes, attack every form of authority by hanging kings, ministers, senators, deputies, prosecutors, lawyers, police chiefs, prefects and the assistants who follow them."[69] They insisted "let us occupy ourselves with chemistry, making bombs, dynamite and other explosive materials that must be used for the destruction of the stinking and ruling bourgeoisie."[70]

Pini's reputation generated such fear in Italian government circles that they believed he planned to assassinate King Umberto during the latter's first trip to the Romagna in 1887.[71] But no *attentat* against King Umberto or any other royal or high government personage was ever committed by Pini or other members of the Intransigenti. The most infamous act of violence committed by Pini and his comrade Parmeggiani was directed not against the state or the bourgeoisie but rather against factional opponents Celso Ceretti, a former Garibaldino and internationalist, and Camillo Prampolini, the prominent evolutionary socialist, whom they tried to assassinate in Italy.[72] Both Pini and Parmeggiani returned to France where the former was eventually arrested and sentenced to a long prison term on Devil's Island, where he died in 1903.[73] While Pini was in the clutches of French justice, Parmeggiani successfully relocated to London, where he persevered in inciting terrorism and engaged in factional attacks, this time against Malatesta.[74] Eventually, at the beginning of the twentieth century, Parmeggiani abandoned the anarchist movement to become a respectable dealer of antiquities in London and Paris and died as a bourgeois in 1945.[75]

The Pini/Parmeggiani assault against Ceretti and Prampolini led to serious debate within the movement about the legitimacy of propaganda by theft. Were acts of theft to be considered acceptable methods of political violence against the bourgeoisie and the state, or did they represent ordinary criminality in the guise of revolutionary action?[76]

In sum, prerevolutionary violence against bourgeoisie property—propaganda by theft—continued to be sanctioned in *theory* as a legitimate form of political action as long as the proceeds were used to benefit the movement. Curiously, however, Italy proved to be infertile soil for individual anarchist or group theft—expropriationism simply failed to develop even as a subcurrent of the movement in nineteenth-century Italy. Nor in the early twentieth century, when more violent manifestations of expropriationism and illegalism emerged, such as the Bonnot Gang in France and the *pistoleros* Buenaventura Durruti and Francisco Ascaso in Spain, did this form of anarchist extremism find practitioners in Italy. But Italy's apparent immunity to expropriationism did not extend to Italian anarchists active abroad. Several of anarchism's most notorious expropriationists in the 1920s were Italians: Severino Di Giovanni and the brothers Antonio and Vincenzo Moretti in Argentina, and Cesare Stami in the United States. They all met violent deaths.[77]

# 3 Bombings, Insurrections, and Cosmopolitanism: Paolo Lega and Sante Caserio

| | |
|---|---|
| A te, Caserio, ardea nella pupilla | Caserio, in the pupil of your eye burned |
| delle vendette umane la scintilla, | the spark of humanity's vengeance, |
| ed alla plebe che lavora e geme | and to the poor who toil and groan |
| donasti ogni tuo affetto, ogni tua speme. | you gave all your affection, all your hopes. |

—Pietro Gori, *Sante Caserio*, ca. 1894

Bombings are traditionally associated with anarchism. Although anarchists in Spain, France, and Italy all resorted to bombings, in the first two countries lethal bombings directed at people were a central characteristic of their activities. In the case of Italy, bombings were directed at buildings as symbols. People were not the intended target. A brief survey of Spanish and French bombings is therefore essential for purposes of comparison and helps illuminate the fact that the minimal toll of deaths and injuries exacted by Italian anarchist bombs was most likely the result of conscious intent.

In Spain the conflict between the government and the anarchists was waged at a level of ferocity and cruelty never approached in Italy. In the land of the Inquisition and armed *pronunciamientos*, the anarchists regarded the Catholic Church and the military as their primary enemies, with the bourgeoisie a close third. Their fight against these oppressive institutions featured the use of explosives calculated to achieve maximum lethality, regardless of who was killed in the process. A leading authority on Spanish anarchism observed that Spain's most notorious bombers, Paulino Pallás and Santiago Salvador, were unconcerned about harming innocent victims as they believed "civilians" were unavoidable collateral damage in class warfare.[1]

The savage cycle of government repression and anarchist retaliation began with an uprising of peasants and artisans in the Andalusian town of

Jerez de la Frontera on January 8, 1892, that was suppressed with customary excess. Four anarchists were garroted in the town square a few weeks later. Retribution followed when Paulino Pallás threw a bomb aimed at Arsenio Martínez Campos, the captain general of Catalonia, during a military parade in Barcelona on September 24, 1893. His intended victim escaped harm but five people were killed and twelve others injured. Pallás was tried by a military tribunal and executed by firing squad on October 6, 1893. To avenge his friend Pallás, Santiago Salvador targeted the elite of Barcelona's bourgeois society attending Gioachino Rossini's opera *William Tell* at the Liceu Theater on November 7, 1893. Salvador hurled his bomb from the top balcony into the orchestra section below, killing more than twenty patrons and injuring around fifty more. An indiscriminate roundup of suspects resulted in the execution of six anarchists who had nothing to do with the bombing. Eventually apprehended, Salvador was garroted in the courtyard of the infamous Montjuich Castle on November 21, 1894. The next episode in the cycle of violence occurred during the Corpus Christi festival in Barcelona on June 7, 1896, when a bomb presumably intended for military and religious dignitaries at the front of the procession was thrown into the tail end, killing six and injuring forty-five common people. This mishap led to speculation that the perpetrator had remarkably poor aim or was a police agent provocateur. The authorities responded with a roundup of three hundred anarchists and numerous republicans and free-thinkers. Scores of anarchists imprisoned in Montjuich Castle were subjected to brutal physical torture, prompting much of Europe's leftist and progressive elements to respond with mass protest demonstrations. International condemnation did nothing to change the savage measures employed by the Spanish military and police when attempting to suppress the anarchists, and the cycle of repression and retaliation continued well into the twentieth century. In the 1890s, Spanish anarchist bombers accounted for more than forty deaths and one hundred injuries, the highest rate for any anarchist movement in Europe.[2]

Rather than the military or the Catholic Church, the hatred of the French anarchist bombers was directed against the bourgeoisie, with Paris their battleground. The cycle of bombings was brief—1892 to 1894—but during that period the Parisian bourgeoisie experienced a degree of insecurity and fear that evoked memories of the Paris Commune. The cycle began when François Claudius Koënigstein, alias Ravachol, a true primitive rebel who previously had committed numerous common crimes, including murder, went on a bombing spree in spring 1892. In an act of retaliation, Ravachol targeted the apartment of Judge Edmond Benoît, who had presided over the conviction of May Day demonstrators in the Parisian suburb of Clichy.

His bomb did not produce fatalities, but he was executed on July 11, 1892, for other murders he had committed. Although most disapproved of his murders, Ravachol's savage rebelliousness and sangfroid before the guillotine mesmerized anarchists in Europe and elevated him to martyr status.[3]

His avenger was Théodule Meunier, a hardworking cabinetmaker described by his comrade Charles Malato as "the most remarkable type of revolutionary illuminist, an ascetic and a visionary, as passionate in his search for the ideal society as Saint-Just, and as merciless in seeking his way toward it."[4] Four days after Ravachol's bomb failed to kill Judge Benoît, Meunier detonated a bomb outside the Lobau barracks in Paris. On March 19, 1892, on the eve of Ravachol's first trial, Meunier bombed the Restaurant Véry, where Ravachol had been arrested, killing the owner and a patron. Meunier was apprehended two years later and sentenced to life imprisonment.[5]

Meanwhile, a twenty-year-old unemployed shoemaker named Léon-Jules Léauthier recently arrived in Paris and, reduced to desperation, confided to the anarchist intellectual Sébastien Faure that he intended to attack members of the bourgeoisie, noting that "I will not be striking an innocent by striking the first bourgeois who comes along."[6] Instead, Léauthier struck higher up the social hierarchy, wounding the Serbian ambassador Georgewitch with a shoemaker's knife on November 13, 1893. Condemned to life at hard labor in the infamous penal colony at Cayenne in French Guiana, Léauthier died within a year while participating in a prisoners' revolt.[7]

Following Léauthier's attack, Auguste Vaillant threw a bomb filled with nails from the gallery onto the floor of the Chamber of Deputies on December 9, 1893. Having lived his entire life in poverty, Vaillant was driven to an emotional breaking point when he could not provide for his wife and child because of chronic unemployment. The intent of his *attentat* was not to kill the deputies but to spur them to pass much-needed economic and social reforms. He failed in his purpose and was sentenced to death despite having killed no one. Pleas for clemency even from bourgeois elements left President Marie François Sadi Carnot unmoved, and Vaillant was executed on February 5, 1894. His tragic circumstances, his eloquent courtroom speech condemning bourgeois society for its craven indifference to the sufferings of France's poor, and his brave defiance in the face of the guillotine earned Vaillant permanent admiration from anarchists throughout Europe. Carnot's lack of mercy, on the other hand, would cost him his life.[8]

The most formidable and ferocious of the French anarchist bombers was undoubtedly Émile Henry.[9] His keen intellect, his cold-blooded approach to class struggle, and the chilling logic by which he justified his deeds distinguished him as unique among all the fin-de-siècle bombers in Europe.

The son of a former communard, Henry was an exemplary student who gained admission to the prestigious École Polytechnique. He abandoned his studies and the comfortable life he could have led when he became a militant anarchist before his twentieth year. Henry's potential for extreme violence soon became apparent to his comrades, one of whom predicted to Malato that "Émile has the temperament of a nihilist; he will perpetrate some horrible deed and end on the scaffold."[10] Malato shared this opinion: "In contrast to Vaillant, who loved the people, Émile Henry only loved the idea. He felt a marked estrangement from the ignorant and servile plebs, a feeling distinctive also of a small number of literary and artistic anarchists." Henry's "aristocratic" attitude, Malato explained, developed from his "frequent intercourse with the romanticists of anarchy, who are more vehement in words than in deeds, and exercised a deplorable influence on his high character. It engendered contempt for human life which Vaillant never felt and Ravachol confined to the privileged classes."[11]

For his first *attentat*, Henry planted a bomb at the office of the Compagnie des Mines de Carmaux (Carmaux Mining Company) on November 8, 1892, a gesture of support for the company's striking miners. He would have preferred the deaths of the mine owners, but when the bomb was transported to the police station and accidently exploded, killing several policemen, Henry was perfectly content. Subsequently, on February 12, 1894, Henry threw a bomb amidst the petit-bourgeois patrons of the Café Terminus at the Gare Saint-Lazare railway station, killing one and injuring more than twenty. Arrested after an intense police investigation, Henry displayed his lethal ideas and personality during his trial in the *cour d'assises de la Seine* on April 27, 1894. The judges and observers were shocked by his calm demeanor and declaration of regret at having killed so few in the Café Terminus: "I wanted to kill as many as possible. I counted on 15 deaths and 20 wounded."[12] He also explained that he had targeted the office of the Carmaux Mining Company because it, too, was occupied solely by bourgeois individuals. During his final speech to the jury, Henry elaborated upon his antibourgeois fixation, echoing Léauthier by maintaining that "there could be no innocents" among the bourgeoisie: "The bourgeoisie, in its entirety, lives by the exploitation of the poor; it must, in its entirety, pay for its crimes."[13] The bourgeoisie always persecuted the anarchists collectively, he maintained. One man, Vaillant, had thrown a bomb in the Chamber of Deputies, but the anarchists—90 percent of whom did not know him—were persecuted collectively. "So long as you consider an entire party responsible for the acts of a single man, and attack them *en masse*, we, too, will attack you *en masse*." He further explained that he had not targeted judges, deputies, or other officials, because "all these men are instruments; they do not act on their own behalf; their functions were created by the bourgeoisie for its own defense; they are no more guilty than the others." His deepest hatred was reserved for the petite bourgeoisie because they were satisfied with the existing system; they applaud the repressive acts of the government and were therefore its accomplices. That was why he chose the Café Terminus and threw his bomb into the midst of the customers rather than target specific victims. "It is necessary that the bourgeoisie understand that those who are suffering are tired of their suffering; they show their teeth and strike as brutally against those who are brutal with them."[14] Indifferent to his fate, Henry shouted "*Vive l'Anarchie*" before the guillotine severed his head on May 21, 1894.[15]

After eleven bombings in Paris, which accounted for nine deaths and numerous injuries, the cycle of French anarchist bombings ended with three important events that cumulatively affected French anarchism: Sante Caserio's assassination of President Carnot on June 24, 1894; the three "*lois scélérates*" passed between December 1893 and July 1894, specifically designed to suppress the movement; and the government's failed attempt to link the intellectual elite of the movement (Jean Grave, Sébastien Faure, Paul Reclus, Émile Pouget) with a gang of illegalist anarchists in the famous Trial of the Thirty in August 1894. The movement began to recover and flourish, however, in 1895, when anarcho-syndicalism emerged as the primary ideological orientation of most anarchists in France, with emphasis on labor militancy, strikes, and the mythological "general strike." Paris was no longer terrorized by anarchist bombings.

From a statistical perspective, the number of bombings perpetrated by—or questionably attributed to—Italian anarchists between 1890 and 1894 (the period best documented) was rather prodigious. At the outset of the decade, the labor agitation that resulted in conflict between police and workers employed at the naval arsenal base in La Spezia caused the authorities great concern because the facility was vital for the military. To crush the local movement, an agent provocateur was used to embroil several anarchists in a phony conspiracy to bomb the Politeama Duca di Genova, a theater popular with the local aristocracy and high-ranking military personnel. Typically, when the prosecution failed to establish the guilt of the anarchists at their trial on October 7–9, 1890, a dozen of them were imprisoned nonetheless for allegedly constituting an "association of malefactors." In Palermo on April 28, 1891, a bomb was placed outside the barracks of a cavalry regiment, followed by one more on January 4, 1892, detonated in the palace of the prefecture of Grosseto (Tuscany) for which two men were arrested and condemned. Another bomb exploded in the palace of the subprefecture of Faenza (Romagna) on April 27, 1892. Damage to the building was considerable, but no one was injured. Three days later a bomb scarcely more powerful than a firecracker exploded on the Corso Vittorio Emanuele in Rome. That same day a package with dynamite exploded in front of the municipal building in Voghera (Lombardy), causing minor injury to three people. On May 20, 1892, a bomb exploded in the palace of the subprefecture in Terni (Umbria). Two men accused of perpetrating the bombing were sentenced to two years of imprisonment. In Tolentino (Marche) on August 10, 1892, two bombs exploded separately: one lightly damaged a private home and bruised two people, the other churned up some pavement. Two men were condemned to ten and six years, respectively. On September 11 of that year a bomb exploded in the telegraph office in Bologna, seriously injuring a journalist. Twelve anarchists stood trial for the bombing but were acquitted. But as usual, since evidence for serious crimes was lacking, the anarchists were convicted for establishing an "association of malefactors." The Spanish Consulate in Genoa was targeted on October 3, 1892. On December 20, 1892, a bomb exploded in Pesaro (Marche), leading to the trial of six men, one of whom had been injured by the blast. All were acquitted.[16]

The failure of the authorities to prevent such acts of violence continued into the next year, as bombings had much the same pattern as in 1892.[17] On January 20, 1893, a bomb exploded in the courtyard of the Palazzo Marsili in Rome, causing light damage to the walls. Six days later a small bomb exploded on the Via del Quirinale, without causing harm to anyone. The Public Security office in the capital's Monti district was targeted on February 10, but only the steps were damaged. The villa of Senator Corrado Tommasi-Crudeli was hit ten days later, with shattered windows the only result. That same day the home of Deputy Enrico Ferri (a socialist) was also targeted; only a door and several windows sustained damage. On March 17, a bomb caused light damage to the grand staircase of the Palazzo Antici-Mattei, followed on March 20 and 21 by bombs detonated in the Marignoli and Sacchetti Palaces, which broke some windows in each. A bomb blast at the Palazzo Altieri on August 27 did little damage to the structure but killed a young man who was present by chance. For all the bombings in Rome, sixteen anarchists were arrested as an "association of malefactors" responsible for the deeds, but they were released for lack of evidence.[18]

Bombings outside Rome were relatively few in 1893. In Palermo, on February 8, a small bomb exploded in a private house; the individual responsible was sentenced to two years imprisonment. On April 14, in Massa Lombarda, a petard planted by an unknown perpetrator broke windows in a private home. Four days later, in the same town, a bomb exploded in the office of Public Security without causing damage. Six individuals were arrested but released for lack of evidence. On April 20, a policeman found a bomb in the palace of the prefecture in Pisa; it detonated when he attempted to toss it into the river, causing him to lose a hand. In Messina, on the evening of April 23, a bomb exploded harmlessly near a piazza where music was being performed. Three men were arrested. In Villa San Pietro, in the province of Ravenna, a bomb exploded in a parish house on June 5; it succeeded only in breaking windows. The residence of the archbishop of Pisa was targeted on July 9, producing no damage. Two individuals were convicted and sentenced to four months imprisonment. Finally, a big firecracker exploded near several private homes in Pisa on October 12, breaking a few windows. The perpetrators remained unknown.[19]

The bombings in 1894 exceeded in number those committed the previous year. A small bomb exploded under the stage of the Teatro Nuovo in Pisa on February 26, resulting in some broken windows. The perpetrator was sentenced to two years imprisonment. The next day a bomb exploded in Piacenza without causing injury or damage. The deadliest attack took place on the evening of March 8, as a powerful bomb exploded in front of the Palazzo Montecitorio, home of the Italy's Chamber of Deputies, killing two bystanders and injuring six others outside the building. Less than ten days later, a bomb planted by persons unknown exploded beneath the window of the *carabinieri* barracks in Ancona, causing slight damage. In the Teatro Pantera in Lucca on March 18, spectators discovered a devise with a lit fuse in a milk carton; the fuse was extinguished in time to prevent the explosion. On April 8 in Siena, two bottles filled with explosive powder detonated in the home of the colonel who commanded the military district. No one was injured. Two men were arrested. The next day, a bomb placed in the residence of the military command of Pesaro exploded, causing light damage to the windows. Two arrests followed. In Alessandria, on April 13, police discovered a bomb several anarchists had made before they could use it against the municipal building. Six individuals were arrested. A small metallic device was thrown at the former mayor and a *carabinieri* lieutenant in Colle Val d'Elsa on April 17. Neither man was injured; three arrests followed. On April 30, a bomb was detonated near a seminary in Ancona shortly followed by another at the Palazzo Odescalchi in Rome with no casualties. In Adria, on May 26, an explosive device was lit under the window of a local parish priest; he managed to extinguish the fuse in time. On May 28, during a religious procession in Cremona, an anarchist threw a noxious brew derived from plant material at the priests. Despite his having missed his targets, the perpetrator was sentenced to eighteen months. The next day, in Messina, a bomb exploded on the staircase of the police chief's headquarters. An eighteen-year-old boy was arrested for the crime. Soon after a bomb exploded on a second-floor window sill inside the Ministry of Justice and another damaged a wall and windows on the second floor of the Ministry of War. Neither explosion injured people.[20]

None of the Italian bombers left calling cards to identify themselves. Nevertheless, in a great majority of cases, the anarchists were the first to be arrested and tried, insufficient or complete lack of evidence notwithstanding.[21] After a bombing in Piacenza, for example, the local prefect informed Rome that "despite [the fact that] one can say the anarchist party here is almost non-existent, active measures to discover the culprits will be undertaken."[22] Even the nonexistence of anarchists did not preclude their assumed culpability. Acquittals at trial did occur, but absolution did not always translate into liberty. The accused anarchists as often as not might be found innocent of bombing but condemned nonetheless as "*malfattori*" and consigned to *domicilio coatto*.

Regardless of legal outcomes, to ascribe responsibility for the bombing solely to the anarchists is untenable, especially during a period of economic hardship, popular rebellion, and intense political repression. Inevitably, there were anarchist bombs, socialist bombs, republican bombs, disgruntled bombs, and the bombs of agents provocateurs. Malato, who was very knowledgeable about the Italian movement, asserted that many of the bombings were committed by disgruntled individuals whose motives were not ideological but personal, frequently the result of ill treatment by the police.[23] However, to whatever extent the bombings were actually the work of anarchists, it was no coincidence that their frequency was highest during 1892 and 1894. Repression of the movement spurred by the May Day riots in Rome and other cities in 1891 continued throughout much of 1892, with the conviction and harsh sentencing of Amilcare Cipriani and other May Day leaders providing incentive for bombings. The year 1894 was when Francesco Crispi's government imposed martial law in Sicily and the Lunigiana, utilized "exceptional laws" to arrest thousands of rebellious peasants and workers, dissolved the Socialist Party and its auxiliary institutions, and condemned hundreds of anarchists to *domicilio coatto*. The bombings at the Ministries of War and Justice on May 31, 1894, for example, occurred on the same day the conviction of the Sicilian *fasci* leaders was announced in Rome.

Italian bombers caused only three deaths between 1890 and 1894 and a total of five during the entire decade, all of them unintentional. A chief factor in the meager death toll was the minimal explosive power of the bombs. Malato attributed this deficiency to the bombers' scant knowledge of chemistry.[24] Deficient expertise may have applied to the disgruntled bomb maker, but not the anarchist seriously bent on large-scale killing. Knowledge of lethal explosive devices had been available in Italy since the Risorgimento, when Orsini bombs made their debut. And by the 1890s more powerful bombs made with dynamite and gelignite could be fabricated readily from bomb manuals, although serious errors were sometimes included in the formulas. One such manual, perhaps circulated by the Parmeggiani group of *individualisti*, featured a typically extremist title: *Studio igienico alla portata dei lavoratori: Viva il furto e la dinamite! Abbasso l'organizzazione e la morale* (Hygienic study accessible to workers: Long live theft and dynamite! Down with organization and morality!) Also around 1890, the Italian anarchist chemist Ettore Molinari had written a bomb manual entitled *Guerra all'oppressore* (War on the oppressor), from which lethal devices could have been produced had the designers so intended. Indeed, based on Molinari's work, the bomb manual *La salute è in voi* (Health is in you) was employed by the Galleanisti in the United States with deadly effectiveness in 1919–20.[25]

The far more likely reason for the comparatively low toll of deaths and injuries in Italy was the anarchists' disinclination to harm innocent people, an explanation confirmed by Malato.[26]

A significant majority of the fifty or more bombings perpetrated between 1890 and 1894 targeted symbols of the state and the ruling classes: the Palazzo Montecitorio (home to the Chamber of Deputies) and the Palazzo di Giustizia in Rome, the luxurious homes of aristocrats, police stations, military barracks, and the occasional church. The same reluctance to harm innocent people also explains why the Italian anarchists did not bomb cafés, restaurants, national celebrations, religious processions, and other activities and locations that attract large numbers of people, especially elements of the bourgeoisie. The exclusion of such targets would have made no sense had the Italians shared the same degree of hatred toward the bourgeoisie as their Spanish and French comrades.

The difference is attributable in large measure to the fact that the Italian anarchists considered the struggle against the state of more immediate importance than the struggle against the bourgeoisie and private property. Malatesta had advanced this position at the International Anarchist Congress convened in London from July 14 to 20, 1881, ostensibly for the purpose of resurrecting the moribund Anti-Authoritarian International. The International, he argued, had always preoccupied itself with economic struggle. Hereafter, he insisted, the International's revolutionary program should accentuate political struggles against governments: "I am far from unaware that economic oppression is the principal cause of all oppression, but it must not be forgotten that the State is the guardian of property and that we can only reach [attack] the property owner by passing over the body of the gendarme."[27] Until around 1897, when Malatesta and the *socialisti anarchici* of similar persuasion began to regard syndicalism with greater sympathy, the political antistatist approach retained primacy in Italy.

It appears incontestable, therefore, that the Italian anarchist bombings in this period were primarily antistatist rather than antibourgeois. Symbols or tangible manifestations of state power were the priority targets, not an abstract class enemy of flesh and blood. Such a pattern of violence was consistent with the revolutionary tradition of the Risorgimento as well as the teachings of Bakunin and Malatesta in another key respect. As previously established, since the days of Bakunin and the First International, the majority of Italian anarchists advocated the elimination of the bourgeoisie as a class, not its wholesale eradication as individuals, an objective consistent with their revolutionary mission—succinctly stated by the Emilia-Romagna regional federation in 1874: "the complete emancipation of the entire human race," not just the working class.[28] Thus the belief that revolutionary violence should always be constrained with the limits of absolute necessity became axiomatic to leaders like Malatesta, Merlino, Gori, and numerous others of their generation and the next, such as Luigi Fabbri. Or as Malatesta argued throughout his career, "real anarchist violence is that which ceases when the necessity of defense and liberation ends. It is tempered by the awareness that individuals in isolation are hardly, if at all, responsible for the position they occupy through heredity and environment; real anarchist violence is not motivated by hatred but by love; and is noble because it aims at the liberation of all and not at the substitution of one's own domination for that of others."[29]

Evaluated in contrast with the deadly explosions caused by Spanish and French anarchists, the wave of bombing that periodically rattled the Italian landscape, targeting stone and stucco rather than flesh and bone, hardly constituted terrorism in the modern sense of the term. Devoid of the illusion that the killing of scores of innocents would weaken and destabilize capitalist society, the Italian anarchists in the 1890s utilized explosives principally as a means of retaliation, as extreme measures of protest and resistance against authoritarian and repressive government. Causing death was not their purpose. Even the worst fanatics shrank from pursuing that path.

While anarchist individual acts of violence commanded the lion's share of public attention in the 1890s, some of the most militant elements had by no means abandoned the movement's original form of political violence—insurrection.

No anarchist possessed greater faith in this tactic than Errico Malatesta. The movement's quintessential insurrectionist, Malatesta had not been disillusioned by the failure of the 1870s nor relinquished his faith in insurrection as a means of propaganda or a potential precipitant to revolution. Like Mazzini and Bakunin before him, Malatesta believed that insurrections should be attempted again and again, even if they failed. For even failure could strengthen the resolve of revolutionaries and oppressed masses to do better the next time. Thus, at the same time that the London Congress advocated the "study of chemistry," and when many anarchists in Italy had come to embrace terrorism (in theory) as the most effective revolutionary weapon, Malatesta was again contemplating insurrection.

The obstacles confronting any attempt at insurrection in Italy were formidable. Aside from the likelihood of government intervention and defeat, Malatesta's plans for new insurrections would invariably face opposition from the *anti-organizzatori*, encounter enormous difficulty raising the necessary funds, and could rely upon only a small minority of anarchists willing to risk imprisonment or death by participating in such a venture. Notwithstanding such obstacles, when Malatesta returned to Europe from Argentina in August 1889, insurrection was high on his agenda. In spite of the fact that he was forced into exile, first in Nice and later London, Malatesta did not flag in his resolve.[30]

Several attempts at insurrection, chiefly by the *organizzatori*, were planned and undertaken during this period. These were clandestine endeavors and remained largely hidden from the public eye (with one notable exception), although the authorities knew through their spy network what the anarchists intended almost from the outset. Because of government intervention, a poverty of resources and lack of sufficient participation by the anarchists themselves, all the insurrectionary attempts were failures that generated repression in their wake. But even in failure they demonstrated the irrepressible conviction of some leaders and militants that insurrectionary attacks against the state and bourgeoisie might at any time precipitate a response from the masses capable of expanding into more widespread and intense rebellion.[31] Malatesta believed that a renewed spirit of militancy was pervading working-class circles in much of Europe, and in his new *Programma* of 1889 he urged the anarchists to pursue revolutionary objects by utilizing every means of direct action save terrorism.[32]

Malatesta's return to Europe coincided with the beginnings of the Italian movement's resurgence, the clearest manifestation of which was the national congress convened in the Swiss (Ticino) village of Capolago on January 4–6, 1891. Malatesta, Merlino, and another eighty-four prominent figures had been selected by groups in more than fifty Italian cities and foreign centers of exile, including London, Paris, Marseilles, Lugano, New York, Buenos Aires, Alexandria, and the experimental anarchist communal Colonia Cecilia in Brazil. More than two hundred associations of various kinds registered their adherence to the congress, one-third of them socialist and laborite. The principles and objectives of this resurgent movement were the fight against Andrea Costa and parliamentary socialism; the formation of a Partito Socialista Anarchico Rivoluzionario—Federazione Italiana; a call for a general strike to be launched in Rome on May 1, 1891; and, ultimately, the organization of multiple uprisings throughout the peninsula starting with one to coincide with the May Day demonstration in Rome.[33]

In preparation for May Day, Luigi Galleani and Amilcare Cipriani were entrusted with the task of rallying support for multiple uprisings. However, because of a lack of funds (the movement's perennial problem) Galleani's propaganda efforts did not extend beyond Tuscany, and Cipriani's activities in all-important Romagna terminated abruptly.[34] Prodded by Malatesta, Cipriani resumed his activities in Sicily.[35] Malatesta and Merlino considered Sicily a potential field of action because the island was suffering dire effects from the tariff war between Italy and France (1888–90), which nearly crippled Italian agriculture, particularly in the South and Sicily.[36] Promising to make amends for his failure in the Romagna, Cipriani ventured to Sicily in March 1891 to verify reports that local anarchists were planning to exploit the island's seething discontent and rebel with or without outside support. Cipriani was hailed as a hero by the Sicilian workers and peasants wherever he visited. Popular enthusiasm, however, did not diminish his reluctance to act decisively, and he urged potential rebels to bide their time because they were insufficiently prepared and a premature revolt would fail and precipitate repression. Whether or not Cipriani's immediate assessment was correct, the anarchists had correctly perceived that a mass uprising of Sicilian peasants and workers was imminent, an observation that eluded Italian Marxists for another two years.[37]

Failure to spark a revolt in Sicily in April did not dissuade the anarchists from undertaking their plans for May Day. Economic and financial conditions were deteriorating rapidly throughout the mainland and Sicily, in large measure because of the onset of depression; Crispi's government responded by increasing the duty on imported grain, thereby saving big land owners at the expense of peasants and workers who paid higher prices for bread at the same time as their taxes increased. Conditions for rebellion, meanwhile, seemed especially favorable in Rome where the construction boom of the late 1880s had collapsed, leaving thousands of workers unemployed and without recourse. Many of the unemployed were migrants from other provinces, and it was among this element that the anarchists had acquired a substantial following. Having learned that the anarchists hoped the May Day demonstration would provoke widespread insurrection, authorities readied their forces in Milan, Naples, Genova, Ancona, and Sicily but mainly in Rome while the anarchists proceeded with their plan.[38] In March 1891 in the capital, as a precautionary measure, the police deported eight thousand unemployed workers back to their hometowns.[39] Undaunted by the threat of repression, on May Day several thousand of Rome's workers clashed with army soldiers and cavalry across the city for hours before a measure of calm was restored.[40] Within days of the May Day upheaval, the police carried out hundreds of arrests throughout the city. Leaders who were not arrested were forced into hiding and some into exile.[41]

Malatesta, Merlino, and other anarchists had been prescient in their conviction that Sicily was ripe for rebellion, as they inferred from their exploration of conditions in 1890–91. Economic collapse and oppressive taxation were most keenly felt on the island, where tens of thousands of peasants and other working-class elements joined the Fasci dei Lavoratori (Workers Groups), an eclectic and loosely organized network of labor groups established between 1891 and 1893. Intended to function as instruments of economic and political agitation, the Fasci dei Lavoratori at the end of 1893 by any standard had developed into a mass movement. The majority of the *fasci* were led by legalitarian socialists.[42]

For about two years the *fasci* led numerous peasant strikes against landed magnates in western Sicily, demanding lower rents and higher wages. Strike action achieved appreciable success, a remarkable achievement considering the control of large property owners.[43] In the eastern and central provinces, railroad workers, sulfur miners, and other categories of workers achieved comparable success. By the summer and fall of 1893, however, economic conditions had worsened as tax relief failed to materialize, unemployment increased, and food prices escalated to levels that caused widespread hunger. Desperation had become so acute and widespread that most *fasci* leaders, who consistently advocated popular restraint, lost the support of their membership. Uncontrollable crowds of peasants, workers, artisans, and lower-middle-class proprietors joined together in spontaneous rebellion, unleashing fire and destruction upon town halls, customs houses, tax record offices, and other government properties they perceived as symbols of exploitation and oppression.[44]

Sicily's ruling classes, fearing they were about to be consumed by revolution, demanded government intervention and suppression of the popular protests.[45] Under orders from Francesco Crispi, the newly appointed prime minister and interior minister, the police began shooting into crowds almost at will, accounting for the deaths of at least ninety-two demonstrators by January 1894. Worse still, on January 3 Crispi declared a state of siege in Sicily and dispatched forty thousand troops to enforce submission. Marshal law spelled the death of the Fasci dei Lavoratori and every other working-class society and cooperative summarily dissolved by Crispi. Thousands of protesters and their leaders were arrested and tried by military tribunals, which meted out outrageously long terms of imprisonment for the pettiest of offenses, and almost two thousand who had been placed under *ammonizione* were subsequently condemned to *domicilio coatto*, as usual without a trial. Sicily was transformed once again into a land of silent suffering.[46]

While marginal in Sicily, anarchists were central in the uprising that erupted in the Lunigiana region of northwestern Tuscany on January 13, 1894.[47] Anarchism enjoyed a broad following among marble-quarry workers in the Lunigiana, an area in the Massa-Carrara district of the Apuane Mountains. In fact, the Lunigiana represented the highest concentration of anarchists in the entire country, according to the minister of the interior in 1882: 1,000 out of 5,627.[48] The quarrymen were tough, individualist rebels without distinguishable leaders, who had experienced many cycles of organization (a Federazione Anarchica in 1883), strikes, and repression since the days of the First International. Repeated efforts to stamp out the movement had failed to extinguish the quarrymen's remarkable resilience, cohesion, and tenacity in their movement right up to their insurrection in 1894.[49]

Nurtured for decades on their belief in worker solidarity, quarrymen and sawmill workers felt morally obliged to demonstrate in support of the oppressed Sicilians when Crispi imposed martial law in early January 1894. On the 13th, quarry workers from the hill towns went on strike in order to stage a demonstration in Carrara. Within a matter of hours a full-scale insurrection had begun, spreading quickly to the surrounding area and involving several thousand insurgents. Attacks conducted by bands of quarrymen and sawmill workers, numbering several dozen to a few hundred, targeted police stations, *carabinieri* barracks, customs houses, telegraph lines, and other symbols of the state. But before reaching Carrara, skirmishes with the *carabinieri* occurred, forcing insurgents to seek higher ground in the mountains, where their guerrilla tactics proved ineffective. Carrara, meanwhile, was occupied by several thousand troops, thereby precluding rebel capture of the principal city in the Lunigiana. The decisive encounter occurred on January 16, when a general strike was declared and around four hundred demonstrators attempted to march on Carrara. They were fired upon by the awaiting soldiers and dispersed. The insurrection was effectively quelled, but Crispi was not satisfied. He placed the Lunigiana under a state of siege and dispatched several thousand more troops. The objective was to uproot anarchism from the Lunigiana once and for all.[50]

Considering the anarchists' abject failure to spark insurrection anywhere in Italy, as well as the enormous cost to pay in retribution, logic might suggest that the principal advocates of this tactic—Malatesta above all—would reassess its feasibility or abandon it altogether. That did not happen. In spite of continued failures, Malatesta never ceased to regard insurrection as the primary weapon in the anarchists' arsenal: "The victorious insurrection is the most effective action for popular emancipation. . . . The insurrection determines the revolution," he declared while in Paterson, New Jersey, in September 1899.[51]

Obviously not all anarchists shared Malatesta's persistent support for insurrectionary collective action. On June 16, 1894, accompanied by his private secretary, Prime Minister Crispi set out in a closed two-horse carriage from his home on the Via Gregoriana en route to the Chamber of Deputies in Rome. As Crispi's carriage turned onto the Via di Capo le Case, a short well-dressed figure approached, grasped the door, and fired one shot at the prime minister inside, missing his target. Thrown from the moving carriage, he dropped his primary weapon and then drew a second but was unable to fire because the coachman and several others had pounced on him, beating him about the head until police arrived to take him into custody. Luckily for Crispi, his would-be assassin had been ill equipped for the task, having armed himself only with single- and double-shot pistols. Unharmed and unperturbed, Crispi proceeded on to the Chamber of Deputies, where news of the assassination attempt had already been received. His colleagues greeted him with applause, cheers, and congratulations. Crispi, relishing his role as the chosen savior of the country, calmly declared, "Neither threats nor harm will deflect me from the path I have set for myself."[52]

The most authoritarian of all Italy's prime ministers before Mussolini, Crispi had been the target of a previous assassination attempt in Naples on September 13, 1889, when Emilio Caporali, a twenty-year-old former architectural student from Canosa di Puglia in the province of Bari, mounted Crispi's moving carriage and attempted to strike the prime minister with a rock. He accomplished nothing more than to terrify Crispi's daughter, who was accompanying her father that day. Caporali's life to that point had been a tale of woe. Forced to abandon his studies after the death of his father, Caporali fell on hard times, briefly working as a bricklayer before unemployment forced him to survive by begging and receiving handouts from friends.

Although he claimed to be republican in his sympathies, Caporali acted out of desperation rather than political intent, explaining to the authorities that "Crispi appeared to me as if he were the happiest man on earth, while I am the most unhappy. Therefore I attempted his life."[53] Declared insane at his trial, Caporali was confined in a mental institution until released in 1896. After spending many years abroad, in Africa, Australia, and Brazil, Caporali returned to Italy, where he died in the Nocera Inferior insane asylum in 1937.[54]

Crispi's last assailant—the anarchist Paolo Lega—was a very different character. A twenty-five-year-old unemployed carpenter from Lugo, in the province of Ravenna in Romagna, Lega was born into a poor family and began working as a carpenter's apprentice at the age of nine. Typical of males of his social class and economic circumstances, Lega could not attend school beyond the second grade. Poverty and exposure to the radical tendencies ubiquitous in the Romagna resulted in Lega's becoming an active republican by age fifteen and a staunch individualist anarchist soon thereafter. Because employment in his hometown was scarce, Lega moved to Bologna in 1886, where he worked for three years as a furniture maker in several factories. His perpetual search for employment brought him to Genoa in 1886. In the great port on the Tyrrhenian Sea, Lega participated in strikes, demonstrations, and journalistic activity under the pseudonym of "Marat," functioning in the selfless role of *gerente responsabile* for the single issue of *Primo Maggio 1892*.[55] In that capacity, an alleged infraction of the press laws caused him to be arrested and "repatriated" to Lugo. (Police could rid themselves of subversives and other "undesirables" born elsewhere but unable to find work or establish a local residence by presenting them with a *foglio di via*— a warrant of repatriation.) Returning to Genoa after three months, Lega's activities caught the attention of the police chief, Siro Sironi, a gendarme noted for his suppression of the anarchists and socialists in his jurisdiction. Sironi considered Lega *"un anarchico pericolosissimo"* capable of any act of violence, and ensured that his minions harassed Lega without respite. Lega was rearrested and "repatriated" back to Lugo, thereby preventing his participation in Genoa's May Day demonstration. Unable to find work in Lugo, Lega returned to Genoa in September only to be arrested once more during a roundup of anarchists on the occasion of the king's visit to the city. Repatriated once again to Lugo, Lega lost his father to a heart attack, allegedly brought on by worry and stress over police persecution of his son. On the sole occasion that fortune favored him, Lega was acquitted of pending press violations in a trial before the Court of Assizes in Bologna. Certain that police harassment would continue, Lega opted for exile, staying with French comrades in Nice and then Marseilles. Poor health and inability to find work compelled his return to Genoa, where he was arrested anew and repatriated to Lugo after spending twenty days in jail. Desperately seeking a respite, Lega applied for a passport to emigrate. Rather than bid good riddance to the "extremely dangerous anarchist," the authorities in Lugo refused his request and threatened to place him under *ammonizione* for "idleness and vagabondage," a common device for harassing unemployed radicals. Spared this fate for lack of just cause, Lega returned once more to Genoa, where he again became very active in local groups there and in La Spezia. Considering his presence in Genoa a menace, the local prefect described Lega as "one of the most active and dangerous anarchists, considered even by his co-religionists to be capable of energetic action in any situation."[56] One step ahead of the police, Lega returned to Marseilles, where he frequented an individualist group close to Paolo Schicchi, which could hardly have been a restraining influence. After six months of working alternatively in Marseilles and Bologna, Lega tried to settle permanently in Genoa, where he joined the local Fascio dei Lavoratori and frequented an anarchist group in the Porta Mazzini district. But on June 16, 1893, he was again arrested and repatriated to Lugo. Lega's forced relocations between Bologna and Lugo occurred two more times, on August 19, 1893, and March 7, 1894, and after this last occasion a police search of his lodgings in Lugo discovered a dagger, an offense for which he served sixty days in jail.[57]

It was most likely during his incarceration that Lega resolved to assassinate Crispi. His decision derived from a combination of personal and political imperatives: to retaliate for the relentless persecution he and his Genoa comrades had endured and to avenge the suffering of the Sicilian peasants and workers from Crispi's imposition of a state of siege throughout the island and the mass trials that condemned hundreds to lengthy prison terms. On May 30 he departed for Rome, traveling long distances on foot. During his circuitous trek, Lega visited several important anarchists on route: Emidio Recchioni in Ancona, Francesco Pezzi and his wife Luisa Minguzzi in Florence, and the former Internationalist Domenico Francolini in Rimini. Lega undoubtedly revealed his intentions to Recchioni, a close associate of Malatesta. Recchioni worked as a minor railroad official and had previously published the newspaper called *L'Art. 248* in Ancona. Authorities considered Recchioni one of the most dangerous anarchists in Italy. Now privy to Lega's scheme, Recchioni accompanied Lega to Rome on June 13, perhaps complicit in planning details of the assassination. Two days later, Lega returned to Florence and met with Pezzi and Minguzzi. He may have confided his intentions to assassinate Crispi, but the couple played no role in its execution. Back in Rome, Lega's motivation was fortified by news of further repression in Sicily.[58]

Before Lega's itinerary and contacts were discovered, the authorities suspected his attack against Crispi had been the result of a plot, a suspicion that
crystallized into certainty within a matter of days. Their conclusion was based
on reflex action, the automatic assumption that every act of anarchist violence
was the product of a conspiracy. The prefect of Ravenna conducted an investigation in Lega's hometown and found no evidence of a plot. Nevertheless,
he maintained that Lega was incapable of planning and carrying out the
assassination attempt by himself: "someone profiting from Lega's ignorance,
fanaticism, and brutality drove him to [commit] the savage crime."[59] Belief
that Lega lacked the intelligence and financial means to have acted alone came
to prevail in official circles, thereby reinforcing their prior assumption of a
conspiracy. Information from "confidential sources," confirming the existence
of a plot, soon flooded the Ministry of the Interior. On the basis of such
information, the police chief of Bologna, Ermanno Sangiorgi, affirmed that
because of the repression in the Lunigiana, Merlino's arrest, Cipriani's failure
to intervene in Sicily, and Malatesta's return to London, the anarchists felt
compelled to prove themselves anew by committing "a bloody vendetta," and
Lega was chosen to be Crispi's assassin.[60] The new police chief of Rome, Siro
Sironi, the former bête noire of anarchists in Genoa, echoed his colleague,
maintaining that Lega, although "a fanatic quite capable of the crime," was
not intelligent enough to have planned the *attentat*. Accomplices must have
conceived the assassination and provided encouragement and financial assistance. Information from several informants convinced Sironi that the plot
may have extended to Malatesta, "the head of the revolutionary anarchist
movement," from whom his close friends Pezzi, Minguzzi, and Recchioni
"took their orders." Sironi ultimately concluded that "Recchioni Emidio, an
acquaintance of Malatesta, was chosen to organize the plot because he was
young, not well known, active, and had many associates, especially in the
Romagna." However, he could not have acted without the approval of the
married couple Pezzi [and Minguzzi], "who devote their souls to Malatesta."[61]
In a subsequent report, the police chief of Bologna expressed his belief that
"the *attentat* against Crispi was [an act] of vengeance by the anarchist sect.
Lega was only the arm of this sect. The noted attorney Pietro Gori and Errico
Malatesta gave the order, Recchioni was his accomplice, and the others were
supporters."[62]

Lega's trial was held in the Court of Assizes of Rome on June 19, 1894.
His defense team was led by the noted attorney and criminologist Ettore
Lollini, who often provided his services to anarchists and socialists. Despite
Lollini's valiant efforts, Lega's guilt was indisputable and a guilty verdict a
foregone conclusion. Lega's brief courtroom statement set the pattern for

Italian *giustizieri* ("those who carried out justice") thereafter. He denied the existence of a plot and described his *attentat* as an act of retributive justice against Crispi as a symbol of state power and oppression rather than as a man:

> I cannot express my ideas clearly because I lack education. However, I must say that I did not commit this offense out of malice or personal hatred, but rather to protest against the privileged classes and against the oppressors. . . . I considered the deeds that have taken place in Italy, the massacres ordered by the government, and decided to commit an act of social vindication. . . . I decided to strike a man who is responsible for so many evils, but not him as a man but rather as the most important personage of the State.[63]

In his final words to the judges and jurors, Lega warned, "Now I await your verdict. Condemn me, I do not care, but I warn you that I will not be the first nor the last anarchist who sacrifices his life."[64] Found guilty with extenuating circumstances, Lega was condemned to a prison term of twenty years and seventeen days, to be served in a prison in Sassari on the island of Sardinia. But Crispi was not satisfied. Thus a campaign to link accomplices to Lega's *attentat* had been launched immediately after the deed; it concluded with the trial at the Court of Assizes in Rome (November 7–30, 1895) of the anarchists with whom he had had prior contact: Recchioni, Pezzi, Minguzzi, Francolini, Claudio Nardi, Luigi Legni, and several others were arrested that August and variously charged with complicity to commit attempted murder or providing the material means for the crime. Lollini again served as defense counsel.[65]

The evidence consisted of prefectural and police reports based on information from "confidential sources" (i.e., spies), which focused primarily on Recchioni, because he was presumed to have directed the plot, and because he had accompanied Lega to Rome on June 13 and stayed with him for two days, leaving Rome "convinced of Lega's resolve to commit the deed."[66] One piece of evidence Police Chief Sironi believed would clinch the case against Recchioni was a confiscated letter he had written to Pezzi and Minguzzi, expressing satisfaction that Crispi's life had been attempted, but which lacked any statement directly associating himself or Pezzi and Minguzzi with Lega's deed.[67] Still scrambling for evidence to solidify the government's case, the prosecution summoned Lega from prison to testify, hoping he might reveal his accomplices in exchange for better treatment. But Lega reaffirmed that he had acted alone. On June 30, 1895, to the surprise of the anarchists and the consternation of Crispi's government, the jurors acquitted the defendants for lack of evidence. Acquittal in Crispi's Italy, however, was no assurance defendants would go free. Just two days after their trial, all the anarchists the state had accused of being Lega's accomplices were consigned to *domicilio coatto*. Returned to prison in Sardinia, Lega died on September 25, 1896. The official version claimed that he had died while confined to an agricultural penal colony near Cagliari. Recchioni, now in exile in London, reported instead that Lega had died because of mistreatment from his guards at the Sassari penitentiary, but there was no evidence to confirm this suspicion.[68] In comparison with their writings about other *attentatori*, Italian anarchists wrote little about Lega in the years that followed. Perhaps he would have been elevated to the pantheon of anarchist martyrs had he been a better shot.[69]

Eight days after Lega's attack on Crispi, the president of France, Marie François Sadi Carnot, was struck down by another Italian anarchist in Lyon. The fourth president of the Third French Republic, Carnot was a rather stiff-necked bourgeois and bureaucrat who graduated from the École Polytech-nique and who had held office since 1887. He was visiting Lyon that June 24 to officiate at the Universal Exposition devoted to industrial and commercial enterprise, a typical presidential function. After attending a public banquet and delivering the requisite speech, Carnot set out in his open carriage on Rue de la République, heading for the Grand Théâtre to see Racine's *Andro-maque*. Seated beside the president were two generals and the city mayor. Accompanying the carriage was a platoon of mounted cuirassiers, but none was riding close enough to provide immediate protection, a serious derelic-tion considering that Carnot had received several death threats since the executions of Vaillant and Henry. Nor was he wearing the protective vest fitted for him after Henry's rendezvous with the guillotine. With both sides of the street lined with cheering citizens, the president's guards were caught by surprise when a young man bolted from the crowd bearing what seemed to be flowers wrapped in a newspaper. But the newspaper contained a dag-ger, not flowers, and upon mounting the steps of the carriage, the presumed admirer plunged his weapon deep into Carnot's abdomen, lacerating his liver and intestines. The president died three hours later from internal bleeding.[70]

Italians living and working in France were targeted for retaliation once the national identity of Sadi Carnot's assassin became known. Motivated by xenophobia and the employment of Italian migrants who undercut the wage scales of native workers, the French had been extremely hostile to resident Italians since the Franco-Italian tariff war of 1888–90, which had proved so disastrous for agriculture in the Mezzogiorno. The worst of many episodes of ethnic violence was the confrontation between Italian and French workers at the salt evaporation ponds in Aigues-Mortes near Marseilles in 1893 that left at least thirty Italians dead. This latest tragedy saw the Italian consulate in Lyon besieged by mobs of enraged demonstrators, shouting "Down with the Italians!" Only the mobilization of troops and police prevented the demonstrators from ransacking the building. The next morning mobs numbering in the thousands turned their wrath on the districts where Italian workers and tradesmen lived, looting, burning, and destroying Italian-owned shops and homes. Anti-Italian rioting extended to other French cities, such as Grenoble and Marseilles, resulting not only in property damage and personal injury but the discharge of thousands of Italian workers. A mass exodus of displaced men and their families fled back to Italy out of fear and the need for work. Their numbers easily approached ten thousand.[71]

The Italian whose deed precipitated this renewed bout of ethnic violence was Sante Geronimo Caserio. Born in Motta Visconti in Lombardy on September 9, 1873, Caserio and his five brothers belonged to a very poor but close-knit family. His father came from peasant stock and worked as a bargeman on the Ticino River in summer and as a woodcutter in winter. The extreme poverty of the Caserio family was characteristic of economic conditions in Motta Visconti, twenty miles southwest of Milan, where child mortality was high and diseases associated with poverty like scrofula, malaria, and pellagra were endemic. Caserio's father, Antonio, was alleged to have suffered from epilepsy, but Sante never manifested signs of the disease, contrary to assertions by Lombroso and others that he had inherited the malady. Antonio's death in 1887 caused the family greater hardship and strengthened Caserio's ties with his mother Martina, a bond that remained intense until his demise. As a youth Caserio was known to be very gentle and caring; he was also a fervent Catholic, serving as an altar boy at the local church and playing the part of Saint John in the annual procession devoted to the patron saint of the town. Of normal stature, with blond hair and bright blue eyes, Caserio retained the appearance of a boy even when he reached maturity. Like most youths of his social class, Caserio's education was terminated after the second grade, and by age eleven he was working to assist his mother and brothers, first as a shoemaker's helper, then as a shop boy in his uncles' wine store in Milan. At age thirteen Caserio was apprenticed at Milan's renowned Tre Marie bakery, where he toiled for very long hours at night. The owner considered him a very hardworking and reliable employee. Caserio eventually joined the bakers' mutual aid society, where he met anarchists and socialists, and began voraciously reading their newspapers and pamphlets and attending their lectures. More than subversive literature, however, it was Caserio's acute sensitivity to the dreadful conditions suffered by the Milanese proletariat and the hardships of his own life that transformed him into an anarchist. Pietro Gori, who knew him well, described Caserio's personality: "His sensitive and affectionate nature was already predisposed to take the part of the oppressed and the exploited, of whom he was one," and when he embraced anarchism, he did so with the devotion and fervor of "born believer."[72] "He lived for the cause, and he was prepared to die for it."[73] Already devoted, Caserio's commitment become more militant after the suppression of the protestors during Rome's May Day demonstration in 1891. He became a very active member of an anarchist group in the Porta Romana district and then formed his own group in the Porta Genova district. Like most anarchists in Milan, Caserio's group drew close to Pietro Gori, who published his own newspaper, *L'Amico del Popolo*, for a few weeks between December 1891 and January 1892, before its suppression by the police.[74]

That Caserio's conversion predated his meeting Gori is significant because the renowned anarchist attorney and poet laureate of the movement would later be falsely accused of having been one of the *cattivi maestri* (bad teachers), who allegedly inspired the young man's *attentat*. The suspicion expressed in the bourgeois press extended also to Ada Negri, a noted poetess of subversive persuasion, who had founded a progressive school in Motta Visconti, which Caserio never attended. Even Caserio's favorite novel, Victor Hugo's *Les misérables*, was considered a contributory factor. Gori did know Caserio perhaps better than anyone and he regarded the young anarchist with considerable affection and admiration. Had Caserio related his intention to him, Gori would undoubtedly have attempted to dissuade the young Lombard. But neither Gori nor anyone else who knew Caserio considered him capable of an *attentat*; they believed him too gentle and kind to commit such an act. Filippo Turati, who knew Caserio as one of the anarchists who frequently attended socialist meetings in order to dispute theory and practice, attested to his excellent character and gentle manner: "He had nothing of the insolent aggressiveness that characterized some of his comrades. On the contrary, he was meek, pensive, taciturn, notoriously affectionate and hardworking; he revealed a nature that deeply embraced the sentiment of duty and sacrifice."[75]

When not engaged in propaganda activities, Caserio spent all his free time reading anarchist newspapers, pamphlets, and other literature. His lifestyle was ascetic. He rarely smoked, never drank, and abstained from sexual activity. Asked by Gori if he ever made love to women, Caserio explained that he once did but would refrain until he found the right girl to be his companion. One evening, while in the company of Gori, Caserio encountered a group of acquaintances just as they were emerging from a brothel. Caserio reproached them for abusing women by purchasing their flesh, to which one of them replied that they had relieved their misery with payment for their services. Angered by the sarcastic reply, Caserio sprang up the stairs, gave one of the women a lira, and then returned without saying a word. Exceedingly generous, he was often observed distributing anarchist literature and fresh loaves of bread to workers outside the Camera del Lavoro (Chamber of Labor)—bread and pamphlets purchased with his own money. He explained to Gori that "it would be an insult to give printed matter to a person thin from hunger rather than satisfy his stomach before reading; this way they are better able to understand what they read."[76] Gori also noted Caserio's extraordinary empathy for human tragedy, even when it befell class enemies. One evening, while he and Gori attended Paolo Giacometti's *Maria Antonietta* at the Commedia di Milano Theater, Caserio's eyes overflowed with tears during the last act, when King Louis XVI and his despised spouse Marie Antoinette were led away to the guillotine.[77] Nothing up to that point suggested that Caserio was capable of violence. Gori observed only two occasions when a flash of genuine anger emanated from his young comrade, both associated with thoughts about his mother: once when he learned that a comrade's mother had died of a broken heart upon hearing of her son's arrest, and again one frigid night in Milan when he and Gori were walking past a posh hotel. Caserio's attention fixed upon an old and ill-clothed woman seated outside. Her job was to remain there all night and "guard against thieves." Caserio pressing some coins into her frozen hands and in a trembling voice declared: "A society that permits such infamy deserves no pity."[78]

The beginnings of the inner turmoil that transformed Caserio from a gentle youth into an angry and desperate man capable of assassination began when the police of Milan became aware of his propaganda activities. Although he hardly qualified as a "dangerous anarchist," the police followed him constantly, searched and ransacked his room regularly, and persistently pressured the owner of the Tre Marie bakery to discharge him because he was an anarchist. After refusing several times, the proprietor finally succumbed to police pressure and dismissed Caserio from his employ. Caserio secured work at other bakeries, but police harassment continued unabated. Finally, on April 26, 1892, he was arrested for distributing the antimilitarist pamphlet, *Giorgio e Silvio*, to soldiers at the Porta Vittoria Bridge and for urging them not to fire upon workers during the coming May Day demonstration. Caserio was convicted and sentenced to imprisonment for eleven months. Pietro Gori, now acting as his attorney, pleaded for leniency and issued a prescient warning: "it is not by chains and imprisonment that an idea can be stifled, that persecution can only embitter a struggle for principles. I concluded by saying that if they confirmed the sentence hatred might take root in this gentle character, and thus would they only have made one more relentless enemy. For bloody and terrible are the vindications of oppressed thought."[79]

Caserio's sentence was confirmed, but he was released under "provisional liberty" pending incarceration. Imprisonment was not nearly so threatening to Caserio as his conscription into the army upon his release. He knew that anarchists in the army were routinely brutalized by their officers, a prospect that had driven many to migrate permanently abroad or seek temporary refuge in exile with the hope of returning to Italy in the future. Deciding to go abroad, Caserio returned to Motta Visconti to request a passport, but the town mayor refused because he suspected Caserio was seeking to avoid the draft. Lacking a viable alternative, Caserio fled to Switzerland with the assistance of comrades, to begin the harsh life of a political exile.

Upon arriving in Lugano, Caserio applied for a passport at the Italian Consulate, but he was refused on orders from police back home. After a few weeks, he returned to Milan to confer with Gori to determine whether he qualified under a forthcoming amnesty after having already been condemned in absentia as a draft dodger. Gori explained that he was ineligible because he had not served his jail sentence for distributing antimilitarist pamphlets. Without proper papers or money, Caserio made it back to Lugano, where he remained for three months, desperately searching for employment. He might not have survived if not for the assistance provided by local comrades.[80]

Swiss police, meanwhile, arrested Caserio and held him in jail for five days because he had no passport. They almost turned him over to Italian authorities but desisted because his offenses were political. They brought him instead to Lausanne, whence they expelled him over the French border. Caserio returned to Lausanne, in a futile attempt to find work, and then made his way to Geneva on foot. At one point Caserio contemplated resorting to theft; however, as he wrote in one of his letters, "I do not feel that I have the strength to take a bourgeois by the throat and make him give me his money. I will end up selling my arms to the first exploiter who comes along." His postscript suggested a different reaction in the future: "I am not afraid. If I do not have the courage to strike down a bourgeois now, when the day of vengeance comes, I will be there. And the vengeance will be terrible."[81]

From Geneva, he ventured by the same means to Lyon in France, trying to avoid police en route lest they arrest him because he lacked proper papers. He remained in Lyon at the end of July 1893, working as a porter for two weeks. His inability to speak French made it impossible for Caserio to find steady employment in Lyon, and depending upon comrades for assistance humiliated him. From Lyon he went on to Vienne, working briefly as a baker, and finally to Cette (later changed to Sète) in October. There he found work as a shop boy at a bakery for fifteen franks a month plus food and lodging. Three months after his arrival, Caserio became sick ("the air here caused me to fall ill") and spent thirty-eight days in the local hospital without a definitive diagnosis. Bereft of funds, Caserio left the hospital and found new work as a baker, luckily at twice his previous pay. However, as he had not fully recovered, the cost of doctor visits and medicine left him without money to buy clothes. Despite his poverty, Caserio sent money to comrades in worse straits whenever he could.[82]

Although a fair number of Italians, mostly from Piedmont and Tuscany, worked in Cette, Caserio's deep longing for his home and family could not be assuaged, and he felt negligent that he could not conduct propaganda activities as before. He repeatedly asked comrades in Italy to send him anarchist newspapers and pamphlets and queried them about the movement's progress in Milan, and whether the bakers were joining the cause.[83] But he was too much the devoted anarchist to remain politically idle even in exile. Anarchists eschewed nationalist parochialism, and Caserio regularly attended the meetings of French comrades in Cette, which usually convened at the *Café de Gard*. Limited by his rudimentary French, Caserio expressed considerable frustration: "I am pained because I cannot speak at meetings and can do little for our idea."[84]

French authorities were aware of Caserio's presence in Cette, and although the Ministry of the Interior had labeled him "a very militant anarchist" when he first arrived, the local prefect did not consider him dangerous and left him unmolested. Caserio, of course, was unaware that he was not in danger of imminent expulsion, and fear of expulsion remained an incessant preoccupation.[85] And yet he ruled out returning to Italy voluntarily. Several weeks prior to his *attentat*, a comrade in Italy urged him to return home because his mother and brothers were so distressed by his absence. As if anticipating some personal disaster, Caserio explained that no matter what course of action he took, his mother and brothers would inevitably suffer on his account. Even if he completed his prison sentence, service in the army still awaited him, a prospect he viewed with dread: "You know my character. I would not be capable of putting up with the bullying the officers inflicted on poor soldiers, and you know well that when one has a loaded rifle in one's hands one would quickly shoot at an officer. Who would save me from death or imprisonment for life?"[86] Even if he were free to remain in Italy, Caserio affirmed that "the pain of my mother and brothers would not end. I cannot tolerate the injustices of modern society. I must protest at all cost." Many were the nights that Caserio cried himself to sleep thinking about the suffering of his family, but the responsibility, he concluded, was not his: "It is not you who causes your mother's pain; it is the entirety of present-day society; the bourgeoisie are the cause of their pain; it is necessary therefore to fight against society without thinking about the tears of my mother and brothers. . . . No, no, I must not think of my mother's tears; I must think of my duty and fight against present society, to destroy these harmful insects who are the exploiters. As for me, I will always cry: War, war against the exploiters. Long live anarchy! Long live the social revolution!"[87]

Caserio's letters do not indicate that he was contemplating an *attentat*, but signs of his mounting rage and desperation were evident. Caserio's commitment to wage "war against the exploiters" was undoubtedly stimulated by the recent *attentats* committed by Spanish and French anarchists and the executions of the perpetrators. The postscript to his letter of May 15, 1894, indicated his preoccupation with these events: "Long live the [French] Republic and the guillotine for our comrades. Long live Spain and her rifles that shot six comrades. One day we will avenge them. Death to the bourgeoisie! Long live anarchy!"[88]

For however long the emotional tempest within was accelerating toward a fatal climax, Caserio's decision to strike a blow against the class enemy was ultimately spontaneous, prompted by news that the president of France would soon be officiating at the Universal Exposition in Lyon. The key incentive was the identity of the prospective victim. Carnot was the perfect candidate for assassination. He was France's highest-ranking politician, a symbol of the state, and he was especially hated by the anarchists because he had refused to commute the death sentence of Auguste Vaillant, despite the fact that the anarchist had a wife and child and that his bomb had killed no one. Once resolved to assassinate Carnot, Caserio pursued his quarry with relentless determination. After obtaining his wages from his employer and purchasing a dagger, Caserio departed from Cette on the morning of June 23, making a number of short hops by train to Montpellier, Tarascon, Avignon, and Vienne, but having exhausted his funds by then, he traveled the last leg of his journey to Lyon, some twenty miles, on foot. Upon reaching Lyon, Caserio learned the president's itinerary from a local newspaper, found his way to the Rue de la République, and secured a place among the crowd near the Palais de la Bourse, from which Sadi Carnot would exit before heading for the *Grand Théâtre*. A few minutes later Sante Caserio became the first Italian anarchist to assassinate a head of state.[89]

Caserio's trial in the Court of Assizes of the Rhône lasted a mere two days (August 2–3, 1894) albeit with enough troops surrounding the building to fend off a new attack from the German army. Hostility toward the defendant pervaded the atmosphere. The presiding judge's statement to the jury at the outset was that his "mission" was to secure a guilty verdict and, thus, that jurors could "count on me" for proper guidance.[90] Caserio's reluctant defense attorney was a Swiss citizen named Alfred Podreider, who spoke Italian and French and had been recommended to the defendant's family. He planned to argue extenuating circumstances—hereditary insanity—but Caserio eschewed this strategy and rejected Podreider's services: "If I killed the President of the Republic, it was not because I was mad but for my anarchist idea."[91] Finally, after all local attorneys refused to take the case, the court appointed the president of the corporation of attorneys, Monsieur Auguste Dubreuil, to assume the thankless task. An interpreter was also provided, although he had difficulties understanding Caserio's Lombard accent.[92]

Despite his client's wishes, Caserio's attorney would claim extenuating circumstances on several grounds: the defendant's father had suffered from epilepsy; Sante had been manipulated by his "master," Pietro Gori; and the crime did not fit the young man's personality.[93] Caserio adamantly contradicted his defense attorney, insisting that he was not insane and had acted alone, and he became angry when his attorney argued that Gori had influenced his behavior, a claim repeated by the presiding judge: "He was not my master! I will not allow you to say that!"[94] He also became incensed when his attorney insisted that Caserio was the victim of anarchist literature that he had scarcely understood. His outburst prompted the presiding judge to threaten him with expulsion from the courtroom, to which Caserio shot back: "Well, I would rather go than listen to such nonsense." His attorney closed with a futile plea for mercy.[95]

Dubreuil's contention that Gori's influence had contributed to Caserio's action followed the line of attack pursued by presiding judge Georges Henri Breuillac from the outset. The French government was convinced (or pretended to be) that Carnot's assassination was the fulfillment of a vast anarchist plot of which Gori was the likely mastermind.[96] Several times the presiding judge sought to catch Caserio off guard by accusing him directly: "Are you not the agent of an anarchist plot?" Caserio calmly replied: "No, I am alone, and I came alone to carry out my act of justice."[97] Ultimately, the judge's attempt to attribute Carnot's assassination to an anarchist conspiracy went nowhere.[98]

Breuillac compensated for his failure to uncover an anarchist conspiracy by denigrating Caserio at every turn. But the young anarchist was not easily bested by the judge's attacks. When Breuillac spoke condescendingly about his lack of formal education, Caserio replied: "I am the first to regret it. If I had been educated, I would have been stronger and better, and would have given more to the ideal than my poor life."[99] Continuing to goad the defendant,

Breuillac reproached Caserio with a reminder that the day he assassinated Sadi Carnot, June 24, was the anniversary of the Battle of Solferino in 1859, when French and Piedmontese troops fought together against the Austrians. Caserio, as is not surprising, viewed the famous battle that contributed to Italian unification strictly from a class perspective, as "serving the interests that were not those of the proletariat, in obedience and service to the calculations of Bonaparte [Louis Napoleon] and [the House of] Savoy."[100] The judge sought next to shame Caserio by asserting that his fixation with anarchism made him forget the debt of gratitude he owed France for having extended hospitality and work to an exile. Caserio responded, "As for the hospitality of labor, you are one of those who alone benefit from work without merit, Mr. President. Instead, I am the one who without respite and blame suffer only torment and humiliation. . . . If a debt remains unpaid, it is a sacred debt of hate, vengeance, extermination; and do not delude yourself, we will settle accounts one of these days."[101] During these jousts, Caserio occasionally scored with a clever retort, as when Breuillac asserted that the defendant had once claimed he would assassinate the king and the pope. Caserio quipped in response: "Not both a once. They never go out together!"[102]

Caserio had maintained his composure until Breuillac accused him of violating his own standard of justice. "You disavow the laws of men but you readily acknowledge the higher law that forbids killing. . . . [Yet] you, a boy of twenty-one, appointed yourself prosecutor, judge, and executioner."[103] As a good anarchist, Caserio believed that when magistrates referred to a "higher law" forbidding murder, their notion of the sanctity of human life extended only to bourgeois life. Moreover, he rejected modern society's inherent belief that state violence in defense of bourgeois interests was morally legitimate while proletarian violence was not. Caserio countered Breuillac thusly: "Do not governments cause the death of millions and millions of men? I am young, yes; I am twenty-one years old, the age of soldiers who also kill, who kill on the orders of the governments." Breuillac became exasperated by this answer and charged that "you have killed not only a head of State but the best of husbands and fathers of a family." Caserio bristled at the judge's sole concern for Sadi Carnot and his family, a narrow focus that once again underscored the double standard of the bourgeoisie toward life and violence: "Fathers of families? There are other [fathers] who are killed by poverty and work. Was not Vaillant also the father of a family, did he not have a wife, a child? Henry had a mother, a brother."[104]

As was customary whenever anarchists faced certain conviction, Caserio hoped to utilize the courtroom as a forum for propaganda by presenting a powerful speech that would explain and defend his *attentat* as an act of retaliatory justice. But Caserio's speech, written in Italian during his incarceration, was translated into French and read aloud by a court clerk in a rapid monotone to an indifferent audience. Any impact it might have had in court was lost. Moreover, the presiding judge prohibited public circulation of Caserio's statement document on the grounds that it "constituted a danger to public order."[105] Nonetheless, an Italian reporter attending the trial had taken stenographic notes, and Caserio's statement was published in *La Sera* of Milan and other European newspapers.[106]

Caserio's words lacked originality because it was so imitative of Émile Henry's final declaration. He described how his exposure to the suffering of the poor and his own travails had convinced him to embrace anarchism, the only hope for humanity. The incurable ills of bourgeois society and government persecution of the anarchists drove him to commit an act of retaliatory justice against Carnot. "Why, if the governments use against us guns, chains, and prisons, should we Anarchists, who have to defend our lives, remain skulking at home? Should we renounce our idea, which is the truth? No, on the contrary, we will answer those governments with dynamite, bombs, and daggers. In one word, we must do all we can to destroy the bourgeoisie and the governments. Émile Henry threw a bomb into a restaurant; I avenged myself with a poignard." Echoing Henry's final warning, Caserio declared, "Gentlemen of the Jury, you are the representatives of bourgeois society; if you want my head take it; but do not believe that in so doing you will stop the Anarchist propaganda. Take care, for men reap what they have sown."[107]

Upon hearing the sentence of death imposed upon him, Caserio shouted *"Vive la révolution sociale!"* His execution was carried out by France's master of the guillotine, Dr. Diebler, at 5:00 a.m. on August 16, 1894. Prior to the grisly ceremony, Caserio was visited by the Italian priest who had known him as a child and altar boy in Motta Visconti. The latter's supplications to return to the True Faith were rebuffed, and Caserio met his death as a devout anarchist.[108] Caserio's courtroom interrogation and final declaration suggest his motivation for assassinating Carnot was a desire to rank, like Vaillant and Henry, among the martyrs of the anarchist movement, to be perceived by his comrades as having struck a great blow for the cause of social revolution. Yet, in the final analysis, another motivating factor may have driven him to act—indirect suicide. In his final letter to his mother, Caserio wrote

> I write you these few lines to inform you that my punishment is the death penalty. Do not think ill of me, dear mother. Think instead that if I committed this deed it was not because I have become, as many will tell you, a criminal or an assassin. You know my goodness of heart, the tenderness that I had when I was

near you. Well, I still have that same heart even today. If I have committed this deed it was precisely because I was tired of living in such an infamous world.[109]

Caserio's testimony at trial substantiated the fact that his thoughts of imitating and avenging the anarchist martyrs had been gestating for months. The possibility cannot be excluded, however, that Caserio's *attentat*—as the letter to his mother suggests—was also an indirect suicide, a self-conscious act of self-destruction that would end his suffering.

Discussion of Caserio's *attentat* among anarchists in Italy was muted in public because their press was silenced by the "exceptional laws" initiated by Crispi in July 1894. But Pietro Gori's interviews with the bourgeois newspapers *La Sera* and *La Tribuna* were widely read and helped elevate Caserio to martyr status literally within weeks of the young anarchist's death. Gori's impassioned and eloquent explanation represents a classic vindication of Caserio's *attentat*:

> All of the great love that Caserio felt for oppressed humanity was converted into hatred for the tyrants of the earth. His hatred must have been intense, because no one can hate deeply if they have not loved deeply. He did not have any personal resentment toward Sadi Carnot; but Carnot was the political representative of the French bourgeoisie, on whose account he had signed the death warrant for the guillotined of Paris. The tragic cry of "Courage, comrades! Long live anarchy!," communicated to each other from the scaffold of suffering by those knights of death, seemed to contain the roar of the torment of hate, made more intense not from the word of anarchist agitators, but rather from the bloody provocations of the bourgeoisie: the injustices committed and thrown like a challenge to misery and hunger.[110]

Caserio's popularity among Italian anarchists derived from his willingness to sacrifice his life in devotion to the Idea, his gentle and childlike personality, and the nature of his victim. Thereafter he ranked as one of the most revered *giustizieri*, celebrated yearly in commemorative newspaper articles and other vehicles of veneration, especially the mournful song "Sante Caserio," written by Gori that remains a classic in the anarchist repertoire to the present day.[111]

# 4 Crispi and the "Exceptional Laws"

| | |
|---|---|
| Siamo coatti e baldi | We are coerced but bold |
| per l'isola partiamo | for the island we must depart |
| e non ci vergognamo | yet we are not ashamed |
| perchè questo soffrir | because our suffering |
| è sacro all'avvenir. | portends a better future. |

—Pietro Gori, *Canto dei coatti*, 1896

Back in Italy, anarchist bombings along with the *attentats* of Lega and Caserio provided the perfect pretext for an intensification of repression. Indeed, all the country's progressive forces—republicans, socialists, and anarchists, above all—would suffer Francesco Crispi's draconian rule for two years, with thousands subjected to *ammonizione*, imprisoned after trials conducted by military tribunals, and consigned by fiat to *domicilio coatto* for periods of four to five years.

By the end of March 1894, well before the trials of the Sicilian and Lunigiana rebels began to fuel criticism of his authoritarian methods, Crispi was planning to demand even more repressive measures than those already employed to suppress political subversion and popular unrest. An essential step toward establishing the authoritarian government he envisioned was passage of "exceptional laws" to eradicate with greater facility and permanence the "*associazioni di malfattori*" supposedly stalking the land.[1]

Accomplishing this objective required constant underscoring of the myth of the *patria* in mortal peril by the internal enemy—the anarchist *malfattori*, demonizing them as malevolent creatures unfit to reside in civil society. Now more than ever, Italy had to be saved from these depraved and bloodthirsty men without conscience, whom ordinary laws were insufficient to defeat. Crispi therefore went before Parliament to propose how the anarchist menace should be eliminated, employing paranoid hyperbole calculated to generate fear and loathing:

A collection of mad men which prides itself on having no country, aims openly at subverting and destroying every social regulation. They want the sacred ties of the family broken, property violated, the peace and life of the citizens undermined. They seek to achieve this end . . . not to stem the evils and pain of the disinherited class, but to propagate hate and havoc, to destroy everything without building anything. They want to renew the world with dynamite and dagger. Everyone feels the need to stem this savage propaganda by invoking a vigorous repression and an effective preventive remedy. . . . When society is threatened at its foundation, it is the duty of any civilized government to protect and defend it. . . . It must hasten to sanction measures capable of exorcising these iniquitous attentats.[2]

In order to "vigorously fight this new, terrible enemy, anarchism," Crispi called for passage of exceptional laws that would enable the authorities to extend the use of *domicilio coatto* and *ammonizione* (discussed in chapter 2) to an unprecedented scale.[3]

The parliamentary debate on the exceptional laws Crispi demanded echoed the discussions that followed Nicotera's plan to suppress the anarchists under Article 248 ("Association of Malefactors") in the wake of the May Day 1891 demonstrations and the later imposition of martial law in Sicily and the Lunigiana in 1894. Opposition to Crispi's proposals was voiced only by the Socialists and the Extreme Left, who immediately recognized the exceptional laws for the repressive instruments the prime minister intended. Their protests did not arise out of concern for the anarchists. The Socialists, fearing with good reason that Crispi's exceptional laws would eventually be used against the Italian Socialist Party (PSI), went to great pains to emphasize—in the words of Enrico Ferri, the future leader of the party's centrists or "integralists"—that "a profound and substantial disagreement exists between anarchism and socialism."[4] The leading champions of the Extreme Left, the radical Felice Cavallotti and the irredentist Matteo Imbriani, once again attacked Crispi as the destroyer of liberty. Only Giovanni Bovio, the republican philosopher, defended the right of men to believe in anarchism. As long as it remained within the realm of thought rather than action, he maintained, anarchism represented a utopia that should not be persecuted as a crime.[5]

Crispi dismissed these fears and criticisms as being wholly without cause. The government had only one objective in mind, he declared: "to ask for the necessary weapons against individuals who do not constitute a party, but, who, scattered throughout the land and united for one purpose alone: to attack the safety of the family and of property."[6] Feigning umbrage that resistance to his proposals had been offered at such a time of crisis, Crispi put the final touches to his portrait of the anarchist nemesis, depicting him as "outside of ordinary law," and insisting that "whatever provisions you enact against him will be legitimate."[7]

Here, at last, was the culmination of the demonizing process launched by Giovanni Nicotera in 1876. Against the anarchist—the ultimate *malfattore*—against this incarnation of evil and menace plotting against society, any means of repression was justified. But Crispi was still not satisfied. Once the exceptional laws had been implemented, Crispi expected Parliament to prepare still another "effective law, a law that can destroy this pestilence that spreads among the people, and against which the defensive weapons of all the governments of the world are ready."[8] Just what kind of "effective" law Crispi envisioned can be surmised from his earlier consideration of a plan for the permanent banishment and settlement of two thousand anarchists in the Italian colony of Eritrea or on an island in the Red Sea.[9] But the plan proved unworkable. In the event, all that was required to deal effectively with the anarchists was a little fine tuning of Italy's existing machinery for political repression.

Thus the exceptional laws (Nos. 314, 315, 316), passed without serious opposition by Parliament on July 19, 1894, were more than sufficient to suppress the anarchist movement; they were to remain in effect until December 31, 1895, at which time the effectiveness of the laws would be reassessed.[10] Already under consideration for several months, Law No. 314 addressed the issue of bombs, specifically the advocacy, defense, instigation, or perpetration of crimes against persons, property, or the public order by means of explosives.[11] Law No. 314 subjected the manufacture and sale of explosives to regulations that seemed to be more stringent but that could still be easily circumvented if so desired.[12] Moreover, the law was punitive rather than preventive and would never have thwarted the intended kind of *attentat* if the Italian anarchists in the 1890s had shared their Spanish and French comrades' proclivity for bomb throwing.

Far more threatening to the anarchists was Law No. 315, which dealt with instigation of delinquency and apology for crimes by means of the press. During the debates in the Chamber of Deputies, Crispi had sought to minimize opposition to his proposal by arguing that Law No. 315 was not a political much less an exceptional law: "it only fills the lacunae that are found in our legislation."[13] Of course, it was nothing of the kind. Crispi placed great importance on dangers inherent in the written word, especially in the form of newspapers available to the working class. Evidencing the class bias of Italy's bourgeois and aristocratic rulers, Crispi insisted that it was one thing for the prime minister and his social peers to have read Proudhon, "but when you speak of the atheist state, of anarchy, of property that is theft, the plebeians take these words literally, and they revolt against the bourgeoisie that is depicted as their enemy."[14]

Law No. 315 was specifically designed, therefore, to prevent the anarchists from dissemination of their ideas to the working class by silencing their press, an easily attainable objective because the law covered such offenses as apologies for acts considered criminal under the law, incitement to disobey the law, and inciting hatred between the classes. Virtually every anarchist newspaper contained material that could be judged in violation of these provisions, a task entrusted to the magistrates of a provincial tribunal rather than a jury of a court of assizes. The only offenses that came under the jurisdiction of the latter were those aimed at subverting the army. In practice, Law No. 315 ensured that anarchist newspapers could be suppressed at will and their editors sent to jail merely for expressing ideas.

In point of fact, Law No. 315 amounted to overkill: the anarchist movement's principal newspapers—*L'Ordine* (Turin), *Sempre Avanti* (Livorno), and *La Favilla* (Mantua)—had already been suppressed in January 1894. *L'Art. 248* (Ancona) managed to publish only nine issues between January and March as a result of police harassment. Only *Il Pensiero*, edited by Camillo Di Sciullo in Chieti, survived into the era of exceptional laws, its final issue appearing on September 30. Consequently, when Crispi demanded the means to prevent the anarchists from disseminating their doctrines by means of the press, he neglected to mention that the sole source of contagion in Italy was a solitary newspaper published in a small provincial town in the Abruzzi.[15]

Law No. 316, concerning exceptional measures for public safety, was unquestionably the most powerful and repressive of the three. Anyone considered a danger to public safety who had violated the provisions of *ammonizione* and special police vigilance on two previous occasions could be sent to *domicilio coatto* for a period of one to five years. Likewise destined for a comparable sojourn on the penal islands were those guilty of a single offense against "public safety and order," defined as instigation to commit crimes, delinquent association, inciting class hatred and civil war, and formation of armed bands. As in the past, deportation to *domicilio coatto* was an administrative rather than criminal procedure now under the purview of a provincial commission composed of the president of a criminal tribunal, the district prosecutor (*procuratore del re*), and an adviser from the Prefecture. The commission could also recommend that persons be sent to *domicilio coatto* "who have manifested the deliberate resolve to commit acts against the social order." The minister of the interior, on the advice of an appeal commission, made the final decision of whether the accused had manifested "deliberate resolve." Those thus condemned could be confined in the penal islands for a term of one to five years. With consignment to *domicilio coatto* under the "exceptional laws" an administrative procedure, Crispi had no further need for public trials conducted before a jury in a court of assizes, thereby eliminating the possibility of acquittal and support for the accused. And finally, as a portent of worse to come, all associations and meetings having as their objective the subversion of the social order by means of deeds were prohibited.[16]

Once Parliament acceded to Crispi's proposals, the exceptional laws intensified the campaign of government repression that had been ongoing since January and even earlier, and within a few months every Italian anarchist of importance was either in *domicilio coatto*, in prison, or in exile. Indeed, the ease and speed with which the anarchist movement was suppressed invites the inevitable question: how much of a threat did the anarchists truly represent? No doubt ruling class paranoia about a possibility of a revolt of the masses elevated fear of the anarchists far beyond their real capacity for undertaking collective action of any sort. Crispi genuinely shared this irrational fear; but at the same time, serving as his own minister of the interior, he must have known from prefect and police chief reports that the anarchists represented minimal danger easily contained by the police and judiciary with the instruments already at hand. Against whom else, therefore, were the exceptional laws intended? This legislation, despite Crispi's parliamentary harangues about the anarchists, was completely vague about their intended target, the word *anarchist* never appearing. Thus Crispi had at his disposal the means to pursue bigger game—the PSI. After passage of the exceptional laws on July 19, the Socialists—despite Crispi's previous assurances—were increasingly harassed, arrested in greater numbers, and condemned to *domicilio coatto* and had their newspapers confiscated. The big blow came on October 22, 1894, when Crispi ordered the PSI and all affiliate organizations (more than three hundred) dissolved. Even socialist deputies, despite their parliamentary immunity, were arrested. Persecution of socialists as well as anarchists was now the order of the day.[17]

Establishing the exact number of men (and there were a few women, like the anarchist Luisa Minguzzi) sent to *domicilio coatto* during the Crispian reaction is problematic because government documents pertaining to the subject are contradictory and frequently do not indicate specific political affiliation. Perhaps as many as seven thousand individuals were originally destined for *domicilio coatto*, but the small islands utilized for this purpose could not accommodate such numbers.[18] Limitations of space and potential costs, not government moderation, reduced the size of the target group. A special report on *domicilio coatto* compiled for Crispi placed the number of *coatti* at 3,560 individuals at the end of 1893 and 4,672 one year later, an increase of 1,112.[19] An inspector for the Ministry of the Interior reported that there were 3,592 *coatti* by mid-1894 and more than five thousand by the end of the year, with 1,894 having been condemned under the exceptional laws.[20] Another such report on the *coatti* confined to the main penal islands at the end of 1894 again indicated a total of 3,592: Ustica (662), Favignana (536), Pantelleria (531), Lipari (597), Lampedusa (617), Ventotene (330), Ponza (319).[21] Neither report noted the five hundred anarchists originally consigned to the fortress of Monte Filippo overlooking Porto Ercole on the Argentario peninsula in southern Tuscany. Overcrowding forced the authorities to divide this group, mainly Tuscans, placing two hundred in the citadel and one hundred fifty in the fortress, shipping the remaining men to other penal colonies, including the island of San Nicola in the Tremiti group (usually referred to simply as Tremiti), off the coast of Puglia, which is not accounted for in the government documents. Also omitted from government calculations were the penal colonies at Ischia, Porto Maurizio, and a few others.[22]

The great majority of the *coatti* were nonpolitical prisoners: common criminals and unfortunate wretches entrapped by the vagaries and class bias of Italy's public security regulations, which weighed most heavily on the poor and unemployed. As of July 1895, the number of anarchists originally denounced for consignment to *domicilio coatto* under exceptional law No. 316 was 1,009, of whom 665 were ultimately condemned.[23] A list compiled by the Ministry of the Interior, indicating the provinces from which the majority of anarchist *coatti* originated, provides an excellent map of the movement's principal areas of strength: Florence (84), Ravenna (83), Genoa (65), Livorno (57), Milan (49), Forlì (36), Pisa (36), Perugia (35), Rome (32), Ancona (23), Arezzo (19), Massa-Carrara (19), and Bologna (13).[24] The seventy-two occupational categories indicated for the anarchist *coatti* reveal the overwhelmingly working-class and artisanal nature of the movement. The occupations practiced by the highest number of anarchists included shoemakers (44), laborers (35), carpenters (33), peasants and *braccianti* (32), mechanics (22), dock workers (21), printers (20), marble workers (19), bakers (19), and tailors (16). Only twenty out of 665 belonged to occupational categories definable as middle class and, of those, three were students.[25] Save for the few, like Pietro Gori, who managed to flee into exile, and those imprisoned for conspiracy or delinquent association prior to the exceptional laws, the *coatti* included almost every important anarchist in Italy: Emidio Recchioni, Cesare Agostinelli, Aristide Ceccarelli, Gigi Damiani, Luigi Fabbri, Giovanni Gavilli, Ademo Smorti, Ettore Sottovia, Pasquale Binazzi, Camillo Di Sciullo, Roberto D'Angiò, and Virgilio Mazzoni, to name but a few. They were soon joined by anarchists whose prison sentences had been served or commuted, such as Luigi Galleani, Eugenio Pellaco, and Galileo Palla.[26]

The islands that served as Italy's detention centers were small, desolate, volcanic rocks located off the coasts of Sicily and southern Italy. The largest, Pantelleria, had a perimeter of forty-six kilometers, with a local population of 6,100; the smallest, Ventotene, a perimeter of four kilometers, with a population of 1,250.[27] Several island penal colonies had previously been used for similar purposes by the Bourbons, a source of shame for Italy, notwithstanding other considerations. The local inhabitants were poverty-stricken, subsisting mainly by fishing, and uneducated, a factor authorities hoped would immunize them from the ideas of the political prisoners. The primary advantage of *domicilio coatto* over prison was the nature of the confinement. The *coatti* were not held in jail cells; they were housed at night in barracks. During the daytime, they were usually allowed to go about the island in relative freedom, interacting with each other at taverns, playing cards, singing songs, and working at odd jobs if they were able to find them. There was no prohibition against interacting with the local inhabitants, who generally respected the political prisoners for the dignity and pride with which they comported themselves. Intimate relationships between *coatti* and local women were not uncommon. The anarchists invariably formed close-knit groups that organized political discussions, sang revolutionary songs (the *Inno dei lavoratori* and the *Canto dei malfattori*), and frequently organized protests against living conditions. On San Nicola, they formed a commune that published a newspaper and operated a small school for intellectual self-improvement. Instructional classes were conducted on every island, teaching a variety of subjects, including Italian to those conversant only in a dialect. On the penal island of Ventotene, the anarchist Adamo Mancini even taught French. These classes were always open to the local population, a few of whom were converted to anarchism.[28]

Despite the relative "freedom" of movement, the conditions under which the *coatti* lived were utterly squalid and occasionally dangerous. The political prisoners were significantly outnumbered by criminal elements who sometimes abused and intimidated their co-islanders, although the latter generally realized that confrontation with the anarchists was probably not a good idea. But short of risking death, the *coatti* could do nothing to prevent the brutal treatment and abuse they constantly received from the guards—"among whom there were many venomous reptiles," as the journalist L. De Fazio observed. The worse place to be sent was the citadel of Porto Ercole known as the Rock and the nearby fortress of Monte Filippo, a hellhole often compared to Spielberg, the infamous prison where the Habsburgs had confined Italian patriots like Silvio Pellico during the Risorgimento. Like the island colonies, the prisoners in the fortress were quartered in makeshift dormitories, but at

Monte Filippo the disciplinary cases—usually anarchists—were caged in sub-terranean cells. Upon entry to the Rock or Monte Filippo they were provided only with a straw pallet and a thin bedspread for protection from the cold and damp walls that surrounded them. Sanitary conditions were deplorable. The well that provided the water supply for the Rock was contaminated from the refuse discarded by the wine shop. Medical care was almost nonexistent; the colony was visited by a physician only once a week and the infirmary was totally ill equipped to treat any serious malady. Several prisoners died from tuberculosis and other diseases. The biggest problem facing the *coatti*—and their primary source of discontent—was food, inadequate in quantity and quality. The food ration consisted of two hundred grams of soup and three hundred grams of bread distributed at midday and another three hundred grams of bread in the evening. The soup included pasta or rice with some vegetables, although it was frequently served with just the latter. Only on Sunday did the prisoners receive two hundred grams of poor quality meat and one hundred fifty grams of white bread. These terrible conditions were further aggravated by the fact that at Porto Ercole the *coatti* were not permit-ted outside the Rock or Monte Filippo, much less to find work.[29] On the less restrictive island colonies, better food and drink was available from local inhabitants if the *coatti* possessed the money to buy them. But money sent to the *coatti* by their families for supplementary support was routinely stolen by the guards. And despite the freedom to seek work, employment on these barren islands was rarely available, save for a few barbers and shoemakers serving the needs of other *coatti*. According to one ex-*coatto*, out of the 5,043 individuals confined in *domicilio coatto* in 1894, 4,283 were completely idle for lack of jobs.[30] And because of the government's perennial desire to keep the costs of *domicilio coatto* low, the allowance paid the prisoners as an in-come supplement was grossly insufficient. The wives and children left behind without means of support inevitably became destitute. Thus *domicilio coatto* spelled great economic hardship not only for hundreds of prisoners but for many thousands of innocent people on the mainland. Indeed, the net loss of productive labor to the entire country was not insignificant.[31]

With discontent widespread and intense, escape attempts, hunger strikes, and protest demonstrations among the *coatti* became common despite the risk of retaliation from the *carabinieri* and army troops assigned to guard them. Invariably, it was the anarchists who conducted the most important episodes of resistance, some of the most famous of which occurred at Monte Filippo, which was under the command of the corrupt Raffaele Santoro, a personal friend of Crispi. Besides being corrupt, Santoro was a petty despot, who at one point ordered the *carabinieri* to fire upon the courtyard full of *coatti* because they had not removed their hats when he appeared to harangue them. The *carabinieri* did not comply. On March 18, with the little money available to them, the anarchists organized a celebration to commemorate the anniversary of the Paris Commune. By nightfall, they had succeeded in ascending to the top of the fortress, where they placed the black-and-red flag of the anarchist movement. For several days thereafter the *coatti* waited for a response to the flood of telegrams they had sent to the Ministry of the Interior protesting conditions and the lack of work. When no response was forthcoming, Galileo Palla of May Day fame, whose letter had requested a transfer to the prison in Massa so he could be visited and helped by his family, decided to undertake a dramatic gesture of protest that would embarrass the government. On the night of Sunday, March 24, after all the prisoners were asleep, Palla and six other comrades managed to escape from Monte Filippo and make their way to Orbetello, where, as a gesture of protest, they walked as a group in plain sight down the main street at 10:00 p.m. Palla and his comrades got as far as the nearby town of Cecina, where they surrendered to the *carabinieri* who had been dispatched to track them down.[32] It was suspected that Santoro had facilitated the anarchists' escape in order to collect the reward money for their recapture. Removed from his position in March 1895 and charged with various crimes, Santoro wrote a report to the Republican leader Felice Cavallotti, a fierce opponent of *domicilio coatto*, describing the wretched conditions of *domicilio coatto*. He had hoped to save his skin by condemning the institution, but when the charges against him were not dropped, Santoro fled to France.[33]

Another penal colony that experienced constant anarchist agitation was Tremiti. From the outset, as the first anarchists were disembarking in chains, the director of Tremiti wrote to the Ministry of the Interior to oppose the idea of establishing a colony on his island chain: "I am convinced that as a practical matter establishing a colony of anarchists in this island is not only difficult but impossible. Such people who do not recognize laws or regulations, that are capable of acts of audacity and violence, cannot be governed if confined together."[34] As predicted, one hundred anarchists working at domestic services went on strike that September, protesting the lack of work available to the *coatti* and the inadequate food.

The agitation on Tremiti became even more intense and widespread when expectations of liberation went unfulfilled. On March 14, 1895, on the occasion of his birthday, King Umberto decreed the release of prisoners condemned by military tribunals to terms of less than three years and a reduction by one-third of those serving longer sentences, a measure that affected a few hundred men. The decree did not apply to those condemned to *domicilio coatto*, however. Then Crispi ignored his own legislation—which specified that the exceptional laws would be lifted on December 31, 1895—and extended them for an indefinite period in order to keep the anarchists in *domicilio coatto*. Not knowing when or if they would ever be released, the anarchists organized a protest strike joined by all three hundred *coatti*. The government attempted to quell the agitation by transferring approximately eighty anarchists under armed guard to other islands, but on March 2, 1896, fifty anarchists refused to come out of their barracks and sang subversive songs in defiance of orders. A riot ensued and the *carabinieri* opened fire, killing and wounding several of the *coatti*. The incident prompted the director of Public Security, Giuseppe Sensales, to remove the director of Tremiti from his post. Similar events took place in other penal colonies, sometimes resulting in the replacement or transfer of the bureaucrats in charge.[35]

Crispi was always fully informed about the dismal conditions in the penal colonies and the protest agitation they generated among the anarchists and other *coatti*. But once the institution became recognized even by moderates as a national disgrace, he was obliged to address the situation. On April 11, 1895, Crispi appointed a special commission to investigate conditions and recommend reforms; its members included Tancredi Canonico, senator and section chief of the Rome Court of Cassation; Martino Beltrani-Scalia and Carlo Guala, state counselors; and Francesco Leonardi, a high-ranking official in the Ministry of the Interior.[36] The commission's report to Crispi was unequivocal in its description of "the horrible state in which we now find the colonies of *coatti*."[37] Concerned primarily with the legality of the institution, the head of the commission, Canonico, recommended, "either provide *domicilio coatto* with a juridical and correctly disciplined basis or abolish it altogether."[38] This would have meant changing the consignment of people to *domicilio coatto* from an administrative to a juridical procedure handled by special courts. But Crispi did nothing to reform *domicilio coatto* or remedy the deplorable conditions existing in the penal colonies. As he informed King Umberto, Crispi remained inalterably committed to the institution of *domicilio coatto*: "One of the most effective means of prevention that our laws allow for the defense of public security and order is without doubt *domicilio coatto*."[39]

Political opposition to Crispi, which had already intensified with the passage of the exceptional laws, was further crystallized after the revelations about *domicilio coatto*. Hostility to Crispi's repressive policies was still centered among the radical and republican leaders of the *Estrema sinistra*: Matteo Imbriani, Giovanni Bovio, and especially Cavallotti, now the prime minister's most tenacious and hostile critic. The voice of this parliamentary opposition was enhanced further as it entered in a strategic alliance with the Turatian elements of the PSI in October 1894. After Friedrich Engels provided theoretical sanction for tactical alliances with bourgeois parties, Turati sought to make common cause with elements of the *Estrema sinistra* against Crispi, especially now that the government's dissolution of PSI and other socialist organizations presaged a full-scale attack against the movement. With this in view, Turati and other moderate socialists joined the Lega italiana per la difesa della libertà (Italian League for the Defense of Liberty) founded in Milan by Cavallotti and the radicals in October 1894. Although the Lega grew rapidly in numerous cities, attracting perhaps one hundred thousand adherents, the alliance set up by Cavallotti and Turati did not become a national focal point of opposition to Crispi. The different philosophies and objectives that motivated the numerous factions composing Italy's political world could not be reconciled. Nevertheless, the new willingness of the socialists to unite with bourgeois elements in a common struggle in defense of democracy paid off handsomely at the polls. In the national election of May 1895, the socialists received 77,000 votes and gained twelve seats in the Chamber of Deputies, considerable gains over the election of 1892, when they received 27,000 votes and won only six deputy seats.[40]

On their own initiative, the socialists conducted a significant campaign against Crispi and his *liberticide* (liberty-killing) laws with every means available to them under oppressive circumstances. A favorite tactic was to elect incarcerated leaders like Giuseppe De Felice and Nicola Barbato to Parliament and to argue (in vain) that their status as deputies warranted their release. The socialists even sought to enlist the anarchists in the running of protest candidates for election to communal government. Thus Andrea Costa exercised his considerable influence in Romagna to elect to the communal government of Imola his old anarchist comrade Adamo Mancini, then in *domicilio coatto* on the island of Ventotene. In typical anarchist fashion, Mancini refused to compromise his abstentionist principles and accept the post, even if so doing would have secured his release. Costa continued to campaign for the release of Mancini and other former comrades, but his efforts were not appreciated. When Costa offered to share with the anarchists in *domicilio coatto* some of the funds for political victims collected from Italian emigrants in Argentina, 180 anarchists in Tremiti signed a statement refusing to accept aid from "a man like Costa with whom we no longer have anything in common."[41] Even when he visited Mancini on Ventotene, Costa received a cold reception from the anarchists, and upon departing the island on a ship with the colony's director—named Porchi (plural for pig)—Mancini overheard one of the anarchists exclaim: "Oh, if only the ship with director

Pig and the Internationalist traitor would sink!"[42] No matter how much good work Costa attempted on their behalf, the anarchists never forgave what they saw as his betrayal of the movement in 1878 when he embraced legalitarian tactics.

But neither the independent campaign of the socialists nor their combined efforts with their radical associates in the League for the Defense of Liberty could dislodge Crispi from power. This outcome Crispi achieved almost all by himself. The Banca Romana scandal had entered its last phase during summer 1894, revived by the acquittal in July (on the same day the *fasci* leaders were convicted in Palermo) of the main culprit, bank director Bernardo Tanlongo, a verdict probably influenced by pressure from the prime minister. Up to this point, suspicion of complicity with bank officials had weighed heavily upon former prime minister Giovanni Giolitti, an appearance of guilt that fostered aggressiveness by his archenemy Crispi. But that September Giolitti obtained a packet (*plico*) of documents that proved Crispi's personal transactions with the Banca Romana (secret unpaid debts incurred by himself, his family, and his friends), which he had effectively covered up during his first term as prime minister. Giolitti submitted the *plico* to the president of the chamber on December 11, and a committee of five deputies, including Cavallotti, was selected to evaluate the material. Their report of December 15 indicated that Crispi's political integrity and personal ethics had been severely compromised by his dealing with the Banca Romana, a revelation that prompted demands in Parliament for a judgment of his conduct. Crispi responded in his customary authoritarian manner, this time by proroguing the chamber for an unprecedented period of five months. During this time and the rest of 1895, Crispi survived because his opponents—now including elements on the right, center, and left—could not unify to bring him down in the face of the support he enjoyed among conservatives, especially in southern Italy, still fearful of social revolution or of a government controlled by radicals.[43]

Crispi was ultimately unseated but not by his parliamentary opponents; they merely delivered the coup de grâce. The death blow to Crispi's political power and career was dealt by the Ethiopians. Italy had been a late comer to the scramble for Africa conducted by the great powers of Europe. As a second-rate power, few pickings were left to satisfy the egotistical craving for empire that drove King Umberto, the Royal Court, and a host of would-be imperialists. Not content with the acquisition of Eritrea, Crispi and his imperialist cohorts now coveted the only significant piece of African real estate not under European control—Ethiopia. Italian encroachments on Ethiopian territory had resulted in several military defeats in the early 1890s, thanks to the money and weapons furnished to the Ethiopian chieftains by the French, who sought to prevent the Italians from interfering with their own quest for a North African empire extending from coast to coast. But Crispi remained inflexible, determined to conquer this huge and inhospitable country at all costs. The ultimate cost was intolerably high: an Italian army of 16,500 men (one-third of whom were *askaris*, or Eritrean troops) was overwhelmed by an Ethiopian force of 100,000 well-armed men at the battle of Adowa on March 1, 1896. Some 9,000 escaped the battlefield, but more than 5,000 Italian troops and *askaris* lay dead and 1,900 were captured.[44]

Anti-Crispi demonstrations erupted in Rome, Milan, Naples, and other cities when news of the humiliating defeat reached the public. Italy's imperialist ambitions in East Africa had come to an ignominious end—at least for the next forty years, until Mussolini succeeded where Crispi had failed. Parliament reacted to the defeat with frenzied condemnation of the prime minister, who resigned on March 5, 1896, before his angry colleagues could vote for his dismissal. Crispi's political career was over.[45]

The big question for the anarchists and other political prisoners languishing in *domicilio coatto* was whether Crispi's repressive policies and methods would end with his exit from office. His successor was the Marquis Antonio Starabba Di Rudinì, who had previously held the premiership from February 1891 to May 1892. His assumption of office was accompanied by an amnesty issued by King Umberto on March 14, 1896, which liberated those prisoners in *domicilio coatto* not considered dangerous, a qualification that continued the confinement of many anarchists condemned under Crispi's exceptional laws until their original sentences expired. Di Rudinì proposed legislation in 1897 that would have "reformed" *domicilio coatto* by transferring decision-making power to judges rather than administrators and the police, but the widespread demand to abolish the institution altogether resulted in the bill's defeat in Parliament. Thereafter, government efforts to reform or abolish *domicilio coatto* moved more slowly than glaciers, and the institution survived to serve as a major instrument of oppression under Mussolini's fascist regime.

# 5 Anarchist Assassins: Acciarito, Angiolillo, and Lucheni

| Francia all'erta, sulla ghigliottina | France alert on the guillotine |
|---|---|
| tronca il capo a chi punirla vuol; | chops off the head of who wants to punish it; |
| Spagna vil garrotta ed assassina; | cowardly Spain garrotes and murders; |
| fucila Italia chi tremar non suol. | Italy shoots those who do not tremble. |
| | |
| In America impiccati, in Africa, sgozzati | Hung in America, slaughtered in Africa |
| in Spagna torturati a Montjuich ognor; | in Spain tortured at Montjuich; |
| ma la razza trista del signor teppista | this sorry race of thugs |
| l'individualista sa colpir ancor. | the individualist knows how to strike. |
| | |
| E a chi non soccombe si schiudan le tombe, | The graves open for those who do not succumb, |
| s'apprestin le bombe, s'affili il pugnal. | prepare the bombs, sharpen the dagger, |
| È l'azione l'ideal! | It's the deed, the idea! |

—Anonymous, *Inno individualista*, s.d.

April 22, 1897, marked the twenty-ninth wedding anniversary of the reigning monarchs of Italy, King Umberto I of Savoy and Queen Margherita. The festivities scheduled for the day included the royal derby horse race at the Capannelle track just outside Rome. The winner's purse would amount to the substantial sum of 24,000 lira, furnished by Umberto to promote the sport. Around 2:00 p.m., the king left the Quirinale Palace in a small, open Milord carriage in the company of his coachman, Arcangelo Serpe, and his aide-de-camp, General Emilio Ponzio Vaglia. After a rapid ride through the city, the king's carriage reached the Ponte Lungo on the Via Appia Nuova, a point nearly two miles from the Porta San Giovanni. A young man suddenly sprang upon the vehicle and struck at Umberto with a homemade dagger he had concealed near the Porta Furba the previous day after learning of the king's plans from newspapers. The king dodged the blow, and before the assailant could strike a second time, he was thrown to the ground by the momentum of the carriage. Tossing his weapon aside, the would-be assassin tried to escape but was apprehended by the *carabinieri*. Umberto and his companion descended from the carriage to examine the agitated young man. Asked his place of birth, the young man replied "Artena," an agricultural district in Lazio near Rome. Confused by the youth's Romanesco dialect, the aide-de-camp misunderstood "Artena" for "Atene" (Athens), and expressed surprise that the young man was Greek. Equally perplexed, the fellow responded, "What Greek?" King Umberto, who would have preferred life as an army general, asked his assailant if he had served in the army. His negative response ended the interrogation. Umberto and his aide-de-camp mounted the carriage once more and proceeded to the horse race. Unruffled, Umberto was reputed to have said that such incidents represented "*gli incerti del mestiere*" (the risks of the trade).[1]

The inevitable "risks of the trade" had been heightened by the remarkably inadequate security measures employed to protect the king. After an investigation, Prime Minister Antonio Starabba, Marquis Di Rudinì informed the director general of public security that "all functionaries were deficient in zeal." Everyone from the police chief down to the king's special bodyguard had demonstrated "complete lack of competence."[2] The most egregious example of institutional dereliction involved police inspector Leopoldo Galeazzi, whose assignment was to follow directly behind the king's carriage whenever His Majesty ventured out of the Quirinale. Although the House of Savoy spent one-quarter of Italy's annual budget on the military, providing the king's protector with a suitable horse and wagon to fulfill his special duty was evidently considered an unnecessary expenditure. Whenever Umberto left the palace, Galeazzi was obliged to hire a horse and buggy in the Piazza Quirinale, but the old nags belonging to the local cab drivers could not keep pace with the magnificent French steeds that pulled the royal carriage along at a fast trot. Galeazzi's missions had exhausted so many horses—one even dropped dead from overexertion—that Roman cab drivers considered him their nemesis and often refused their services. On the morning of the suspected attack, Galeazzi made a special plea to the municipal guards for a reliable horse, but the beast they provided was no faster than the usual specimens he hired. When Umberto was set upon by his assailant, Galeazzi and his tired horse were staggering along two hundred meters behind the royal carriage. Nor were the *carabinieri* assigned to patrol the route near the scene at the critical moment. To cover up the near disaster, the two *carabinieri* who overtook the assailant were awarded gold watches for their heroism.[3]

Umberto's failed assassin was a twenty-five-year-old blacksmith and iron-monger named Pietro Acciarito. His father, Camillo, a faithful monarchist of peasant stock, could never find steady employment in his hometown of Artena, and so in 1888 he transferred his wife and three sons to Rome where he toiled at menial jobs before finding steady work as a concierge. The collapse of Rome's housing construction boom in 1887 seriously depressed the capital's economy, limiting employment possibilities for migrants such as the young Acciarito, whose prospects were already limited by his lack of education and meager intelligence. Despite the dire poverty of Rome's working classes, the Italian government provided nothing by way of unemployment insurance, food relief, or any other form of succor. Such willful neglect led directly to the violent rioting of Rome's unemployed in the Piazza Santa Croce di Gerusalemme on May 1 of that year.[4]

Whether Acciarito participated in the rioting is unknown, but he undoubtedly shared the hostility toward the authorities and upper classes that was widespread and intense among Rome's poor and unemployed. His disposition toward authority did not improve when he was arrested in 1893 for carrying a "dangerous weapon"—an awl. He was released without penalty because the "awl" was actually an ordinary compass he used while briefly attending a school for design. Not even the police chief could later explain the circumstances of this ludicrous incident. Fortunately the arrest was not recorded and did not preclude his finding work as a blacksmith with the Bank of Naples. His employment at the bank lasted until 1895, when he was hospitalized for several months with tuberculosis. Upon returning to his job, Acciarito found that conditions at the bank had deteriorated dramatically. The Bank of Naples in 1895 was immersed in numerous irregularities, and as a cost-saving measure hired outside contractors to replace its employees. Corrupt, like Italy's entire banking system, the contractors padded their pockets by exploiting their workers, reducing wages and withholding payment for many months. After complaining angrily about nonpayment of wages, Acciarito was discharged in November 1896, rehired, and permanently dismissed by his boss ("my first assassin") in February 1897.[5]

At this juncture, Acciarito rented a small blacksmith shop at No. 27 Via Machiavelli but became disillusioned and depressed when he failed to attract customers in this time of economic crisis. Acciarito grew even more frustrated because his poverty prevented his marrying Pasqua Venaruba, a poor young woman who had become his lover the previous summer. Despondent to the point of psychological breakdown, Acciarito may have contemplated suicide as he indicated to friends; but had he chosen that solution to his problems, he would have done so (he later claimed) in a manner benefiting the working class—by sending a message to Italy's rulers: "the government must provide for the poor people!"[6]

A few days prior to his *attentat*, Acciarito closed his shop and sold his tools and harnesses, a sign that he had given up hope for the future. For several days, neighborhood acquaintances had observed Acciarito in a highly agitated state and heard him mutter that he intended to kill a big shot ("*capocione*") or himself. Acciarito's behavior prompted his father to report him to the police for his own protection. Orders for Acciarito's arrest were issued, but he could not be found; he apparently spent the night in a hotel near the train station or hid outdoors after friends told him the police were seeking his arrest. Alarmed by this threat, the police chief of Rome informed all the officials involved with ensuring His Majesty's safety to be on the alert. Nevertheless, by the afternoon of April 22, 1897, Acciarito was still free and determined to kill the king.[7]

Ironically, Acciarito's failed attempt proved a godsend for King Umberto and the House of Savoy, whose popularity and prestige were at an all-time low in the wake of Italy's humiliating defeat in Ethiopia the previous year. Telegrams congratulating the king on his escape poured into the Quirinale, and the piazzas overflowed (at least according to police reports) with grateful subjects organized by monarchists to celebrate Umberto's good fortune. Even the Vatican, despite its official estrangement from the Italian state, permitted the *Te Deum*, thanking God for saving the monarch from an assassin's blade, to resound throughout the churches of Rome.[8]

Behind closed doors, government officials were focusing on how best to exploit Acciarito's failed *attentat* for the benefit of the monarchy, government, and propertied classes. Domenico Farini, the president of the senate, conferring with Prime Minister Rudinì the day after the *attentat*, proposed the strategy the government should pursue: "belief in the existence of a plot would be an excellent means to impel this weak society to defend itself."[9] The menace from which the "weak society" needed defending was the anarchists. As usual, anarchists would furnish the pretext to suppress the threatening tide of popular discontent and agitation now raging across the land.[10] Thus a nefarious and widespread "anarchist plot" had to be invented.

Engendering fear of an anarchist plot would have been much easier if Acciarito had been a terrifying terrorist like French anarchists Ravachol or Henry or, better yet, if his "accomplices" belonged to a revolutionary conspiracy proven to be national or international in scope. But Acciarito was a pathetic figure, hardly the ferocious nemesis of bourgeois nightmares, and the handful of Roman workers soon designated as his "accomplices" were no more threatening than he. As it happened, Acciarito's initial interrogation yielded nothing to substantiate the authorities' plot thesis. He did not identify himself as an anarchist, denied affiliation with any anarchist group, and made no statements that would have suggested familiarity with anarchist doctrines. The only newspapers he admitted reading were *Il Messagero, Avanti!, L'Asino,* and *La Tribuna*—none of which was anarchist. He insisted that he had acted alone, out of anger and frustration. Asked his occupation, he spat out the word that in his own mind defined his existence: "*Affamato!*" (Starved).[11] His "occupation," he explained, had motivated him to kill the king:

> I mean that those who command make us literally starve to death, and I am indeed one of those who suffer continuously from hunger. . . . Hunger, my friends, is a bad counselor when you see yourself abandoned by everyone. . . . I saw many carriages, many rich and happy people enjoying a splendid day at the races, where the king donated 24,000 lira for the winning horse, while so many unfortunates are dying from lack of food. . . . I lost my head and did what I did."[12]

Acciarito's contact with the movement was primarily through friendships with neighborhood anarchists. In 1890, he had been befriended by Cherubino Trenta, an anarchist who worked on the editorial staff of the socialist daily *Avanti!* in Rome. In fact, at the time of his *attentat,* police initially believed Acciarito's allegiance was to the socialists. Only six months before his *attentat* did he begin to associate with several members of the Gruppo la Rivendicazione in the Esquilino neighborhood, whose members included some of Rome's best-known militants: Ernesto Diotallevi, Aristide Ceccarelli, Ettore Sottovia, Pietro Colabona, Federico Gudini, and others. His activities with them were more social than political, frequenting taverns and singing anarchist songs. Acciarito's "contribution" to the movement consisted merely in his signing an abstentionist manifesto written and circulated by Malatesta, together with nineteen neighborhood anarchists.[13] Acciarito's "comrades," however, were unimpressed with the extent of his involvement, often chiding him for devoting more time to his girlfriend than the movement. And when Acciarito boasted to them that he intended to kill a "big shot," they concluded he was mentally ill and discouraged him from taking such action.[14]

The anarchists understood from the outset that Acciarito was not a *giustiziere* in the mold of Paolo Lega and Sante Caserio. They had made inquiries outside Rome about his identity as quickly as the police and concluded he was not one of their own. Malatesta's group in Ancona expressed the general consensus among comrades: "the act was the work of a poor wretch, exasperated by misery, who had no relations with any party."[15] Even *L'Avvenire Sociale,* the individualist anarchist newspaper in Messina, which generally condoned individual acts of political violence, concluded that "political opinions are extraneous to this deed; today [the perpetrator] is an irresponsible wretch."[16] The veteran anarchist Galileo Palla, still in *domicilio coatto* for his role in the May Day riot in Rome in 1891, wrote, "I am glad this act was done by an irresponsible person rather than an anarchist, because this way everyone can better understand once and for all that there is no cause without effect, and there can well be rebels who do not belong to any party."[17]

To the chagrin of Farini, Rudinì, and other plot seekers, the Stefani News Agency, the information source for so many bourgeois newspapers, had claimed Acciarito did not have accomplices.[18] Nor was much credence being given to official reports regarding the political nature of the crime. Italy's most prestigious newspaper, Milan's *Corriere della Sera*, wrote, "Pietro Acciarito is a product of his environment; he is a phenomenon of the economic moment. The interrogation perhaps exaggerated the political character of the attentat. We prefer to consider it a mark of the moral situation. The interrogation [of Acciarito] . . . quickly made clear, like a thunderbolt, the state of the soul of the proletariat."[19]

Despite the doubts expressed by conservative elements like the Milan daily, the authorities remained committed to the conviction that Acciarito's *attentat* had been the result of an anarchist plot; and animated by this falsehood, the machinery of state repression went immediately into action, targeting the movement's principal center of activity, Ancona, where Malatesta was known to be operating in secret. For the time being, the wily Malatesta eluded capture, but his closest associates—Cesare Agostinelli, Emidio Recchioni, Ruggero Recchi, Angelo Pieri, and Benedetto Faccetti—all of whom served on the editorial staff of his newspaper, *L'Agitazione*, were arrested immediately after the *attentat* and sent to *domicilio coatto*.[20]

The Roman police, zealous in their determination to find accomplices, raided scores of private residences and detained dozens of anarchists, socialists, and republicans, especially those living in Acciarito's Esquilino neighborhood. One man netted in the dragnet, a republican named Romeo Frezzi, aroused particular suspicion because found among his possessions was a photograph of neighborhood friends, one of whom was Acciarito. Held incommunicado in San Michele prison, Frezzi was found dead five days later, beaten to death by guards determined to extract a confession. Felice Cavallotti, the radical party leader, declared in the Chamber of Deputies that Frezzi was a symbol of innocence persecuted by an oppressive regime determined to crush the power of the people. Cavallotti's assessment was widely shared, and protest demonstrations led by leftist elements erupted in cities throughout Italy. Rudinì's first instinct was to prohibit the demonstrations, but popular support for a public funeral honoring Frezzi was so overwhelming that the prime minister decided to permit the procession provided that it remained nonviolent. Rudinì's concession infuriated royalists and conservatives who wanted the demonstrations suppressed. Courtiers observed Queen Margherita in a state of hysterical rage at the thought of the Italian people honoring Frezzi rather than her husband. The ubiquitous Farini lamented to Urbano Rattazzi, the minister of the Royal House: "This is how revolutions begin."[21]

The Frezzi scandal virtually nullified the recent surge of support for King Umberto. Therefore, in hope of shifting public attention back to the assassination plot hatched by the nefarious anarchists, Acciarito was rushed to trial at the Rome Court of Assizes on May 22, 1897. A guilty verdict was a foregone conclusion. The primary objective of the famous chief prosecutor, Eugenio Forni, was to establish that Acciarito's *attentat* was a political crime, one planned and executed with accomplices, and not a consequence of Italy's oppressive poverty. But the show trial failed to realize the government's purposes. Once again, Acciarito denied having accomplices. Indeed, no matter how hard the prosecutor sought to elicit evidence of an anarchist plot, his testimony underscored the fact that the motivational factors responsible for his *attentat* were precisely the economic and social travails besetting the nation, which the authorities hoped to obscure. He declared as follows:

> I committed it [the assassination attempt] because of poverty, like one who commits suicide because of poverty. . . . Responsibility for the poverty in which the workers live belongs to the bourgeois classes who starve the workers. The working people are dying of hunger while millions are spent on Africa and on horse races. These things cause bad blood. The king is the father of the country; therefore, when the country is in poverty the father of the country must provide. . . . We want work, we youths have need of work, but instead we poor wretches are dying of hunger. . . .
>
> I know that I hate all the idle rich. I know that after working hard I was compensated with hunger and treated like a criminal. I did not know if I should kill the King, the Pope, or someone else. I was incredibly enraged; I saw the King and struck at him to vent my feelings.[22]

On May 23, 1897, the jurors took less than five minutes to find Acciarito guilty without mitigating circumstances. He was sentenced to *ergastolo*—life imprisonment; the first seven years were to be served in solitary confinement.[23]

The failure of Acciarito's trial to expose any accomplices did not dissuade the authorities from persisting with their goal of establishing the attempt against King Umberto's life as the work of an anarchist plot. On the contrary, police and administrative officials, like the police chief and prefect of

Rome, who originally had discounted the plot theory,[24] were now in lockstep with the government's efforts to invent an anarchist conspiracy, furnishing whatever information top officials wished to hear. Thus, the police chief of Rome reported to the chief prosecutor of the Court of Appeals on July 24, 1897, that "Acciarito's action was the consequence of a plot, of which he was the designated instrument chosen by lot, or the work of a fanatic whose fervor was studiously excited, sinisterly and tenaciously guided and supported, by others."[25] Information provided by the usual "confidential" and "reliable" sources convinced the police chief "not only of the existence of a plot in Rome, but that it was the desired outcome predetermined by the tactical system of the [anarchist] party." The "head of the plot in Rome was Acciarito's friend, Cherubino Trenta." But orders for the *attentat* originated from the "Commission of the [anarchist] party based in Ancona under the organizing intellect and driving spirit of Enrico [sic] Malatesta."[26] This once again showed how, in the fevered brains of the Italian police, all anarchist conspiracies led back to Malatesta.

The Roman police chief had competition from other police chiefs, prefects, and even Italian consular authorities abroad, each demonstrating their devotion and efficiency by providing the names of Acciarito's accomplices. The consul general in Geneva, for example, furnished Rudinì (he was interior minister as well as prime minister) with the names of seventeen anarchists in Rome who were coconspirators, "proof" residing in the fact that they, together with Acciarito, had signed an abstentionist manifesto written by Malatesta.[27] Rome's police chief was content to select eight among the local movement's most prominent militants: Aristide Ceccarelli, Ernesto Diotallevi, Cherubino Trenta, Pietro Colabona, Federico Gudini, Ettore Sottovia, Umberto Farina, and Ettore Varagnolo. Evidence linking these anarchists to the *attentat* was nonexistent. Diotallevi, for example, was in Greece fighting the Turks when the deed occurred. Such discrepancies did not deter the authorities from indicting him and his comrades.[28]

Considering that the crown and the highest circles of government were adamantly committed to establishing the existence of an anarchist conspiracy, the Roman judiciary might well have yielded to pressure from above and railroaded the anarchists in custody. Yet to the chagrin of the government and police officials responsible for fabricating a plot, the indictment section of the Court of Appeals in Rome ruled on November 4, 1897, that sufficient evidence was lacking to prosecute any of the eight anarchists suspected of complicity in the *attentat*, each of whom already had spent five months in preventive detention.[29] But the mission to prove Acciarito's *attentat* as the result of an anarchist conspiracy was not abandoned. To secure a conviction of his "accomplices," the prison authorities soon obtained a confession from Acciarito.

Anarchists subscribed to their own code of *omertà* ("silence"), and so implicating comrades in any sort of illegal act was considered unconscionable. But Acciarito was not a militant anarchist, and certainly not a man to endure martyrdom with stoic fortitude. During the early weeks of his confinement in Santo Stefano prison, he still clung to the delusion that he might someday walk through the gates a free man: "I am young," he wrote to his father, "the years pass and things happen daily. I have the hope that I will not leave my bones in this tomb."[30] His optimism quickly lapsed into depression as the reality of his situation finally penetrated and the dreadful conditions of his incarceration began to take their toll. "At first my cell was dark and without air, and I was treated like a dog. The water was filled with vermin and the soup stank. I thought I would die like a dog," he later related.[31] Soon it became apparent to his jailors that this extremely gullible and self-centered young fellow, faced with his ultimate demise in a hellish dungeon, might eventually pay the required price for liberation—the betrayal of his friends.

Toward that end, prison authorities—with the full knowledge and encouragement of Prime Minister Rudinì and his successor Luigi Pelloux—embarked upon a truly devious subterfuge to prove that an anarchist plot had been responsible for Acciarito's assassination attempt. Under direct orders from Martino Beltrani-Scalia, director general of prisons, to check on Acciarito in his dungeon confines, Inspector Alessandro Doria, attached to the General Direction of Prison, met with the famous prisoner on July 13, 1897, and after some initial small talk, turned the subject to Acciarito's "accomplices." When informed that his friends had been arrested, Acciarito revealed the bitterness and resentment that would become so easily exploited by the authorities. Doria related to the police chief of Rome that Acciarito "never affirmed their innocence; on the contrary, he indicated that he was pleased that they should suffer as he was suffering."[32] After the interview, Doria reported to his superiors that "a few more months in the dungeon of Santo Stefano will convince Acciarito to return to the new path on which he had already started in moments of true and profound emotion."[33] For now, however, no inducements to confess were offered the prisoner. Doria and Beltrani-Scalia were both confident that "solitude and reflection will perhaps awaken in his conscience remorse for the crime he committed, and these sentiments will counsel him to make spontaneous revelations in the interests of justice."[34]

Solitude and reflection failed to evoke a crisis of Acciarito's conscience, much less elicit the names of accomplices. Evidently on the order of Rudinì (who later denied knowledge of the intrigue), Beltrani-Scalia decided that a new approach to extracting a confession had to be conceived, and on Doria's recommendation, the prison director selected an official expertly qualified to undertake this "special and delicate . . . mission of persuasion"—Alfredo Angelelli, the vice director general of prisons in Catanzaro.[35] Angelelli could have been the prototype for Puccini's "Baron Scarpia," the unscrupulous gendarme who took sadistic pleasure in his work. Known for his devotion to the House of Savoy and professional zeal, Angelelli boasted that he would "place anarchy at the feet of the throne." In the process, he and his superiors in government would disgrace the very institution they sought to safeguard.[36]

Whether Angelelli or Doria masterminded the new plan to extract a confession was never determined; each would later accuse the other of authorship. Not that it mattered. Upon assuming command of Santo Stefano on August 18, 1898, Angelelli moved patiently and deliberately, manipulating Acciarito with consummate skill. He was too shrewd to arouse the prisoner's suspicion by prematurely offering him a pardon in exchange for a confession. First, the wretched conditions that Acciarito had endured under continuous protest improved markedly overnight. Next, Angelelli placed another prisoner serving a life sentence, Andrea Petito, in a cell next to Acciarito's so they might communicate. Petito's assignment was to pose as an anarchist, gain Acciarito's confidence, encourage him to confess, and transmit the information to Angelelli, which he did in some fifty letters. Furthermore, to verify the "accuracy" of Petito's reports, several prison guards were strategically located to overhear what passed between Acciarito and his false comrade.[37]

Acciarito was brought to Angelelli's office some eighty times starting in late August 1898. During conversations lasting four or five hours, the prison director nourished his "plant" (his term) with ample quantities of wine, hoping that the ancient aphorism—*in vino veritas*—would prove true. He eventually discovered that compassion was a more potent fertilizer for the soil he wished to cultivate than alcohol, and he began to profess paternal affection for Acciarito and the desire for his "moral regeneration." At the same time, like holding a bone before a hungry dog, Angelelli steadily insinuated that Acciarito stood a "98 out of 100" chance of receiving a pardon from his merciful king. However, as Umberto could not grant a pardon unless he knew the full extent of the crime, Acciarito would have to name his accomplices. And to make the deception even more palatable, Angelelli added that because the government already knew the identity of his accomplices, Acciarito could obtain a pardon for them as well by revealing their names in a personal petition to His Majesty. Acciarito still provided no names.[38]

Since the plant had not borne fruit, prison officials devised a new and utterly cruel stratagem by mid-November 1898—convince Acciarito that his lover, Pasqua Venaruba, had given birth to a son. The idea was instilled in his credulous brain by the prisoner Petito on orders from Angelelli, who later attributed authorship of the stratagem to Inspector Doria.[39] Belief that he had fathered a son became an obsession for Acciarito, as did his fear, instilled by Petito, that the boy would be killed unless he cooperated by naming accomplices.[40] Encouraged by Acciarito's tormented state of mind, Angelelli reported to Doria that "the blackbird will sing."[41] Having "lost his head over the boy," Acciarito informed Angelelli that he wished to write a letter to Pasqua to learn more about his son's welfare. Realizing that the non-existent child was the key to Acciarito's soul and the long sought confession, Angelelli was delighted to grant the prisoner's request, even demonstrating his paternalistic concern by providing stamps to ensure that Pasqua's reply reached Santo Stefano without delay.[42]

Acciarito's letter was immediately forwarded to the new director general of prisons, Giuseppe Canevelli, who had been informed of Angelelli's mission upon succeeding Beltrani-Scalia in July 1898. He was pleased to receive a report from Angelelli, indicating that "the noted person had fallen into the trap."[43] Beltrani-Scalia, notified of the positive turn of events, urged Canevelli "to strike while the iron is hot" and furnished him with precise instructions for the writing of a fake letter of response from Pasqua, confirming the existence of Acciarito's son and lamenting their terrible condition. Should the spurious letter not suffice, Angelelli had recommended an even more diabolical ruse—compel Pasqua to visit Santo Stefano with a male child, the sight of which would drive Acciarito crazy with love and convince him finally to confess in hope of a pardon. Inspector Doria sanctioned the ploy.[44]

Her involvement proved unnecessary. The spurious letter—composed in draft form by Petito, corrected and embellished by Angelelli, and penned by the guard Laganà—was forwarded to Canevelli and Doria for approval, and then passed along to the director general of public security, Francesco Leonardi, who sent it to Santo Stefano by registered mail on November 29, 1898. Arriving the next day, the letter was read to Acciarito by Angelelli in the presence of Petito and several guards, all of whom were privy to the deception and feigned empathy with a waterfall of tears.[45] The letter read in part

> I find myself in great poverty with your child [Pietrino] to support. Oh, adored Pietro, if you only knew of my suffering and the suffering of your child. I do not have enough milk to feed him. From your friends, for whose cause you

are sacrificed, I have never received any help; none of them ever come to see me, yet they know you have this son who would have his bread and your assistance if you were free. . . . If you revealed their names they would perhaps be doomed and driven out by their comrades, while you would be able to see your son and not remain for eternity at the bottom of a prison from which you exit only to go to the cemetery.

How happy we would be if you were now free. Each morning you would be the first to kiss his pure face, and in the evening after work, he would run to greet you, and you would take him in your arms and play with him on your knee. On Sunday you would take him outside the city, while now we are grieving and miserable. . . . I go almost crazy with the thought that soon I will have to lose this jewel of our love, the only memory I have of you, because he is emaciated and malnourished. . . . We are abandoned by everyone. They all think of themselves, while you are in the depth of a prison.[46]

When provided with a draft of the letter, Leonardi decided it was unnecessary that the version intended for Acciarito be written in a woman's hand, because Pasqua was illiterate.[47] The fact that she could not have written the letter by herself, however, did not arouse Acciarito's suspicion. Instead, the remarkably naive prisoner was emotionally devastated by the letter: "I lost all peace, could no longer sleep, and dreamed only of my son."[48] He soon asked that the child be brought to Santo Stefano, but Angelelli refused to grant the request unless Acciarito cooperated.[49] Now completely malleable, Acciarito signed a petition on December 2, 1898, beseeching a pardon from King Umberto. Affixed to the document were the names of two "accomplices," Diotallevi and Ceccarelli, against whom his resentment had been brewing for months, because—as Angelelli repeatedly reminded him—they were at liberty while he was in prison. Several weeks later, having received no response from His Majesty, Acciarito signed a second petition, to which he added the names of Colabona, Gudini, and Trenta. Such was the nature of Acciarito's "confession."[50]

That Acciarito had been deceived by this ruse attested not only to the desperate state to which he had been reduced but to his limited intelligence and casual association with the anarchist movement and its doctrines. Even after his second petition produced no pardon, Acciarito continued to delude himself and feed false information to the authorities concerning his friends and "their part" in the *attentat*.[51] No experienced anarchist would have been duped into believing the king would pardon anyone guilty of attempted regicide. And for their part, the authorities—from King Umberto down to Inspector Angelelli—would never for an instant have seriously entertained granting Acciarito a pardon, no matter how many names he designated as accomplices. This foolish wretch was just another tool in the state's arsenal of repression, a reality he still had to learn.

The trial of Acciarito's alleged accomplices began on June 21, 1899, in the Rome Court of Appeals. Their number had been reduced from eight to five: Aristide Ceccarelli, Ernesto Diotallevi, Pietro Colabona, Federico Gudini, Cherubino Trenta, the last in absentia. Ceccarelli, a twenty-seven-year-old tinsmith who had already spent two years in *domicilio coatto*, and Diotallevo, a twenty-three-year-old carpenter, were the two most important anarchists in Rome, now that Pietro Calcagno had taken refuge in London. Conviction of these two militants would deal a severe blow to the local movement, and serve as well the political purposes of the crown and the government, still seeking pretexts to continue the repression of the Left, which had escalated so dramatically after the bloody *Fatti di Maggio* in Milan the previous year (see chapter 6).

Nothing went according to plan. Ceccarelli and Diotallevi were the first defendants to be interrogated. Both men acknowledged that on several occasions during the weeks preceding the *attentat* Acciarito had expressed a desire to commit some act of violence, preferably the assassination of King Umberto. They insisted that they had done their utmost to dissuade him from attempting such a deed, as it would lead only to disastrous consequences for the anarchist movement. They emphatically denied any involvement with the *attentat*. Colabona and Gudini likewise proclaimed their innocence, admitting only that they were with Acciarito on the morning of April 22, having come to warn him that the police were searching for him.[52]

The prosecution hoped the key to convicting these "accomplices" was Acciarito himself. Brought to Rome from Santo Stefano to testify, Acciarito was immediately queried by the president of the court about the motives that had driven him to commit his *attentat*. His response once again unveiled the fundamental cause of his action, in his own words: "continuous poverty and unemployment."[53] Asked to comment on the testimony of Ceccarelli and Diotallevi, Acciarito—as previously instructed by Angelelli—claimed that the two anarchists were his principal associates in the crime: "Since hunger compelled us to start a revolution, we thought to avoid a great slaughter by assassinating the king. . . . I was to commit the attentat and Diotallevi was to provide me with the means."[54] Against Colabona and Gudini, Acciarito testified with some reluctance, and in explaining why, made a revelation that opened the door for the defense to counterattack: "I was compelled to accuse you Colabona and Gudini. But here we are dealing with a request for a pardon from His Majesty [so] it is necessary to be sincere. I am sorry to have accused you, Colabona, because you are a poor wretch, and you, Gudini, are a boy."[55]

Mention of the petition for a royal pardon set into motion the collapse of the prosecution's entire case. Asked by Defense Counselor Di Benedetto if he had left the names of his accomplices blank, Acciarito revealed that Inspector Angelelli had filled them in. Di Benedetto then posed a question that left the courtroom dumbfounded: "Are you convinced, Acciarito, that you have a son?" "I believe so," he responded in total honesty. Shifting back to the issue of the petitions, Counselor Lembo asked Acciarito if he hoped for a pardon. "And why should I not hope?" he replied. "Is it true that the director [of Santo Stefano] promised you a pardon after the condemnation of your accomplices?" Lembo continued. Still not realizing that he had been lured into a trap, Acciarito responded: "It was told to me that His Majesty could not pardon if he did not know the crime first." Counselor Ciraolo delivered the finishing blow: "In the name of the defense and in the interests of justice, I call upon the president [of the court] to take the blindfold off of Acciarito and inform him that it is not true that he has a son." Acciarito leaped to his feet in hysterics, crying out: "It is truly barbarous if I have been made to believe that I have a son that does not exist. Not only did they make me believe I had a son, but I received a letter from [Pasqua] at home." Once Acciarito mentioned the spurious letter from Pasqua, the prosecution could not block the defense lawyers' demand that the letter be presented and entered into the record as evidence. Audible gasps and expressions of outrage and dismay emanated from the audience and jurors as the letter was read aloud.[56] Seizing the occasion, the defense attorneys demanded to know why Chief Prosecutor Eugenio Tofano had failed to voice any protest against "this system of torture in our prisons that is called investigation."[57] An honest answer from Tofano would have been self-incriminating, for when he and Judge Sebastiano Caprino conducted the judiciary investigation that resulted in the indictment of the anarchists, the two officers of the court already knew about the forged letter and Acciarito's subsequent compliance. But this flagrant irregularity did not discourage them from ordering the trial of his "accomplices." In fact, Caprino had been shown a copy of "Pasqua's" letter by Angelelli but omitted it from the official documents attached to the trial proceedings, considering it extraneous to the case.[58]

Attention focused next on the master manipulator, Angelelli. The director of Santo Stefano acknowledged that Pasqua's letter was a forgery but denied authorship. Further interrogation revealed the extent of Angelelli's machinations despite his evasive answers, outright lies, and attempts to place the burden of blame on the prisoner Petito. The defense attorneys demanded that Angelelli be charged with having abused the powers of his office to the detriment of the prisoner in Santo Stefano. But Chief Prosecutor Tofano had no interest in calling Acciarito's persecutor to account. Tofano's concern at the Rome trial was "justice," which required that he demonstrate the existence of a plot. To accomplish that end, Tofano called Pasqua Venaruba to testify, knowing full well that the young woman was still under the illusion that co-operation with the authorities might help her man. When Pasqua appeared in the witness box, Acciarito went wild, jumping out of the prisoner's dock in an attempt to embrace her, but he was thwarted by his guards. Pasqua's testimony, however, did nothing to strengthen the prosecution's case. The next few sessions were dominated by battles between the defense attorneys and the chief prosecutor over procedural matters, which were invariably decided in favor of the latter. Having finally reached the limits of their frustration, the defense attorneys threw down their robes and stormed out of the courtroom in protest. The court appointed a new team of lawyers to conduct the defense, but they refused to proceed, arguing that they did not know the details of the case. With the proceedings at an impasse, the chief judge suspended the trial on July 3 and ordered its resumption somewhere other than Rome.[59]

Exposure of the devious methods employed by Angelelli and his minions to manipulate Acciarito generated outrage even among conservative elements outside government. There were still some who believed in the sanctity of the judicial process. The *Corriere della Sera* declared, "the system adopted and exposed by the current trial in Rome has in its cold, laborious, and refined hypocrisy something repugnant and illegal." Comparing the psychological torture employed to extract a false confession from Acciarito to the methods of the notorious Spanish Grand Inquisitor Torquemada, Italy's most pres-tigious newspaper described the affair as an "atavistic perversion" that "is truly and profoundly deplorable."[60] *La Nazione* of Florence, denouncing "the immoral principle that the end justifies the means," declared that the conduct of the officials involved harkened back to "the obscure times of Philip [II] of Spain."[61]

The damaging publicity generated by the trial prompted the Court of Cas-sation to transfer the proceedings to the small provincial town of Teramo in the Abruzzo, where public scrutiny might be less intense and more credulous jurors available. Proceedings resumed on March 17, 1900, with a new group of attorneys for the defense, including the famous socialist Enrico Ferri. The interrogation of witnesses continued to underscore the inconsistencies and falsehoods in Acciarito's earlier testimony. His new recounting of the details concerning the spurious letter and his appeals for pardon shifted the trial's focus more sharply on the villainy perpetrated by Angelelli and other officials. Acciarito related, "I wanted to ask a pardon for myself alone, because I had faith in His Majesty and did not think that so many schemes had been made to the detriment of myself and others in order to bring half of Italy to trial."[62] He further revealed that Angelelli had wanted him to implicate the noted anarchist attorney and theorist Francesco Saverio Merlino in his crime. When he refused on the grounds that Merlino had nothing to do with the *attentat*, Angelelli responded, "It does not matter; indict him anyway."[63] Under continuing interrogation from defense attorneys, Acciarito eventually repudiated all his previous testimony alleging the complicity of his friends. He admitted that he was the sole perpetrator of the *attentat*. Subsequent testimony from Pasqua, Angelelli, the defendants, and some of Acciarito's acquaintances proved anticlimactic and unrevealing. By the end of the proceedings, it was apparent that the state had failed to produce any real evidence of a plot involving the defendants. Moreover, the damage to the prosecution's case had become irreversible largely as a result of the revelations concerning Angelelli's machinations. In his final summation, the new chief prosecutor, Paletti, sought desperately to counter the image of Angelelli as an archvillain, arguing that "Angelelli should be thanked even for the invention of the baby, if that was capable of touching Acciarito's heart."[64] But the jury believed otherwise and acquitted the defendants of all charges on April 5, 1900.[65]

As the Teramo trial was drawing to a conclusion, Acciarito was reputed to have said, "Now everything has collapsed; I have discovered every deception; I understand full well that the only remaining hope I have is a royal pardon."[66] That Acciarito, at this last stage of the affair, could still entertain the fantasy of a king's pardon only underscored the poor man's amazing naïveté and total ignorance of political reality. After the Teramo trial, Acciarito was returned to a dungeon, not at Santo Stefano, but at Portolongone, the ill-famed prison where the renowned revolutionary Amilcare Cipriani had languished for six years in the 1880s. Upon completion of his term of solitary confinement in 1904, Acciarito was transferred on orders from the ministry of the interior to the asylum for the criminally insane at Montelupo, a not uncommon practice for isolating notorious political prisoners. For once labeled mentally unstable, any embarrassing testimony he might offer in any future legal proceedings could be easily challenged. Acciarito's travail at Montelupo did not end until his death on December 4, 1943.[67]

Although Acciarito acted out of desperation shaped by personal economic destitution, in contrast, Michele Angiolillo's *attentat* displayed the characteristics of the anarchist cosmopolitan *giustiziere*. Like Caserio before him, Angiolillo's assassination of the Spanish prime minister, Antonio Cánovas del Castillo, was a deliberate act directed not simply at a symbol of privilege and exploitation but, in a show of solidarity with foreign comrades, an act of retribution against an individual directly responsible for acts of violence against the innocent.

On June 7, 1896, Corpus Christi Day, Barcelona held its traditional celebration of the Eucharistic sacrament with a long procession snaking its way through the main avenues and streets of the city. At the head of the procession were the archbishop of Barcelona, the new captain-general of Catalonia, Valeriano Weyler y Nicolau (soon to become known as the "Butcher" for his atrocities in Cuba), and other religious and political notables. As the marchers proceeded along the Calle de los Cambios Nuevos, a bomb was hurled from an upper-story window into the procession, killing seven people and wounding forty-five others. What distinguished this bombing from others was the social status of the victims. The bomb did not explode at the head of the procession, where it would have harmed the religious and political elite—logical targets of an anarchist *attentat*—but at the tail end, where the victims were six workers and a soldier. Suspicion immediately focused upon the Brigada Social, a special police unit known for its ruthlessness, which may have executed the bombing in order to justify a new wave of repression against the anarchists. Anarchist leaders Ricardo Mella and José Prat became skeptical of this interpretation, concluding that the perpetrator might have been a misguided anarchist. Several years later, anecdotal evidence related by the journalist Luis Bonafoux implicated a French anarchist named Jean Girault, who escaped from Spain to Argentina after the bombing.[68]

The *agent provocateur* theory continued to be advanced in some quarters, but most anarchists accepted the disquieting likelihood that the perpetrator was one of their own. The true identity of the bomber was irrelevant as far as Spanish authorities were concerned. The Corpus Christi tragedy furnished the ideal pretext to strike against all subversive elements and the ensuing repression constituted the most ferocious one undertaken by Spanish authorities during the fin de siècle. Workers' organizations and newspapers were immediately suppressed, and hundreds of anarchists, republicans, Free Masons, anticlericals, free thinkers, and sympathizers were arrested and incarcerated in the dungeons of the Montjuich, the imposing military fortress overlooking Barcelona's harbor that had been converted into a prison for political subversives and workers. The jailors at Montjuich, led by Lieutenant Portasso, believed their mission was to obtain confessions proving the existence of a vast anarchist conspiracy that plotted the Corpus Christi bombing. Anarchists and other suspects were starved and deprived of sleep for many hours in overcrowded, fetid cells; their limbs were bound tightly with ropes and chains to cause extreme pain; they were also flogged repeatedly with whips and beaten with iron rods. When such measures proved insufficient— or when their sadistic tormentors wanted to entertain themselves—some victims had pieces of wood hammered beneath their fingernails and toenails and then pulled out with pliers. Others had their testicles twisted by wire or slowly crushed, rendering them permanently damaged. Several prisoners died from these tortures; the others inevitably confessed to whatever crimes the authorities claimed they had committed.[69]

The government intended originally to transport—without benefit of trial—three hundred anarchist suspects to Río de Oro, a desolate patch of the western Sahara considered as hellish a place as France's Devil's Island, but abandoned the plan in the face of widespread criticism. Meanwhile, eighty-seven anarchists were brought to trial at Montjuich on December 11, 1896, including the alleged masterminds of the *attentat*: Tomás Ascheri, José Molas, and Antonio Nogués, well-known militants who had nothing to do with the bombing, but confessed to the deed under torture. Their fate was determined by a military tribunal thanks to a new antiterrorist law of September 1896, which applied retroactively to the Corpus Christi affair and gave special powers to the army in cases involving bombs. Trial by military tribunal in Spain virtually guaranteed convictions and draconian sentences because they could act arbitrarily with complete impunity.[70] Knowledge that confessions had been extracted by torture did not trouble them in the least. When the prosecuting officer delivered his final statement, he allegedly declared, "Given the enormity of the crime and the number of the accused, I close my eyes to reason and, despite the lack of proof, consider all of the accused as authors and accomplices."[71]

By now, word of the atrocities committed at Montjuich was circulating throughout Spain and the rest of Europe as newspapers of every political persuasion reported the gruesome details. Letters smuggled out of Montjuich were often written by several of the movement's most important figures, such as Fernando Tarrida del Mármol, Anselmo Lorenzo, and Federico Urales, and therefore given total credence. Tarrida was the scion of a renowned family in Barcelona and director of the Polytechnic Academy. Family connections secured Tarrida early release, enabling him to write articles reprinted in France and England and to publish his famous book, *Les inquisiteurs d'Espagne* which graphically described the infamies committed at Montjuich. Meanwhile, the noted French journalist Henri Rochefort published photographs of the mutilated bodies in his newspaper *L'Intransigeant*, together with other revealing documents and Ascheri's letter to his mother describing the tortures he had endured. The letter was quickly reprinted in other newspapers, including the anarchist *La Scintilla* of Messina.[72] But Rochefort went even further, parading one of the victims naked in the streets of Paris so the handiwork of the *Brigada Social* could be directly observed. The most impressive protest demonstration, organized by the Spanish Atrocities Committee, took place on May 30, 1897, in London's Trafalgar Square, where around one thousand people gathered to hear speeches from anarchists, socialists, and republicans, members of the Independent Labour Party and Fabian Society, and even from some victims of Montjuich.[73]

As the scandal and protest campaigns increased in scope and intensity, the Spanish government headed by Prime Minister Cánovas del Castillo decided to show "mercy" to those convicted of the Corpus Christi bombing. Although the prosecutor had demanded death sentences for twenty-eight anarchists, only five were ultimately executed by firing squad in the courtyard of Montjuich on May 4, 1897: Tomás Ascheri, José Molas, Antonio Nogués, Juan Alsin, and Luis Más. The remaining anarchists were condemned to sentences ranging from eight to twenty years at hard labor. Eleven were acquitted, only to be sent to Spain's penal colony in Río de Oro. Of the remaining three hundred anarchists arrested within days of the bombing, some eighty were expelled from Spain, the majority taking refuge in London.[74]

A crystal ball was not required to predict that the barbarities inflicted upon Spanish anarchists at Montjuich would be avenged. The logical target was Cánovas del Castillo, the prime minister who presided over the state's terror campaign against the anarchists. The barbarities inflicted at Montjuich were merely the last in a long list of practices and policies that earned Cánovas the enmity of the entire Left. An opponent of the first Spanish Republic (1873–74), Cánovas had been instrumental in the restoration of the Bourbons. As head of the Conservative Party, he opposed democracy, religious freedom, and free thought. His tenure as prime minister coincided with the final collapse of Spain's empire, and in his vain effort to maintain control of Cuba and the Philippines, Cánovas ordered the brutal campaigns that attempted to suppress the national insurgencies in both colonies. Therefore, as Henri Rochefort wrote, "if ever a man ought to have expected to find someday some bullets shot into his head or body, that man was Cánovas."[75]

The anticipated assassination of Cánovas del Castillo occurred on August 8, 1897, by the twenty-six-year-old Italian anarchist Michele Angiolillo. Born in Foggia (Puglia), Angiolillo was the only Italian anarchist avenger of the 1890s whose family roots were petit-bourgeois, albeit of modest means. His father Giacomo, a man of liberal principles, was a printer by profession. His mother Maria, a devout Catholic, enrolled "Lilio" in a seminary at age six or seven, with the intent of making him a priest. Despite blandishments and punishment, Angiolillo proved a recalcitrant novice and eventually continued his education at an *istituto tecnico*. His childhood friend, the individualist anarchist Roberto D'Angiò, described the adolescent Angiolillo as tall and good-looking, mild-mannered, and even-tempered. Like Caserio, he seemed an unlikely candidate for an assassination. On reaching his eighteenth year, he enrolled at the University of Naples, where he regularly attended the lectures of the republican philosopher Giovanni Bovio. He may also have read the anarchist Proudhon at this time, but his political orientation was republican, and in 1891 he joined and became secretary of the Aurelio Saffi society in Foggia, so named in honor of the Triumvir of the Roman Republic of 1849. Self-conscious and reserved, Angiolillo rarely spoke at meetings but developed excellent writing skills, as his private letters and manifestos reveal. One such manifesto protested Italy's celebration of "Venti Settembre," the day the Italian army seized Rome from Pope Pius IX on September 20, 1870:

> No, people! Rome, the true Rome has not been seized; it is still not free; it is in the hands of false preachers of liberty and justice who serve themselves on your back and on the bodies of your brother victims to ascend the throne of an autocracy that they have deposed in order to install themselves in its place, changing only the system and leading always to the same end.
>
> People, awake! We need another 20 September that will be true; a 20 September that will destroy government and property and transform the world into a single country.[76]

Prior to his conversion, during the many political discussions between him and his volatile anarchist friend Roberto D'Angiò, the latter always advocated violent revolution, while Angiolillo invariably supported a peaceful and evolutionary approach to the social question. His attitude would change dramatically in 1892 once he entered military service in the army, the institution responsible for the creation of so many Italian anarchists. Based in Naples, Angiolillo served for six months as an officer cadet but was demoted to ordinary soldier when the army learned of his radical persuasion. One version holds that his difficulties began when he helped organize a meeting for the radical deputy Matteo Imbriani; another maintains that he was unjustly blamed for an article mocking Queen Margherita. Whatever his offense, Angiolillo was assigned to a disciplinary company based in Parma and then Capua for the next year and a half. As a result of the harsh treatment meted out to "disciplinary" cases, together with his association with anarchists and other radicals compelled to serve, Angiolillo emerged from the army a convinced anarchist in 1894.[77]

After returning briefly to Foggia to regain his health (exhaustion, weight loss, and untreated illness were commonplace in disciplinary units), Angiolillo resumed his studies at the University of Naples but was obliged to withdraw because of his family's financial problems. Back in Foggia, Angiolillo found employment at a print shop and lost no time before plunging into anarchist activities—and into trouble. On the occasion of the general elections of 1895, as a gesture of protest against Crispi's exceptional laws, Angiolillo edited a manifesto supporting the candidacy of Nicola Barbato, one of the imprisoned socialist leaders of the Sicilian Fasci dei Lavoratori. Under the same legislation, Angiolillo's manifesto violated the new press law, resulting in his arrest and indictment for "inciting hatred between the classes," a charge the authorities regularly employed to suppress anarchist literature. Provisionally released on July 27, 1895, Angiolillo experienced another encounter with the state a few weeks later when he accompanied a female relative to the courthouse in the nearby town of Lucera on a matter pertaining to an inheritance. Although the issue was extraneous to politics, the local prosecutor, who knew Angiolillo because of his Barbato manifesto, intervened in the case for no other purpose than to insult and denigrate him. The prosecutor then ordered Angiolillo and his relative from the court without addressing the matter for which she had sought redress. Angiolillo responded to this abusive treatment on August 31, 1895, with a letter to the ministry of justice, denouncing the prosecutor's behavior in scathing terms.[78] He understood, however, that this gesture of defiance had compounded his offense and had sealed his fate; therefore, to escape the punishment he knew would result, Angiolillo took advantage of the provisional liberty granted to him after his arrest for the Barbato manifesto to go into exile in September 1895. He was subsequently convicted in absentia to eighteen months imprisonment and three years in *domicilio coatto* for his two offenses.[79]

Angiolillo's life in exile typified that of most anarchists on the run. He had extreme difficulty finding employment, was always in need of money, and suffered constant harassment from police. The result was a peripatetic existence, condemned to expulsion from one country after another because of his political beliefs, joblessness, and lack of proper papers. The first stop on Angiolillo's odyssey was Marseilles, where he remained for two months before settling in Barcelona. He was aided by Italian and Spanish comrades in the Catalan capital and became active in their circles. His years as a student had taught him neither a profession nor a trade, but he eventually found work in the print shop of Ciencia Social. His situation remained precarious, however, as his presence in Barcelona was known to both Spanish and Italian authorities. After Cánovas's government launched its campaign to crush the anarchists in the wake of the Corpus Christi bombing, Angiolillo wisely decided that he, like any anarchist, was vulnerable to arrest as an "accomplice." He left

Barcelona in August or September 1896. The Italian government hoped he would return to Italy, where imprisonment and *domicilio coatto* still awaited him, but Angiolillo opted instead for Marseilles.[80]

Within days of setting foot on French soil, Angiolillo was arrested by police for traveling under a false name without proper papers and for defying a previous expulsion order, which, in fact, had never been issued. Released provisionally on September 17, he wrote to his parents requesting what little money they could spare and various items of clothing so that he could look respectable while seeking employment. But French authorities availed him no respite. Arrested once more, Angiolillo was incarcerated for nearly two months before an expulsion decree was finally issued. Given a choice of adjacent countries, Angiolillo chose Belgium, never expecting that the trip from Marseilles to the border at Briey, in Lorraine, would take twenty-two days, during which he was caged in a mobile cell for periods ranging between eight and twenty-three hours a day. He finally reached the Belgian frontier by way of Luxemburg on November 20, 1896.[81]

After a few days in Liège, Angiolillo set out for Brussels. Here, as in Barcelona, he was handicapped by his lack of manual skills. Not even the intervention of a university professor known to his family sufficed to secure him a decent position. Only after a long search for employment was Angiolillo hired by the printing establishment owned by the widow of the old Belgian socialist and internationalist Désiré Brismée. He was well liked by his fellow workers whose recollections, published in the radical daily *Réforme*, described Angiolillo as a gentle, polite young man who always returned to his small room after work to read books. Although Angiolillo's behavior had been exemplary, Belgian authorities knew him to be a foreign anarchist previously active in Spain and expelled from France. That information was sufficient cause for the police to harass him. Rather than await the inevitable removal decree, Angiolillo departed Brussels for London at the end of March 1897. Left unmolested by Scotland Yard, he was able to find work as a printer in the Typografia association, a branch of the British typographers union that employed only foreigners and published a monthly journal in Spanish and French that dealt with commerce and industry.[82]

London was the largest and most cosmopolitan haven for anarchist exiles in all Europe, providing the environment in which Angiolillo associated with Italian, Spanish, German, and other anarchists, including Malatesta and the noted anarcho-syndicalist Rudolf Rocker. Rocker described Angiolillo as a very intelligent and learned young man who cut an elegant figure, with glasses, a trim beard, and delicate hands that gave him the appearance of a physician. Neither his personality nor philosophy suggested him capable of violence, and "if not for the terrifying horrors of Montjuich, Angiolillo probably would have lived out his life in peace," according to Rocker.[83] But Angiolillo's stay in London coincided with the arrival of many Spanish anarchists who had escaped the post–Corpus Christi roundups or had been subsequently released on condition that they leave Spain, like Juan Montseny. Rocker recalled that at one meeting victims of Montjuich related the horrors they and other prisoners had endured, causing Angiolillo to become terribly upset. His emotional reaction to Montjuich atrocities was subsequently intensified by his presence at the mass demonstration convened in London's Trafalgar Square on May 30, 1897, to protest against Spain's inquisitional treatment of Montjuich prisoners. Besides speeches by eminent anarchists, socialists, republicans, and liberals, the demonstration organized by the Spanish Atrocities Committee featured actual victims of Montjuich, some of whom exhibited their naked bodies to reveal the physical damage and scars left by Spain's modern inquisitionists. At some point, the stories he had heard directly from Spanish victims, the mass protest meeting with its exhibition of lacerated bodies, and his reading of Fernando Tarrida's *Les inquisiteurs d'Espagne* all combined to offend his sense of human dignity and convince Angiolillo that he must exact revenge for the horrors of Montjuich.[84]

Angiolillo left London for Paris toward the end of September 1897, posing as "Emilio Rinaldini," a book salesman and correspondent for the Italian newspaper *Il Popolo* of Milan. In Paris he attended several meetings at which various figures of note, such as Charles Malato and Henri Rochefort, were present. They remembered the young "journalist," but were entirely ignorant of his intentions. More mysterious meetings were held with Dr. Ramón Emeterio Betances y Alacán, head of the Parisian branch of the Cuban Delegation, that is, the Cuban revolutionary party that was fighting for independence from Spain. Many Italian leftists were supportive of Cuba's liberation movement, contributing funds and even volunteering to fight.[85] Angiolillo's visit to Betances gave rise to speculation that he may have entered into a conspiracy with Cuban revolutionaries to eliminate Cánovas and that Betances allegedly provided him with a thousand francs to pay for traveling expenses to Spain.[86] Evidence for that interpretation is entirely anecdotal and far from convincing. Angiolillo left Paris in mid-July and reached Madrid by the end of the month. That he arrived in Madrid virtually penniless undermines the credibility of a munificent contribution by Cuban revolutionaries and any conspiratorial understanding between them. His destitute condition was confirmed by José Nakens, the republican editor of the Madrid weekly *El Motín*, whom Angiolillo visited in his office. They discussed the Cuban situation, Tarrida's *Les inquisiteurs d'Espagne*, and the issue of propaganda of the deed, Angiolillo defending such violence and Nakens rejecting it. When he departed, Angiolillo supposedly told Nakens of his plan to assassinate Cánovas. The Spaniard did not believe him; he felt sorry for the young Italian and gave him five pesetas so he could eat.[87]

Tracking the prime minister's movements in the press, Angiolillo learned that Cánovas would be vacationing with his wife at the Santa Águeda spa in the Basque countryside in August. Upon arriving at his destination, Angiolillo registered at the hotel posing as a journalist who wished to interview the prime minister. For several days he did nothing, patiently awaiting an opportunity to confront Cánovas when his wife was not close by. On Sunday, August 8, after Cánovas returned from mass and was sitting on a bench reading a newspaper, Angiolillo approached his quarry. Anticipating a greeting, Cánovas looked up from his newspaper only to receive a bullet in his temple and two more in his chest and back. His spouse, who had been chatting with friends nearby, ran to the scene and started beating the young man about the face with her fan and screaming "murderer" and "assassin." Angiolillo allegedly told the imminent widow: "I have nothing to do with you madam. I am no murderer, I have only avenged my comrades tortured and murdered by your husband in the fortress of Montjuich."[88] Angiolillo made no attempt to escape before police arrived to arrest him. He had completed his mission and was resigned to his fate.[89]

Angiolillo was tried by military tribunal in the Basque town of Vergara on August 14–16, 1897. The verdict and sentence were never in doubt for a moment. Nevertheless, concerned lest Angiolillo's trial testimony constitute effective propaganda for the anarchists, the military tribunal prohibited open access to the proceedings and publication of his statements. But someone among the observers—evidently a soldier—defied the prohibition and wrote down Angiolillo's final statement. Soon published in the French anarchist newspaper *Le Libertaire* (Paris) and reprinted in *L'Agitazione*, *Freedom*, and other newspapers, Angiolillo's self-justification was a classic depiction of political assassination as an act of retributive justice, beginning with his opening declaration—"*Signori, voi non avete dinnanzi un assassino, ma un giustiziere*"—"Gentlemen, you have before you not a murderer, but someone who has carried out justice."[90]

Angiolillo described the suffering and misery of the poor he had observed throughout his travels, focusing on Spain, "where I learned . . . with horror, that in this country, . . . classic land of the Inquisition, the race of torturers was not dead." Because of the arrests and banishment of so many anarchists, the tortures inflicted upon them in Montjuich, and the execution of five innocents, "I said to myself that such atrocities should not go unpunished."

He determined that retribution should be directed at the man who was not merely the symbol of state power and oppression in Spain, but at the political leader widely considered directly responsible for the atrocities—Cánovas del Castillo.

> "I felt from the bottom of my heart an unconquerable hatred against this states-man who governed through terror and torture; against this minister who sent thousands of young soldiers to their deaths; against this criminal who reduced to misery, by crushing them under the burden of taxes, the population of Spain, which could be prosperous in this magnificent country so fertile and so rich; against this heir of the Caligulas and Neroes; this successor of Torquemada; this emulator of Stambuloff and Abdul Hamid; against this monster that I am proud and happy to have rid the world of—Cánovas del Castillo.
>
> "Is it a bad action to strike down the bloody tiger whose claws are tearing human hearts, whose jaws are crushing human heads? Is it a crime to crush the reptile whose bite is lethal? For the carnage he committed my single victim was worse than a hundred tigers, worse than a thousand reptiles. He personified in their most hideous features, religious ferocity, military cruelty, the implacability of the magistracy, the tyranny of power, and the cupidity of the landowning class. I have eradicated him from Spain, Europe, and the entire world!" At this point, he repeated, "This is why I am not an assassin, but someone who has carried out justice."[91]

Having explained "the motives which have impelled me," Angiolillo tried to discuss "the probable likely consequences of my act from a social and general point of view, and from the point of view of Spain in particular." The presiding officer was disinclined to listen to Angiolillo's didactic discourse and prevented him from speaking further. Minutes later the inevitable verdict of guilty was rendered, and Angiolillo was sentenced to be executed by garrote on August 19, 1897. Like Caserio and other anarchists before him, Angiolillo rejected the ministration of Catholic priests to save his soul. Defiant to the end, the last word he uttered before the garrote stifled his breath was "Germinal!"[92]

Of all the assassinations and failed attempts perpetrated by the Italian anarchists prior to Angiolillo's, his was the *attentat* motivated overwhelmingly by a moral decision to exact political retribution from the tormentors of innocent victims. Unlike Paolo Lega, the element of revenge for personal suffering at the hands of police did not factor into his decision. Nor is there evidence to suggest Angiolillo was experiencing the kind of despondency and emotional breakdown that contributed to Sante Caserio's deed. His letters to parents and friends describe the travails he endured in exile but contain no indication of an impending crisis that would have caused a violent reaction.

And there was certainly no trace of the deep resentment and self-pity caused by personal poverty characteristic of Acciarito's deed. Angiolillo was Nemesis personified, or in his own words, a *giustiziere*. Indeed, Angiolillo was the quintessential *giustiziere*, having committed a classic act of retributive anarchist justice. As such, Angiolillo occupies the highest rank in the pantheon of anarchist martyrs.

If on a scale of political and moral consciousness Angiolillo's *attentat* represents the highest level, the lowest place is occupied by the assassination of Empress Elizabeth of Austria struck down by Luigi Lucheni on September 10, 1898.[93] Born Elizabeth Amalie Eugenie, of the House of Wittelsbach in Bavaria, the empress (nicknamed "Sissi") was married at age sixteen to Franz Josef of Austria in 1854, a dynastic union she regretted. She found life in the Habsburg court oppressively dull and fossilized, much like her husband. Eventually she escaped the suffocating confines of royal palaces by indulging in horseback riding, marathon walks, love affairs, and endless traveling throughout Europe. Considered a great beauty, Elizabeth was meticulous about maintaining her svelte figure and sustained herself with strenuous and bizarre diets that did more harm than good. Eventually, a series of family tragedies plunged Elizabeth into a deep depression from which she never fully emerged: the drowning death of her insane cousin, Ludwig of Bavaria; the execution in Mexico of her brother-in-law, Maximilian; her sister Helene's death in a fire; and above all her son Rudolf's famous suicide with his young lover at Mayerling. By age sixty, Elizabeth had become physically frail and so drained emotionally that she was said to have longed for death.[94] Lucheni was eager to oblige.

Although she had been critical of the Swiss for granting asylum to anarchist exiles, Elizabeth had come to love Switzerland late in life, especially Geneva, with its beautiful lake and the cosmopolitan atmosphere that afforded the anonymity she craved. Traveling with her companion, the Hungarian Countess Irma Sztáray, Elizabeth registered at the Hotel Beau Rivage under a false name to ensure her privacy. She refused security-guard protection from local police for the same reason. Unfortunately, news of her visit to Geneva was leaked to the press, as was the name of her hotel, thereby providing Lucheni with just the information he needed. Having planned a trip to the spa in Montreux, Elizabeth and the Countess Sztáray stood waiting at the wharf to board a steamer at around 2:00 p.m. Lucheni, meanwhile, had maintained a vigil outside the Hotel Beau Rivage, awaiting the exit of his intended victim. After trailing Elizabeth and her companion to the dockside, Lucheni struck without hesitation when the opportunity presented itself. Experiencing shock more than pain, Elizabeth's first reaction was to think that her assailant had wanted to steal her watch. Upon regaining her composure, Elizabeth boarded the boat unaware of the extent of her injury, and within minutes of embarkation she collapsed. The empress was transported back to shore and driven to her hotel room. The small trickle of blood that first appeared on her bodice had disguised the gravity of her wound. The weapon—a triangular file Lucheni had sharpened to a fine point and to which he had affixed a makeshift handle—had punctured her left lung and cut a small hole in the left ventricle of her heart, causing blood to leak slowly into the pericardium. Elizabeth died quietly within an hour of the attack.[95]

Who was Elizabeth's assassin? Luigi Lucheni's formative years as a boy had been wretched. His mother, Luigia Lucheni, a servant girl of eighteen impregnated by her employer or his son in a village near Parma, was paid to disappear. She eventually ended up in Paris, where she gave birth to a son on July 22, 1873. Bereft of means to care for a child, she entrusted the newborn to the Hospice de Saint Antoine, which soon shipped him off to the Ospizio degli Esposti in Parma. The orphanage traditionally paid families to serve as foster parents, and Lucheni at thirty months was taken in by Ferdinando Monici and his wife Folgia in the village of Melegari near Parma. Age sixty-two, Monici worked as a shoe smith but drank to excess; Folgia, age fifty-nine, was a washerwoman, usually absent during the day. According to Lucheni himself—and contrary to Cesare Lombroso's study,[96] from which considerable misinformation has been derived—he was well treated by the Monici couple until 1881, when they returned him to the orphanage because of their advanced age. The director of the orphanage was unconcerned about the suitability of foster parents and now with some financial encouragement entrusted Lucheni a year later to the Nicasi family in the village of Varano de' Melegari. An agricultural laborer to neighboring tenant farmers, Nicasi was shrewdly adept at increasing his income by exploiting Lucheni as he would a slave. Instead of the family hovel, the boy slept in a makeshift barn with the animals and legions of lice. He was never fed bread, only polenta. After performing an assortment of tasks, like collecting dung from the roads, Lucheni was rented to a blind man, whom he served as a guide. Nicasi's next renter was the village priest, Don Giuseppe Venusti, described by Lucheni as the greediest man he ever met. The avaricious cleric not only exploited the boy; he even prohibited him from attending church services save for one day of the year. Lucheni was last outsourced to the family of Angelo Savi in the village of Rubiano. For two years he worked taking care of a flock of sheep and goats. He was well treated there—actually eating dinner at the same table as the family, something he had never experienced with the Nicasis. During his boyhood, Lucheni sporadically attended classes both at the orphanage and at the local elementary school, where he had no friends and was often addressed as the "Parisian" or "bastard." Lucheni was not unintelligent, and despite the wretched circumstances of his existence, he achieved good grades and won a prize—an apple. Ultimately, at age fourteen, Lucheni ran away from his local exploiters and found work as a day laborer on the railroad between Parma and La Spezia.[97]

Six years of rootless wandering through Switzerland, Austria, and Hungary followed. Unable to find work in Budapest after six months, he appealed to the Italian consulate for help in July 1894 and was issued a provisional passport for passage to Fiume. Just before his departure, Lucheni was arrested for vagrancy and expelled to Trieste, where the Italian consulate refused him a passport upon discovering that he had been denounced as a draft evader back in Italy. Handed over to Italian authorities on August 22, 1894, Lucheni was given a choice: imprisonment or military service. He chose the latter.[98]

Whereas Caserio envisioned military service with dread, for Lucheni it proved to be the only satisfactory period of his life. As a private attached to the Monferrato cavalry regiment, Lucheni and his unit remained in Italy until shipped off to Eritrea in spring 1896. Luckily, Lucheni was not part of the invading force that suffered a humiliating defeat at Adowa in Ethiopia on March 1, 1896. Transferred back to Italy in July, Lucheni was discharged from the army with a clear record, the draft evasion charges having been expunged. Lucheni was considered a good soldier by his captain, Prince Raniero De Vera d'Aragona, who hired him as a manservant after his discharge. During his service with the prince in Palermo and Naples, Lucheni conducted himself properly and was appreciated for his affectionate treatment of the family's children. But in March 1898 Lucheni abruptly quit the prince's employ because the latter refused him permission to attend a horse race. From Palermo, Lucheni went to Genoa and then on to Lausanne in Switzerland, where he found work as a manual laborer. Dissatisfied, he wrote to Prince d'Aragona in May, requesting to return to his employ. The prince declined, considering Lucheni too insubordinate. Princess D'Aragona felt sorry for Lucheni, who continued to write her in hope she might change her husband's mind.[99]

Lausanne hosted the largest community of Italian workers in Switzerland, employed primarily in the construction industry: the skilled as stone cutters, the majority as manual laborers. Among these workers was a contingent of anarchists, the first Lucheni had ever met. The extent of his involvement with the anarchists in Lausanne cannot be established with certainty. To a friend in Naples, Lucheni wrote, "The anarchist idea is making amazing progress here. I beg you, do your duty toward the comrades who are not yet well informed."[100] Yet there is no evidence that Lucheni was particularly active among the Lausanne anarchists save as a drinking companion when they frequented local taverns. They remembered him as a seemingly intelligent and literate man, preoccupied above all with his physical appearance. Guests at his *pension* recalled that he was generally quiet but given to boisterous singing of anarchist songs (he carried an anarchist songbook in his pocket) when drunk, a not infrequent occurrence. But there is no question that Lucheni was exposed to anarchist and socialist ideas during his Lausanne sojourn, mostly through his reading of newspapers: *Il Socialista*, *Avanti!*, *Le Père Peinard* (Paris), *Le Libertaire*, *L'Égalité* (directed by the French socialist Jules Guesde), and *L'Agitatore*. Published by Giuseppe Ciancabilla and Giuseppe Colombelli, *L'Agitatore* was the voice of a number of individualists who had taken refuge in Neuchâtel. On at least one occasion, Lucheni went to Neuchâtel to attend an anarchist meeting. Whether he ever met with Ciancabilla, an avowed advocate of terrorism, is not known. Lucheni never mentioned Ciancabilla during his interrogations or trial, and considering that only twelve issues of *L'Agitatore* were published between July and September 1898, how much could he have learned about anarchist ideas and principles? The few articles Ciancabilla wrote about the need to overthrow the House of Savoy hardly sufficed to create an assassin. Nevertheless, his contacts with anarchist workers and exiles in Lausanne, his reading of anarchist literature, and the various claims of being an anarchist he made after his arrest, certainly suggest that Lucheni was influenced by anarchist ideas.[101]

By September 1898 Lucheni had become fixated with assassinating a high personage so that his deed would be featured in the newspapers and bestow permanent notoriety upon him. His first choice was King Umberto, but Lucheni lacked the necessary funds to return to Italy. The victim he selected, therefore, was the Prince Henri d'Orléans, an inconsequential pretender to the defunct French throne who was visiting Geneva. But Prince Henri had already left the city when Lucheni arrived on September 5. Undeterred, Lucheni scanned local newspapers and discovered the availability of a much more exalted victim—the Empress Elizabeth of Austria.[102]

His mission accomplished, Lucheni attempted to flee the scene (a reaction inconsistent with his desire for notoriety should he have escaped) but was overpowered by two coachmen who had observed his attack. He offered no resistance when police arrived to take him into custody. On the contrary, flanked by two gendarmes on route to police headquarters, Lucheni was photographed exhibiting a big, self-satisfied grin, a facial expression he assumed whenever cameras appeared. He even broke into song as he strutted along, until ordered to desist. At the police station, Lucheni calmly described his deed and expressed satisfaction when informed that Elizabeth had expired: "So much the better. I did my duty, the others will do theirs. There are many anarchists in Lausanne and Geneva."[103]

Transferred to St. Antoine Prison, Lucheni was interrogated by Procurator Georges Navazza, Geneva's most celebrated prosecutor. Lucheni responded to Navazza's request to know the motivation for his deed, saying, "The great Bakunin showed the way. You are a bourgeois, you cannot understand. I believe in propaganda of the deed, and there are thousands of men like me."[104] Navazza observed that Lucheni insisted with obvious pride that responsibility for the *attentat* was entirely his, as though the existence of accomplices would have diminished his newfound fame. Despite his reference to Bakunin, Lucheni declared he had never belonged to an anarchist or socialist society: "I am an 'individual' anarchist, and, wherever I have been, have always associated only with those of the same thinking."[105] Questioned why he had assassinated Empress Elizabeth, Lucheni replied, "As part of the war on the rich and great. A Lucheni kills an empress, but would never kill a washerwoman."[106] From these responses, Navazza concluded, "Lucheni is inspired by the true megalomania of crime. I have never come across such a criminal before in my whole career. He is proud of his action and never ceases to lament that he cannot be brought to the scaffold for it."[107]

Very concerned about his public image, Lucheni became incensed prior to his trial when the monarchist newspaper *Don Marzio* in Naples depicted him in Lombrosian terms as a born criminal. Allowed to respond to *Don Marzio*, Lucheni insisted he was not insane—an assertion he would make numerous times—and explained the motivation behind his crime:

> It is necessary to finish with rulers and bosses. The blows must come one after another without pause. After Carnot, Cánovas, after Cánovas, Elizabeth of Austria, and after Elizabeth others and still others. It is necessary to kill not only sovereigns, but also the presidents of republics, ministers, generals, and all those who . . . want to command others. Those who wish to eat must work; the rulers and bosses are lazy, exploiters of those who work and sweat.[108]

While his trial was pending, Lucheni petitioned the president of the Swiss Confederation to transfer his case from Geneva to Lucerne, where the death penalty still remained the punishment for murder, unlike Geneva. Concerned that his strange request might be interpreted as a sign of mental illness, Lucheni insisted that the president not consider his petition to be an admission of insanity. To affirm his status as a "very dangerous anarchist," Lucheni signed the petition *"Louis Lucheni, Anarchico ex pericolosissimo."*[109] He also expressed a desire for death in a letter to Princess Dolores d'Aragona, the wife of his former employer: "Never in my life have I found myself so content as now, and I say frankly that, if I should have the good fortune to be judged by the Code of the Canton of Lucerne . . . , I should mount the steps of the Beloved Guillotine without any help from assistants who would push me." If his petition were rejected, however, Lucheni would "beg his judges to have a cave dug under the superb [Lake] Leman, where I could no longer encounter the rays of the sun."[110] This time he signed his missive "Louis Lucheni, Conscious Communist." His head now swelling with illusions of grandeur, Lucheni asserted in another letter to the princess that "My case is comparable to the Dreyfus Case."[111]

Lucheni's supposed longing for death undoubtedly reflected his assumption that martyrdom would establish his reputation as a "very dangerous anarchist" in perpetuity. However, his petition was denied and the trial was set for November 10, 1898, in Geneva's Court of Assizes. Calm and cooperative, with an air of pride and satisfaction, Lucheni smiled at the observers and flirted with some of the women in the audience, giving the impression that he was enjoying himself. Lucheni's answers to his interrogators were replete with cynicism and sarcasms, but he rarely challenged witness testimony that weighed heavily against him, even when it established premeditation. He confirmed the truth of the testimony offered by an Italian friend who asserted that upon reading about Angiolillo's assassination of Cánovas del Castillo in the newspapers, Lucheni had commented, "I too would like to kill [someone] so that my name appears in the newspapers." In that light, the prosecutor and presiding judge sought to establish why Lucheni had chosen Empress Elizabeth for his victim. Lucheni acknowledged with complete candor: "I wanted to kill a high personage, no matter which one." He was able to identify the empress when she left her hotel because he had seen her once in Budapest. Asked about his motive and purpose, Lucheni declared, "Poverty. . . . To strike down the persecutors of the workers." In his final queries, the judge asked Lucheni if he had experienced any remorse since committing his crime, and whether, in retrospect, he would do it again. Lucheni responded indifferently to the first question: "What good would it do? What is done is done." And to the second: "I would do it again."[112]

Unlike the previous trials of the anarchist bombers and assassins, the prosecution did not fixate on the issue of anarchism, even though the authorities had believed initially that Lucheni must have had accomplices from among local anarchists. The arrests that followed the assassination, however, revealed no trace of a plot, and upon questioning in court, Lucheni declared emphatically that he had acted alone. He explained that his first contacts with anarchists occurred after he had quit the employ of Prince D'Aragona. Asked whether he had been converted to anarchism by his comrades, Lucheni replied, "No, I became one by myself."[113] Yet save for a few sporadic comments, genuine evidence of a true anarchist was nowhere present in the trial proceedings. None of Lucheni's comments referred to the basic goals of anarchism—liberty, justice, human redemption—crucial objectives that anarchists invariably sought to interject when speaking from the witness box. Not that it mattered to the jurors one way or another. After fifteen minutes, they found Lucheni guilty of murder without mitigating circumstances. The sentence of the court was life imprisonment in Geneva's Evêché prison. Lucheni greeted the sentences with a cry of "*Vive l'Anarchie! Mort aux Aristocrates!*"[114]

Incarceration in Geneva's Evêché prison produced a remarkable transformation of Lucheni's life far beyond the objective reality of imprisonment. After two years of inconsequential existence, Lucheni came under the tutelage of Ernest Favre, a Christian philanthropist and evangelist, noted for his efforts to rehabilitate prisoners prior to their release. In Lucheni's case, he encouraged the prisoner to utilize his time in productive pursuits that would improve his mind and well-being. Over the next few years, Lucheni taught himself to read and write French and took to reading books voraciously—perhaps five to six hundred during his twelve years of incarceration, including works by Dante, Voltaire, Rousseau, and the Encyclopédistes.[115]

After five years of study, Lucheni embarked upon the project that would become his raison d'être—writing an autobiography. Composed in French in five notebooks, Lucheni's memoirs were meant to provide an account of the experiences that led to his assassination of Empress Elizabeth. The subtitle spoke volumes: *Histoire d'un enfant abandonné à la fin du XIXe siècle racontée par lui-même*. Lucheni was obsessed with the fact that his mother had abandoned him at birth, thereby depriving him of the mother's love he so craved. His resentment toward her was immense. Interviewed by psychiatrists in 1901, Lucheni declared, "beginning the day that vile woman . . . abandoned me, I ceased to be human."[116] Intense feelings of rejection, compounded by the wretched life he endured as a boy in servitude, evolved into an all-consuming hatred of society compounded by an abundance of self-pity. Lucheni would not accept full responsibility for his action. He insisted he was a victim of social injustice, that society—like the mother who abandoned him—was the cause of his misery, that society was his accomplice in the assassination of Elizabeth.[117] Now Lucheni even told the psychiatrists who visited him in prison that he had never been anarchist.[118] He expressed disagreement with

Malatesta's vision of a future society based on liberty, human redemption, and social justice. Social order, Lucheni maintained, could not exist without a master; it required leadership from someone like an enlightened despot.[119]

It is difficult to determine whether Lucheni's retrospections were an honest assessment of the motivations that drove him to murder or a self-serving attempt to deflect responsibility for killing a sad and lonely woman who just happened to be empress. However, the fact remains that regardless of whether Lucheni's initial utterances about his anarchism were sincere or part of a pose, his deed was not the act of an avenger, a reality recognized even by Prosecutor Navazza, who, in contrasting Caserio's assassination of Carnot with the killing of Elizabeth, declared, "You, Lucheni, were not guided by revenge; it was hatred alone."[120] As Pier Carlo Masini succinctly summarizes, "If, on a scale of political and moral consciousness, Angiolillo's deed occupies the highest place, the *attentat* carried out by Luigi Lucheni occupies the lowest."[121]

The conditions of Lucheni's imprisonment at Evêché worsened markedly in 1909, when the new prison director declared that the leniency he had previously enjoyed would end. His mission was to "subdue" Lucheni, not rehabilitate him. When the director ordered all the books removed from his cell, Lucheni protested vehemently, a transgression punished by solitary confinement for five weeks. When he returned to his cell, he discovered the notebooks containing his memoirs were missing, probably stolen by one of the guards. Writing his memoirs had been Lucheni's primary reason for living. After their loss he became increasingly rebellious and unhinged, until finally, on October 19, 1910, the infamous assassin of Empress Elizabeth hanged himself with his belt.[122]

# 6 *Fatti di Maggio* and Gaetano Bresci

| Deh non rider sabauda marmaglia | Do not laugh, you rabble of the house of Savoy, |
|---|---|
| se il fucile ha domato i ribelli, | if the gun has subdued the rebels, |
| se i fratelli hanno ucciso i fratelli, | if brothers have killed brothers, |
| sul tuo capo quel sangue cadrà! | that blood will be on your head! |

—*Il Feroce Monarchico Bava*, anonymous, 1898

The year 1898 was the *annus horribilis* of the 1890s, unprecedented in the scope and intensity of social upheaval as well as the severity and authoritarian direction of government repression. The Italian economy had been in a wretched state well before this momentous outburst of working-class discontent and brutal government reaction. Late industrial development, agricultural depression, technological backwardness, the tariff war with France, financial instability, pervasive corruption, rising prices, widespread unemployment, and the moral indifference and colossal ineptitude of Italian governments throughout the decade had already taken a terrible toll on the peasants and workers of Italy, causing hundreds of thousands of them to migrate abroad in search of survival and a better life and priming the millions who remained for rebellion.

The harvest of 1897 had produced the lowest yield of grain in more than twenty years, one-third less than the average of the previous five years. As bread was still the primary source of sustenance for workers and peasants alike, the grain shortage and rising price of foodstuffs spelled extreme hardship, especially in the south, where the poor lived "a half-day from starvation."[1] The prime minister at the time, Antonio Starabba Di Rudinì, and the finance minister, Ascanio Branca, were both owners of large estates in the South (*latifondisti*) and were therefore loath to reduce import duties despite the crisis, demonstrating once again that Italian governments considered the financial interests of big grain producers more vital than the well-being of the masses. Conditions were exacerbated by higher grain and freight charges imposed by exporters in Argentina. Further increases in the price of bread began in April, the result of the Spanish-American War, which substantially increased the cost of grain from the United States. Additional cuts in grain duties were not forthcoming, and the crisis became more intense with each passing month.[2]

What ensued was the most intense and widespread wave of popular unrest and upheaval in the entire post-Risorgimento period. In Piedmont, Lombardy, and the Veneto in the north, in the Marche, Romagna, Emilia, and Tuscany in the north-central regions; in Lazio and the Abruzzi in the center, and in Sicily in the south, desperate peasants of every kind, artisans, laborers, factory workers, and the unemployed arose in a great "protest of the stomach," as the eminent socialist Napoleone Colajanni observed that year.[3] Already in fall 1897 protest demonstrations and riots demanding "*Pane e Lavoro*" had erupted in many cities and towns in the Marche, Romagna, Tuscany, and in Milan, Naples, and Palermo. By November these and adjacent regions experienced repeated assaults on granaries and bakeries by hungry people, often with women in the vanguard. In Rome even middle-class merchants took to the piazzas to denounce the government's economic policies. Nevertheless, the price of bread continued to rise, taxes remained exorbitant, landowners cut the wages of their laborers. A small reduction in the duty on grain in January 1898 failed to mitigate the crisis, and thereafter the government refused to take emergency measures. Instead, Di Rudinì's government called up forty thousand troops for emergency deployment. Popular demonstrations everywhere were confronted by sizable contingents of soldiers and *carabinieri*, resulting in thousands of arrests and frequent bloodshed. Mass arrests and shootings were considered more effective means of quelling popular unrest than reducing the price of bread.[4]

Ancona was the epicenter of popular agitation at the beginning of 1898 with republicans, anarchists, and socialists cooperating to lead protests against municipal taxes and duties on grain and other consumer goods. From Ancona agitation and revolt spread to the rest of the Marche and Romagna and then in every direction as if ignited by spontaneous combustion. Bari was occupied by troops under the command of General Luigi Pelloux on May 4, and his authority quickly extended to the rest of Puglia, Basilicata, and Calabria. In the north, Parma saw young workers leading demonstrations, cutting telegraph and telephone wires, and confronting troops in the working-class section of the city. In Tuscany rioting erupted between May 3 and 7 in Florence, Livorno, Pisa, and other towns. Almost as an afterthought, Di Rudinì ordered the duty on grain and flour suspended until June 30. His preference, however, was for military suppression. In the port of Livorno, two warships trained their guns on the city, ready to shell working-class neighborhoods.

Agitation, meanwhile, had erupted in Biella, Vercelli, and other industrial towns in Piedmont; likewise in Milan, Pavia, Lodi, and other cities in Lombardy; and the same in Padua and other towns in the Veneto. With the upper classes now quaking in fear of revolution and demanding suppression of their social inferiors, Di Rudinì mobilized an additional eighty thousand to pacify the nation. On May 2 he authorized all prefects to call upon the army for assistance whenever they deemed necessary. Italy's largest cities were to be defended against popular insurrection no matter the cost in blood. Martial law was declared in Bari, Florence, and Milan, while troops assumed quasi-official control of scores of other cities and towns. Military occupation and martial law inexorably intensified already volatile conditions. Confrontations reached their climax in May, the *Fatti di Maggio* (the "May events"), when violent encounters between troops and angry demonstrators—essentially guns versus sticks and stones—resulted in thousands of arrests and hundreds of dead and wounded—nowhere more so than in Milan, the economic capital of Italy.[5]

Although the economic crisis in Milan was not as severe as in other major cities, such as Naples and Bari, tension and anger among Milanese workers had been mounting since Felice Cavallotti, the popular leader of the Radical Party, had been killed in a duel with a conservative deputy on March 6. His funeral was the occasion of huge crowds of protestors demanding action. The fighting mood of the Milanese working class was further stimulated by the fiftieth anniversary celebration of the famous *"Cinque Giornate di Milano"* (March 18–22, 1848), when the population rose up and expelled the Austrian army from the city in the opening days of the Revolution of 1848. The situation in Milan continued to smolder throughout April, and by early May popular wrath had erupted, provoked by the death of Muzio Mussi, the son of Giuseppe Mussi, the popular radical and former vice president of the Chamber of Deputies, shot by police during an encounter in Pavia on the evening of May 5. Demonstrations protesting Mussi's death increased after several workers employed at the Pirelli rubber factory were arrested for distributing a socialist manifesto demanding the restoration of liberty and justice. All were released save one, Angelo Amadio, who remained in custody because he allegedly was arrested with a rock in his hand. His detention became a cause for further agitation by enraged workers.[6]

On Friday, May 6, despite pleas for calm from socialist deputies Filippo Turati and Dino Rondani, an angry throng of more than two thousand striking workers, most from the Pirelli works, demonstrated on the Via Galilei for the release of their comrade, shouting *"Evviva Turati! Evviva Rondani! Abbasso il governo!"*("Long live Turati! Long live Rondani! Down with the government!) The two socialist leaders once again urged calm, but the situation changed abruptly with the approach of two to three hundred people, mostly women and children, singing the *Inno dei Lavoratori*. As the two groups joined together and marched down the Via Andrea Doria, they found their path blocked by a company of troops. When someone threw a rock, the troops responded with a volley of gunfire, wounding many and killing three, one of them a policeman in plainclothes who failed to dodge in time. After one of the wounded workers died en route to the hospital, his comrades battled police for control of their fallen comrade and brought him to the Cimitero Monumentale for burial. That evening, the Piazza del Duomo, the center of the city, was overflowing with demonstrators singing the *Inno dei Lavoratori*. A few tussles and arrests took place, but by midnight the crowd dispersed without further incident. That same night, meanwhile, Giovanni Battista Pirelli, the owner of the famous rubber factory, telephoned the chief of police of Milan to recommend that the imprisoned Amadio be released as a conciliatory gesture to placate the workers. Manifesting the obstinacy and stupidity typical of Italy's public security authorities, the police chief adamantly refused. Then the prefect of Milan, demonstrating even greater irresponsibility than the police chief, telegraphed Lieutenant General Fiorenzo Bava Beccaris to request more troops and an immediate declaration of a state of siege.

The next day, May 7, the Piazza del Duomo was militarily occupied by contingents of infantry, cavalry, and artillery under the command of Bava Beccaris. Major arteries leading to the Piazza del Duomo and the city gates were likewise occupied by troops. But rather than restore peace, the mobilization of so many troops ready to unleash a hail of lead only served as further provocation for the working class of Milan. Confrontations began that day as striking workers in the industrial zones located on the outskirts of the city assembled and marched down the Corso Garibaldi and other major avenues toward the Piazza del Duomo. Responding to threats from the troops, they erected barricades from furniture, metal grilles, and dismantled trolley cars. Such defiance only incited the troops to attack. For most of May 7 and the entire day of May 8, facing workers armed only with stones and roof tiles, the troops went berserk, blasting barricades with point-blank artillery fire and shooting indiscriminately without proper warning. (Three trumpet blasts, the signal for a crowd to disperse, were required before troops could open fire, a rule never observed during the *Fatti di Maggio*.) Much of the gunfire was directed against individuals who could not possibly have been perceived as a threat, including people trying to reach their homes and others looking out apartment windows to watch the drama below. There were also several instances of women trying to block streets with their bodies, believing the troops would not shoot them. They were trampled by cavalry instead. The mounted troops proved unsuccessful against a crowd of two thousand students assembled on the Corso San Gottardo, some of whom had come from Pavia armed with revolvers. The infantry dispersed them with cannon fire. Not content, troops and *carabinieri* continued to fire at the backs of people fleeing the scene. In the grip of excessive exuberance, the troops engaged in actions were more farcical than tragic. Word had spread that the Cappuccini monastery on the Via Monforte was occupied by a nest of revolutionaries. This false rumor precipitated a full-scale assault against the monastery, using artillery fire to blast a huge hole in the wall. Soldiers tugged on the beards of the monks, thinking they were revolutionaries in disguise. The beards and monks both proved genuine, but the baffled monks were arrested nonetheless. By May 9, after troop reinforcements arrived from other parts of Lombardy as well as Piedmont and Emilia, Milan was firmly in the repressive grip of martial law. In other cities, like Florence and Naples, where popular upheavals had also assumed almost insurrectionary proportions, the military effectively quelled the workers' demonstrations, albeit without bloodshed comparable to that spilled in Milan. Throughout Italy the *Fatti di Maggio* were over. The workers of Milan, Florence, Ancona, and scores of other cities and towns had no choice but to return to their factories and workshops in defeat.[7]

The official tally of the casualties sustained during the *Fatti di Maggio* in Milan was 80 civilians and 2 policemen killed and 450 wounded; unofficial estimates have placed the number of dead between 118 and 400. Elsewhere in Italy the fatalities numbered 51, according to the government. Milanesi arrested and turned over to military tribunals for judgment probably exceeded 1,000, and of the 828 ultimately accused of some transgression (224 were minors and 36 were women), 688 were condemned to imprisonment for terms of up to twelve years. All told, the military tribunals in Milan handed down sentences amounting to 1,390 years of imprisonment, 307 years of surveillance, and 33,952 lire in fines. The brutal role played by the army during the *Fatti di Maggio* generated deep feelings of antimilitarism that Italian workers would manifest for decades thereafter.[8]

Unknown at the time, the *Fatti di Maggio* had brought King Umberto to the verge of ordering a coup d'état—"*questa volta facciamo bum!*" ("this time we blast them"), he declared to a few of his advisers on June 15.[9] Later that month, General Luigi Pelloux replaced Di Rudinì as prime minister. According to Pelloux, Di Rudinì and Minister of War Alessandro Marzano had urged Umberto to keep the Rome garrison of sixteen thousand troops in readiness. Though tempted by the prospect, Umberto held back from ordering a coup at that time.[10] For the short term, Umberto and the aristocrats and bourgeois conservatives of Milan and Lombardy had to settle for the suppression of the rabble. And when the echoes of gunfire faded, the upper classes expressed their endless gratitude to the "hero" who had saved them from the "revolutionaries," showering General Bava Beccaris with adoring accolades. No less thankful, King Umberto awarded the general Italy's highest decoration, the Great Cross of the Military Order of Savoy, and on June 6 Umberto congratulated him in a personal telegram for "the great service you have rendered to our institutions and to civilization."[11] Umberto's congratulations to the man who had ordered troops to shoot down scores of innocent workers in Milan seared the collective consciousness of the anarchist movement like a molten hot blade, ensuring that the king—the highest symbol of authority and oppression in Italy—would be held directly responsible for the atrocities perpetrated to save his throne. By his callous indifference to the suffering of his people, and his outrageous approval of their slaughter by rifle and grapeshot, Umberto had effectively signed his own death warrant. It was only a matter of time before an avenger arose to strike.

The *Fatti di Maggio* terrified Italy's middle and upper classes. Domenico Farini, the president of the Senate and intimate adviser to the king, wrote in his diary on May 5, "Rebellion is spreading throughout Italy . . . with barbarous scenes of vandalism and bloodshed. It is a new 'jacquerie.' The havoc and pillaging signal as never before in this country the hatred of the common people for the upper classes that exploit and oppress them."[12] It followed, of course, that the authorities would respond to the perceived "jacquerie" of the lower classes in the traditional manner in which the Italian government had always dealt with mass disturbances waged by its suffering people—repression, but repression that eclipsed even the worst days of Crispi's reaction. Huge contingents of infantry and cavalry were so omnipresent and primed for action that Italy gave the appearance of a country occupied by enemy forces, and states of siege and military tribunals were operative until order was restored. Prefects and police chiefs conducted their countermeasures with optimum enthusiasm and efficiency, dissolving several thousand chambers of labor, trade unions, cooperatives, and workers' societies and suppressing and confiscating newspapers by the score. Countless numbers of private domiciles were invaded and searched by police without proper authorization and invariably without cause. Thousands of arrests resulted and boatloads of victims—primarily anarchists—began departing for *domicilio coatto*. Included among those arrested and imprisoned were socialist deputies such as Filippo Turati, Leonida Bissolati, and Andrea Costa, notwithstanding the fact that such measures strictly violated their parliamentary immunity. Turati and the republican deputy Luigi De Andreis were sentenced to ten years in jail for allegedly preparing and participating in the Milan uprising. Scores of others, including Anna Kuliscioff, Costantino Lazzari, Paolo Valera, and others less notable received shorter sentences. Like De Andreis, not all the victims of government repression were socialists and anarchists; the reaction of 1898 extended its net to entrap republicans, radicals, and even Catholic elements. Among other falsehoods propagated by the government was the claim that the *Fatti di Maggio* had resulted from a plot implemented by "reds" and "blacks" against national unity.[13]

With the suppression of popular and subversive elements continuing apace, a political campaign was taking shape intended to transform Italy from a nominally liberal state into a more authoritarian state with maximum power invested in the monarchy and minimal power relegated to a parliament elected on the basis of limited suffrage. The theoretical basis for this reactionary trend was provided by Sidney Sonnino's famous article, "*Torniamo allo Statuto*" (a reference to the Constitution of 1848) published in January 1897, in which he advocated increasing the king's executive power. Prime Minister Di Rudinì, alarmed at the electoral gains registered by democrats and socialists that March, gave evidence of where conservative thinking was gravitating when he confided to Farini that he "believed more than ever in the need for a conservative Government. If the electoral law is not changed, after three [more] elections everything will blow sky high."[14] With the onset of popular upheavals throughout the peninsula, Di Rudinì introduced legislation in the Senate to contend with political subversives by making consignment to *domicilio coatto* easier to execute, greatly restricting freedom of association, curbing the press with greater censorship, and eliminating the right to elect local officials so that socialist and democratic candidates would be thwarted and control remain in the hands of traditional elites.[15]

*Domicilio coatto*, now more easily administered, would soon become an even more effective weapon for the suppression of the anarchist movement. A new round of harassment had begun with the movement's resurgence early in 1897, when scores of anarchists consigned to *domicilio coatto* during the Crispian reaction were released and Malatesta returned to Italy. Harbored by comrades in Ancona, now the movement's primary center of activity, Malatesta clandestinely assumed the directorship of *L'Agitazione*. His comrade and disciple, Luigi Fabbri, considered Malatesta's stay in Ancona to have been the "most formative" (in a relative sense) period in the evolution of his political thinking, with emphasis on the need for anarchists to organize along federative lines, establish closer ties with the workers' movement, and make greater use of syndicalist tactics.[16]

Alerted and alarmed, the authorities immediately targeted *L'Agitazione*, first by confiscating issues and then by consigning the editors, Cesare Agostinelli and Emidio Recchioni, to *domicilio coatto* and indicting the rest of the editorial staff. After the police finally located his hiding place, Malatesta was arrested on November 12, 1897, but he was released after a few hours without charges filed against him, a virtual admission that his activities since March had been entirely legal. When the rising price of bread caused popular demonstrations and rioting to erupt in Ancona on January 17–18, 1898, Malatesta and the anarchists emerged as the leaders of the agitation. From this position, they hoped to broaden the revolt, but the arrival of troops precluded that possibility. Meanwhile, the police had again arrested Malatesta on January 18, claiming he had orchestrated the upheaval. He and eight comrades associated with *L'Agitazione* were indicted on charges of constituting "an association of malefactors" (Art. 248) and of inciting disobedience of the law and instigating class hatred (Art. 247). The government's depiction of Malatesta as a malefactor precipitated protest demonstrations in London, Paris, and Switzerland. In Italy, more than three thousand anarchists, socialists, and republicans signed a manifesto expressing solidarity with the defendants and denouncing the charge that Malatesta and his comrades constituted an "association of malefactors."[17]

The trial was adjudicated in Ancona's Tribunale Penale from April 21 to 28. The central issue of the proceedings was whether the anarchists were still to be prosecuted as common criminals, as they had been since the Rome Court of Cassation's ruling of 1880, or to be recognized as political subversives under the law. The political implications of the case and the celebrity of the principal defendant and his attorneys generated widespread attention. Superbly defended by Pietro Gori, Francesco Saverio Merlino, the socialist deputy Enrico Ferri, and several other lawyers, and brilliantly persuasive in his own defense, Malatesta was found guilty of the political charges—inciting class hatred and disobedience of the law—and sentenced to serve only seven months in jail and pay a 150-lira fine. His comrades received lesser sentences. The bourgeois jury rejected the government's charge that Malatesta and his comrades had constituted an association of malefactors, maintaining that ever since Malatesta had assumed leadership of the local movement, the anarchists had eschewed violence, organized workers associations, and conducted peaceful strikes. Even more remarkably, the Ancona Court of Appeals and the Supreme Court of Cassation of Rome rejected the prosecutor's appeal to declare Malatesta a malefactor, ruling instead that an association of anarchists did not constitute an association of malefactors under Article 248 of the Penal Code.[18]

The court ruling constituted a great political victory for Italian anarchists, a retroactive moral vindication for every militant previously condemned to *domicilio coatto* or *ammonizione* on the spurious charge of membership in a criminal association. But there was no time to exult. The massive increase in repressive measures launched by the government in the wake of the *Fatti di Maggio* struck the anarchists with the force of a tsunami, sweeping them up en masse and consigning the cream of the movement—Malatesta, Galleani, Agostinelli, Fabbri, and others—to *domicilio coatto* for five years. The total population of *coatti* now languishing on Lipari, Ustica, Lampedusa, Pantelleria, Ponza, Ventotene, and other islands—anarchists, socialists, republicans, and common criminals—numbered several thousand, possibly as many as five thousand.[19] On the mainland and Sicily, meetings of any sort were prohibited and attempted only at great risk. Private domiciles were subject to arbitrary search and seizure of newspapers, books, pamphlets, and letters. The anarchist press—*L'Agitazione*, *L'Avvenire Sociale* (Messina), and several others—was completely suppressed, although a few single issues were published clandestinely. Some lucky enough to escape the police dragnet or to escape from *domicilio coatto*—notably Malatesta and Galleani—joined the diaspora and settled abroad.[20]

With the movement now in a state of virtual paralysis, save for the remarkable fortitude and defiance demonstrated by the anarchists confined to the penal islands, from where they contributed effectively to the emerging campaign to abolish *domicilio coatto*,[21] the fortunes of Italian anarchism seemingly could not sink any lower.

The combination of the carnage of the *Fatti di Maggio* with the increase in repression that followed set the stage for the most momentous of all the *attentats* carried out by an Italian anarchist *giustiziere*. King Umberto I of the House of Savoy arrived at the Royal Villa in Monza on the morning of July 21, 1900, never suspecting that he was soon to become the last victim of the violence that had wracked Italy since troops had fired upon unarmed workers in Milan two years earlier. The aforementioned reactionary campaign led by Prime Minister Luigi Pelloux and Sidney Sonnino to transform Italy into an authoritarian state with greater powers vested in the monarchy had already been defeated in summer 1900 by a temporary alliance forged among socialists, republicans, radicals, and progressive liberals—a development to which his future assassin paid no heed. The king was weary of the battles that had nearly destroyed parliamentary rule during the previous two years, and he seemed content with the reestablishment of normality by the moderate government formed by the seventy-eight-year-old Piedmontese politician Giuseppe Saracco. Monza was Umberto's favorite retreat because it was home to the Duchess Eugenia Attendolo Bolognini Litta ("La Litta"), his first and most cherished mistress. A small path with closely overhanging trees connected the park of the Royal Villa to the adjacent villa of La Litta, providing some semblance of discretion to Umberto's periodic visits.[22]

Besides visiting his lover, Umberto intended to spend his vacation in Monza without engaging the burden of state affairs, but he could not escape the reports from Rome, informing him about the contingent of Royal Marines recently dispatched to China to participate in the suppression of the Boxer Rebellion. On July 29, after rising at 7:30 a.m. and eating a light breakfast, Umberto had his hair cut by his barber before taking his customary walk in the Parco Reale, in the course of which he stopped off to visit La Litta for a half-hour. Back in his study after attending mass at 11:30 a.m., the king immersed himself in official reports, including a telegram from the heir to the throne, Prince Vittorio Emanuele, announcing his imminent return on the yacht *Yela*, aboard which he and his wife Elena, a Montenegrin princess, had visited the Levant. He also learned that his Royal Marines were marching on Peking, a source of pride for the king, who had always resented Italy's minor position among Europe's great powers. Umberto ate lunch in the company of Queen Margherita, whom he invited to accompany him to the gymnastic contest of the Società "Forti e Liberi," scheduled to be held in the royal park late that evening. The contest and accompanying ceremonies, which included speeches from local dignitaries and music from five bands, was a big event for Monza. Nevertheless, the queen declined to attend. He rejoined her for a multicourse dinner at 8:00 p.m., after spending a leisurely afternoon in his room and the villa's garden. Looking forward to the gymnastic contest, Umberto arrived at the Royal Park promptly at 9:30 p.m. in the company of his aide-de-camp, Emilio Ponzio Vaglia, and General Felice Avogadro di Quinto.[23]

The king had always been fatalistic about the possibility of his being assassinated, believing nothing could prevent it if such was his destiny. After Acciarito's failed attempt, however, Umberto was persuaded to be fitted for a protective vest made of steel, but on this hot summer night he refused to wear it. The king had enjoyed the contest and was about to depart when his vehicle was surrounded by gymnasts hailing His Majesty. Also positioned amid the raucous crowd was Umberto's nemesis, a revolver at the ready. Vulnerable in his open carriage, Umberto rose to acknowledge the cheers of the gymnasts, saying "*Grazie, giovanotti, grazie giovanotti.*" At that moment three gunshots cut through the sound of the "Marcia reale" played by the local bands. The king fell across the knees of his aide-de-camp, surprised but barely aware of the three wounds to his chest. Ponzio Vaglia asked the king if he was wounded; Umberto answered, "I don't think it's anything." The royal carriage raced for the king's villa at the gallop but, upon arrival, Umberto was already dead. Consternation quickly spread among the royal entourage, with Queen Margherita shouting above the din in her habitually hysterical manner, "This is the greatest crime of the century."[24] A few days later, at a mass meeting in Bartholdi Hall in Paterson, New Jersey, the anarchist Beniamino Mazzotta offered a different assessment: "The killing of the king was the greatest revenge of the century."[25]

His assailant was a thirty-one-year-old weaver from Paterson named Gaetano Bresci, who had returned to Italy to carry out his long-planned mission to assassinate the king in revenge for the victims of government oppression sanctioned by Umberto's royal decrees. Born in the town of Coiano, on the periphery of Prato (Tuscany), Bresci entered the world on November 11, 1869, one day after the birth of the future king Vittorio Emanuele III—a coincidence considered lucky by the family's neighbors. Gaetano grew up in modest circumstances as the youngest of four children born to Gaspero Bresci and Maddalena Godi, owners of a small property where the family resided in a three-story house and grew grain, olives, and grapes. The eldest son, Lorenzo, was the town shoemaker and an anarchist sympathizer, although he appears not to have had any political influence on his younger siblings. His brother Angiolo received a secondary school education and at age nineteen joined the army, eventually rising to the rank of lieutenant in the artillery. Angiolo's military career would later become a source of contention between him and Gaetano, reaching a point of permanent alienation. The daughter of the family, Teresa, would marry a cabinetmaker, Angelo Marocci, who later opened a small umbrella factory in Castel San Pietro, near Bologna. Each of his siblings would have their lives seriously disrupted by Gaetano's *attentat*.[26]

The family's condition began to decline around 1880, when Italy's agrarian crisis worsened with the importation of cheaper grain from the United States, which greatly reduced the incomes of thousands of small peasant proprietors as prices for their crops greatly declined. For more than a decade thereafter the Bresci family lived in relative poverty. To supplement the meager earnings his farm generated, Gaspero began making shuttles, which he sold to the artisan silk weavers of Prato. Young Gaetano accompanied him on his rounds and also helped out in his brother's cobbler shop. Life assumed a new direction as Prato emerged as one of Italy's major centers of silk weaving. The old cottage industry of independent artisan weavers succumbed to the modern factory system when German industrialists built new establishments in the city in 1888 and absorbed the artisan labor force. One of these manufacturers,

Hans Hosler, wanted to build houses for his German managers and bought a sizable piece of Gaspero's property for that purpose. As part of the negotiation, Hosler took Gaetano into his factory (known locally as the Fabbricone) as an apprentice. Only eleven years old, Gaetano quickly demonstrated talent and on Sundays was permitted to attend a trade school, where he specialized in silk decoration. By age fifteen Gaetano was a fully qualified silk weaver.

By then Bresci already had become an active member of Prato's anarchist group whose most noted figure was Giovanni Domanico, a veteran of the First International. Bresci's conversion resulted from the same factors that produced many recruits for the anarchist cause throughout other parts of Italy. The poverty he and his family had endured generated a natural resentment toward Italy's social order, resentment augmented in turn by the exploitation he observed and experienced firsthand as a factory worker. Hostility for the system he perceived responsible for his suffering translated into overt political consciousness by direct contact with the anarchist artisans and factory workers of Prato, where the movement had enjoyed a sizable following since the days of the First International. His militancy as a young anarchist developed rapidly over the next few years. His work history, at the beginning of the 1890s, appears to have been varied, taking him briefly to Florence, Compiobbi, and Ponte all'Ania in Tuscany. Back in Prato, Bresci took an active role in the 1891 strike against the Fabbricone and demonstrated his willingness to defend those he considered victims of exploitation and arbitrary authority. This propensity caused his first brush with the police.

On the afternoon of October 3, 1892, Bresci and a group of anarchist comrades (police claimed there were twenty) were walking along the Via Ricasoli in Prato when they came upon a young boy in tears. He had been given a summons by two policemen because the butcher shop where he worked had remained open a few minutes after the prescribed hour for closing. According to the police report, Bresci and his comrades intervened, denouncing the officers: "It would be better if you went on your way and left this poor worker alone. Aren't you also workers? Not at all. Today you belong to the exploiters and are a bunch of thieves, spies, and bums."[27] The fracas subsided when an armed plainclothes policeman arrived on the scene. The officers did not attempt to make arrests because they were outnumbered, but Bresci and three comrades were apprehended later. Tried before the pretore of Prato on December 27, 1892, Bresci was found guilty of insulting the officers and refusing to identify himself when ordered; he was condemned to serve fifteen days in jail and pay a twenty-lira fine. Hereafter marked as a "dangerous anarchist" by the authorities, Bresci became a victim of the Crispian reaction of 1894 after joining with other anarchists to organize a strike of textile workers in

Prato. He and fifty-two comrades were condemned to *domicilio coatto* on the island of Lampedusa, where he remained for more than a year before being released along with many other political prisoners, following the royal amnesty of May 1896 issued to mollify public hostility toward Crispi and the Crown after Italy's disastrous defeat in Ethiopia. Like so many anarchists condemned to *domicilio coatto*, Bresci emerged from the experience a more resolute and committed militant, thereby defeating the purpose for which the repression was intended. Once back in Prato, Bresci, blacklisted by his former employer, found work at a woolen factory in Ponte all'Ania. Always a skilled and conscientious worker, Bresci was well liked by his employer and received a promotion after a few months. He was also popular among the women in the factory. Relatively tall and good-looking, with dark wavy hair, a full mustache, and the elegant clothing and jewelry to which he was very partial, Bresci cut an impressive figure and by age twenty-seven had become an inveterate ladies' man. One of his relationships, with a married woman estranged from her husband, resulted in the birth of a son in summer 1897. Bresci was not a candidate for domesticity at this point in his life and he severed contact with the woman after the child died a year later. Whether to escape the responsibilities of fatherhood, to join workers formerly employed at the Fabbricone who had migrated and described better conditions in the United States, or to avoid further harassment from the police, Bresci migrated in December 1897, arriving in New York on January 29, 1898.

By the turn of the century, the silk mills and dye houses of Paterson had attracted some ten thousand Italians, predominantly northerners from Biella and Vercelli in Piedmont, Como in Lombardy, and Prato in Tuscany. Approximately 60 percent of the Italians worked in the silk industry. Those from Biella, Vercelli, Prato, and their satellite towns, with previous experience in textile manufacture (mainly wool) were employed as weavers in Paterson's scores of mills, while those from Como, experienced in silk production, were employed as dyers in the few but large dye works. Southern Italians began arriving in appreciable numbers by the turn of the century and were employed mainly as dyers' helpers, the worst and lowest-paying jobs in the industry. As in other industrial centers in the United States, the arrival of Italian workers was not welcomed by older English-speaking workers, and tensions between them remained high for several decades. As one expert on Paterson has written, "Because Italians were conspicuous, they were saddled with every prejudice, stereotype, and animosity typically aimed in America at exotic newcomers."[28]

Many of the Italian weavers had been radicalized in the course of their previous labor struggles in Italy. Anarchist influences were particularly strong in Biella and its environs, which accounted for the Biellesi constituting the hard-core militants of Paterson's anarchist colony.[29] Many had migrated to Paterson and nearby towns like West Hoboken in order to earn higher wages than were available in Italy; others had fled from political persecution. In July 1900 U.S. sources placed the strength of the anarchists in Paterson at between fifteen hundred and two thousand, a figure probably too high. At the time there were around three or four hundred avowed anarchists and even more sympathizers judging from the fact that one thousand copies of the three thousand published weekly by the local movement's newspaper, *La Questione Sociale*, were read locally.[30] Such numbers signify that Paterson, with an Italian immigrant population of around ten thousand, boasted the highest percentage of anarchists and anarchist sympathizers of any major industrial city in the United States at the turn of the century. Often forgotten by authors preoccupied with the anarchists was the strong presence in Paterson in the 1890s of their main political rivals, the reformist and revolutionary socialists affiliated to the American Socialist Labor Party headed by Daniel De Leon. *Il Proletario*, the official voice of the Italian socialists in the United States, was published in Paterson from 1898 to 1900 and edited by Camillo Cianfarra and Dino Rondani, respectively.[31]

By the mid-1890s, Paterson's most important anarchist group was the Gruppo Diritto all'Esistenza. With a fluctuating membership of between forty and one hundred, the majority of them weavers from Biella and its environs, the Gruppo Diritto all'Esistenza was exceptionally large for an anarchist group. Its most notable members in 1899–1900 included the temporary sojourner Errico Malatesta, Giuseppe Ciancabilla, the multilingual Catalan typesetter Pedro Esteve, Fermino Gallo, Alberto Guabello, and Beniamino Mazzotta. Also included in the Gruppo Diritto all'Esistenza was a strong contingent of women, such as Maria Roda (Esteve's companion), Ninfa Baronio, Ersilia Cavedagni (Ciancabilla's companion), and Ernesta ("Ernestina") Cravello. Rather than defer to their male comrades, as was so often the case even among anarchists, Roda and her female comrades formed a Gruppo Emancipazione della Donna in September 1897.[32] With its size and importance, it was inevitable that the Gruppo Diritto all'Esistenza would sooner or later publish its own newspaper. In September 1895, *La Questione Sociale* was founded with its printing facilities located in a small office on the third floor of 355 Market Street. Antonio Agresti, a well-known figure in Europe, served as its first editor, while rank-and-file militants of the Gruppo Diritto all'Esistenza performed other editorial and administrative functions. The primary contributors of political and theoretical articles at this early juncture were prominent anarchists living abroad and in the United States as temporary sojourners, figures such as Agresti, Pietro Gori, Edoardo Milano, and Oreste Ferrara. Basic news coverage concerning the anarchist and workers' movement was international in scope. Weekly meetings of the Gruppo Diritto all'Esistenza were held every Wednesday night in the back room of *La Questione Sociale*'s office. Larger and more inclusive meetings of local anarchists were held in Bartholdi Hall at 286 Straight Street or in Mazzini Hall. For many years, *La Questione Sociale* remained the most important Italian anarchist publication in the United States. Because of the anarchists' strong commitment to self-education, the newspapers also operated the Biblioteca Sociale Libertaria, which sold a variety of pamphlets and books.

The ideological orientation of the Gruppo Diritto all'Esistenza and its newspaper was Malatestian, the form of *socialismo anarchico* that advocated organizing along federative lines and support of the labor movement whose advocates were known as the *organizzatori*. Members of the group and the editorial position of *La Questione Sociale* invariably supported strikes in Paterson and other textile centers, as well as the efforts of Italian weavers to establish their own unions, such as the Lega di Resistenza and the Lega dei Tessitori, which counted more than five hundred members while it lasted. The group and newspaper were likely involved with the various committees formed among anarchists in many cities to promote revolution in Italy, such as the Comitato Rivoluzionario Permanente and the Comitato per i Moti Rivoluzionari d'Italia. Inevitably, there were other anarchists in Paterson and West Hoboken—the *anti-organizzatori*—who disagreed with the orientation of the Gruppo Diritto all'Esistenza and *La Questione Sociale*. A group of *anti-organizzatori* formed the Società Pensiero e Azione in 1899.[33]

From the early 1890s and beyond, Paterson, like New York, functioned as a major outpost of Italian anarchism both because of the movement's intrinsically diasporic and transnational nature and since *La Questione Sociale* not only enjoyed international circulation but served as the movement's principal voice during periods of repression in Italy when other newspapers had been silenced. Because of its primacy, Paterson in the 1890s and early twentieth century was visited in turn by each of the movement's major figures. Francesco Saverio Merlino, Italian anarchism's most original thinker prior to his embrace of libertarian socialism, arrived in 1892, and together with Luigi Rafuzzi and Vito Soliero founded *Il Grido degli Oppressi*. Merlino wrote eloquently about the poor conditions in which Italian immigrants lived and undertook a lecture tour in eight states, speaking in Italian, French, and English. After he returned to Europe in January 1893, *Il Grido degli Oppressi* was transferred to Chicago, where it survived for only another year.[34] Merlino was followed in July 1895 by anarchism's "knight errant"—the poet, dramatist, attorney, and criminologist Pietro Gori. Not its founder, as commonly believed, Gori wrote articles for *La Questione Sociale* during his three-month stay in Paterson, after which he undertook a proselytizing tour from coast to coast, giving several hundred lectures in Italian, French, and English—sometimes three a day—to audiences that often had never heard of anarchism.[35] With the departure of Agresti and Gori, the editorship of *La Questione Sociale* was entrusted to another temporary sojourner, Francesco Cini, one of Malatesta's closest comrades; he, in turn, was replaced by Pedro Esteve, another former associate of Malatesta's. Esteve also edited *El Despertar* in Spanish, the newspaper that spoke for the Spanish comrades in New York as well as the Spanish and Cuban anarchist cigar makers in Tampa, Florida. The administrator of *La Questione Sociale* at the end of the decade was Francis Widmar—a Slovenian printer who spoke his native tongue, German, Italian, French, and Spanish, but no English. That a Catalan and a Slovenian performed essential roles for *La Questione Sociale* attested to the multinational and internationalist nature of anarchism in Paterson and the close links that bound them to the same cause.[36]

Esteve continued in his dual role as typesetter and editor until the arrival of his replacement, Giuseppe Ciancabilla, who departed from London, where he had sought refuge after his expulsion from Switzerland because of his outspoken approval of Lucheni's assassination of Empress Elizabeth. Ciancabilla was not an original thinker, but at the end of the nineteenth century he certainly qualified as one of the movement's more prominent intellectuals; after his hasty conversion to anarchism under Malatesta's influence, Ciancabilla went on to embrace the ideas of Peter Kropotkin (he wrote the first Italian translation of the latter's classic *The Conquest of Bread*) and French anarchists with whom he associated while in exile in Paris, especially Jean Grave. These influences transformed Ciancabilla into the Italian movement's leading representative of the antiorganizationist current together with Luigi Galleani.[37] He maintained that "organization (not free accord or free association, let us understand) is anti-anarchist."[38] "We uphold the free initiative of the individual. . . . How can anyone who calls himself an anarchist not aspire to the emancipation from every moral and material authority?"[39] With free initiative and free association constituting the alpha and omega of his anarchism, Ciancabilla—like all the *anti-organizzatori*—believed that all forms of organization were harbingers of authoritarianism, and so it followed that Ciancabilla rejected anarchist federations, labor unions, cooperatives, mutual aid societies, formalized programs, congresses, permanent committees, and so on.[40] Inevitably, as its new editor-in-chief, Ciancabilla immediately reoriented *La Questione Sociale* to reflect his own ideological persuasion, but the counterarguments that continued to appear in its pages (he could not bar their publication) did nothing to alter his fixation with free initiative, spontaneity, and authoritarianism and his dogmatic opposition to anarchist organizations and labor unions.[41]

Ciancabilla's stance on anarchist organization and labor unions ran counter to the view of Pedro Esteve and the majority of the Gruppo Diritto all'Esistenza, who adhered to the organizationist current personified by Errico Malatesta. The issues for them were not theoretical abstractions, since most of the members of the group were weavers directly involved with the workers' struggles in Paterson and other textile centers nearby, such as those waged by the Lega di Resistenza and the Lega dei Tessitori.[42] Alberto Guabello, one of the most important anarchists in Paterson and an initial supporter of Ciancabilla, recalled years later that the internal discord generated by the fighting over the issues of anarchist organization and labor unions proved "profoundly detrimental to our movement," as the internecine struggle caused the anarchists to lose ground to their socialist rivals.[43] As Ciancabilla became more intractable in the face of opposition to his editorship, the atmosphere in Paterson, West Hoboken, and adjacent anarchist enclaves became ever more contentious. "It was an ugly period," Guabello related; "our camp was divided into two currents. Many friendships were ruined, and petty personal rancor increased. Instead of the rival activity that should logically have arisen from such a situation, we had to witness a rivalry of insults."[44] Seeking a solution to the conflict—and a replacement for Ciancabilla—Pedro Esteve invited his good friend Malatesta to come to the United States and hopefully assume direction of *La Questione Sociale* in order to heal the strife threatening to split the Italian anarchist movement in Paterson and the rest of the country.[45]

The invitation to come to the United States arrived at a critical time in Malatesta's career. On the night of April 26–27, 1899, Malatesta had escaped by boat from the island of Lampedusa, the penal colony where he had been condemned to *domicilio coatto* for five years. By way of Tunis and Malta, Malatesta returned briefly to London before departing for the United States, arriving in Paterson on August 12, 1899. The primary enticement for his visit was the opportunity to direct *La Questione Sociale*, the movement's only propaganda vehicle save for *L'Avvenire* in Buenos Aires, all others in Italy having been suppressed in the wake of the Fatti di Maggio. The inevitable showdown between Ciancabilla and Malatesta and their respective support-ers came within a few weeks of the latter's arrival. By a vote of eighty to three, the Gruppo Diritto all'Esistenza declared itself in favor of Malatesta's program, thereby leaving Ciancabilla no choice but to resign as editor of *La Questione Sociale*. A new series of the newspaper was initiated under

Malatesta's direction on September 9, 1899. To compensate Ciancabilla for his loss, the Gruppo Diritto all'Esistenza assisted him financially when he launched publication of his own antiorganizationist newspaper, *L'Aurora*, in West Hoboken on September 16, 1899.[46]

In the end, Malatesta's editorship of *La Questione Sociale* did nothing to restore peace and harmony among the contending factions. To the contrary, his powerful presence threatened to assure the permanent ascendance of the *organizzatori*, a prospect that enraged some of the more fanatical followers of Ciancabilla. Thus, while Malatesta was explaining his program at a meeting in the Tivola and Zucca saloon in West Hoboken on the evening September 3, 1899, a young barber and malcontent named Domenico Pazzaglia drew a revolver and shot Malatesta in the leg. Accounts in the U.S. press and some historians misrepresented the incident, some identifying Ciancabilla as the shooter (he was not even present at the meeting), others claiming that "Count Malatesta" was the assailant.[47] Malatesta dismissed the incident as *"una piccola disgrazia"* (a minor mishap)[48] and continued with his activities without missing a beat. On September 23, 1899, Malatesta departed from New York on a propaganda tour lasting four months that brought him to anarchist communities in Pennsylvania, Illinois, Massachusetts, Rhode Island, and Vermont, all the while contributing a prodigious number of articles to *La Questione Sociale*. After brief visits to Tampa and Havana, where he addressed Spanish and Cuban workers, Malatesta departed from New York for London on April 4, 1900, leaving before projects such as organizing an anarchist federation could be completed. Esteve and other local comrades resumed the editorship of *La Questione Sociale* after his departure. Ciancabilla, meanwhile, was obliged for financial reasons to transfer *L'Aurora* to a small mining community in Yogohany, Pennsylvania, and again in December to the mining town of Spring Valley, Illinois. The absence of the two rivals in Paterson and West Hoboken helped reduce the squabbling between *organizzatori* and *antiorganizzatori*, but it was Bresci's assassination of King Umberto of July 29, 1900, that reestablished strong bonds of solidarity among the anarchists as they came under unprecedented scrutiny and attack from outside sources.[49]

When Bresci first arrived in the United States, he settled in West Hoboken and readily found work in a local silk factory; in April 1899 he moved to a better-paying job as a skilled decorator at the Hamill and Booth silk mill in nearby Paterson, averaging fourteen dollars a week. Adjusting easily to his new environment, Bresci was genuinely appreciative of the greater economic security and political freedom he enjoyed in the United States and gave no indication of sharing the goal of so many Italian immigrants, that is, to save money and eventually return to Italy. As he wrote to his brother Lorenzo,

"Here everything is different than in Italy. Here we are free to express our opinions. The police leave us alone, our newspapers can publish what we want, and the citizens of every social class have the same political rights."[50] Nevertheless, Bresci was acutely conscious of the labor strife and exploitation inherent to industrial life in the United States as well as the contempt with which Italians were regarded by the Anglo-Saxons, the Irish, and other ethnic groups that had preceded them. "They even call us pigs," he would later declare at his trial.[51]

Bresci also differed from so many comrades and other Italians who remained insular and isolated within the immigrant community. He aspired to become acquainted with English-speaking Americans, especially women. At a picnic in the woods of Weehawken he met a comely Irish-American seamstress named Sophie Knieland in April 1898. She later claimed that after a courtship of nine months they were married before a justice of the peace; however, they may well have lived together without benefit of state or clergy in a rented house at 363 Clinton Avenue in West Hoboken. In March 1899, Sophie gave birth to a daughter, named Maddalena after his mother, and shortly before Bresci's departure for Italy would become pregnant with another daughter, to be named Gaetanina. Apolitical herself, Sophie had little knowledge of her husband's political activities, much less his plans concerning King Umberto. She knew only that Bresci was an anarchist, but without comprehending the pariah status of that philosophy, later explaining to interrogators that he was an anarchist "in the same way that one is a Catholic or a Protestant."[52] Bresci made no attempt to convert Sophie to the cause. Like so many Italian radicals, Bresci was content to keep his domestic and political lives separate. This dichotomy was facilitated by his living and work arrangement. While Sophie and Maddalena resided in West Hoboken, Bresci boarded at the Bertoldi Hotel in Paterson during the week, returning home to be with his family between Saturday and Sunday evenings. Bresci spent most of his free time in the countryside with his wife and child, indulging in his favorite hobby, taking photographs with a camera that became a constant companion during nonwork days. As in Italy, Bresci was fastidious about his appearance, always well groomed and partial to good clothing and jewelry. Some of his comrades considered his sartorial preoccupation a bourgeois affectation, but their mild disapproval did not deter Bresci from this form of self-indulgence. In all superficial aspects, therefore, Bresci was a model family man, leading a happy and conventional life, giving no trace of possessing the capacity to commit a political assassination. He was the antithesis of the demonic anarchist assassin whose stereotype was so deeply imprinted in the minds of the bourgeoisie, then and later.[53]

The apparent normality and conventionality of his personality and life-style was precisely what made Bresci the most enigmatic of the *giustizieri*. According to Ernestina Cravello, the twenty-year-old woman dubbed the "queen of the anarchists" by New York reporters, Bresci "had been brooding over Humbert . . . ever since he came to America."[54] Yet he gave no inkling that the assassination of Italy's king was already germinating in the darker recesses of his mind, not to his comrades, not even his wife. "He was not a man to confide in anyone," Cravello noted.[55] The very impenetrability of his thoughts and character prevented his comrades from conceiving Bresci capable of assassinating the king of Italy. Giuseppe Ciancabilla, who knew him well, described Bresci as possessing a very stable and ingratiating personality: he was "good, temperate, honest, calm, anything but impulsive, almost phlegmatic, and enjoyed the esteem and affection of his comrades."[56] "Almost phlegmatic," in the sense of his being a man of few words, was considered a defining characteristic by virtually all his comrades. The weaver Luigi Prina remembered him as "a man who never spoke. . . . If you addressed him, he answered; if not, he was capable of remaining silent for an entire day."[57] Pedro Esteve noted that Bresci, "with his habitual calm, could make even the mildest of men lose their patience. . . . We all knew he was not impulsive."[58] The anarchist community in Paterson and West Hoboken therefore reacted with collective shock when news of his deed was received from Italy. Asked by New York journalists whether she was surprised, Ernestina Cravello responded "more than surprised; he seemed like such a good person, so peaceful."[59] Another young woman, Emma Quazza, who had met Bresci aboard the ship that brought him back to Europe and was later interrogated by the *carabinieri*, stated, "I would never have believed him capable of committing such a serious crime, because he seemed to have such a gentle soul."[60] Such was the opinion of nearly all who knew Bresci, whether intimately or casually.[61]

Prior to his assassination of King Umberto, Bresci was by no means a prominent member of the anarchist community in Paterson and West Hoboken, although he had acquired a measure of notoriety in the course of the conflict between Ciancabilla and Malatesta. On that evening of September 3, 1899, when Pazzaglia shot and wounded Malatesta, it was Bresci who disarmed the assailant.[62] Apart from this spontaneous act, Bresci had not distinguished himself in any way save for his taciturn and peaceful nature. A typical rank-and-file anarchist, Bresci had joined the Gruppo Diritto all'Esistenza after his arrival, regularly attended Wednesday night meetings at the Bertoldi Hotel, read *La Questione Sociale*, and purchased a $10 share in the Casa Editrice L'Aurora, the group's publishing operation. He never submitted an article or letter to the newspaper and was not a regular contributor, having donated fifty cents on just one occasion.[63] Whether Bresci was an active or passive participant at weekly meetings is unclear. Commemorative articles suggest he always contributed to discussions, while other sources portray him as generally a silent observer, who, if he spoke at all, reserved his comments for the end of the meeting, when he would ask for the floor by saying "*una piccola osservazione*" ("a minor observation").[64] If aroused, however, Bresci could be passionate and forceful. Many years later, a veteran anarchist who wrote under the name "Marat" recalled an incident that occurred during a meeting of the Gruppo Diritto all'Esistenza, at which Malatesta was discussing issues with his comrades. "Marat," who was not a member of the group, quietly entered the room, curious to hear what the famous anarchist leader had to say. Malatesta, always attuned to the possibility of infiltration by police spies, asked the visitor to identify himself. "Marat" did so by declaring himself a "black sheep," a supporter of Ciancabilla. Sensing unease among the group, "Marat" offered to leave if his presence was unwelcomed, which prompted Bresci to declare, "if that individual goes, I go as well." His bold gesture was unnecessary. Although a supporter of Ciancabilla, "Marat" was nevertheless considered a comrade and invited to remain. The meeting continued without further incident.[65]

Bresci's personality and behavior do not reveal anything decisive about his ideological orientation. Italian and American authorities in 1900—and all conspiracy theorists thereafter—associated Bresci with Malatesta. They believed that Bresci's disarming of Malatesta's assailant became the basis for a close relationship between them. On the one hand, Malatesta's disciple and biographer, Luigi Fabbri, wrote that they became friends after the incident, and Malatesta himself many years later alluded in passing to Bresci as "my close friend."[66] On the other hand, an unnamed anarchist from Paterson, interviewed by a New York reporter, insisted that Bresci and Malatesta were not well acquainted.[67] Bresci himself maintained during an interrogation session that he had attended several of Malatesta's lectures, but insisted that he did not have "friendly relations" with him, noting also that "during a rather animated discussion, I expressed opinions different from his."[68] The possibility that Bresci and other anarchists wished to deflect suspicion away from Malatesta cannot be excluded. Nevertheless, concerning the vital issues of violence and organization, Bresci's ideas were unquestionably closer to Ciancabilla's. Moreover, his differences with Malatesta's ideas may have translated into Bresci's differences with the Gruppo Diritto all'Esistenza, which he claimed to have quit some four or five months before his departure for Italy: "It seemed to me that the members did not profess true anarchist socialist ideas."[69] On the other hand, Bresci may have quit the group much earlier or at least was tending in that direction around the time of Ciancabilla's ouster as editor of *La Questione Sociale*. This possibility is suggested by his one-time contribution of fifty cents in support of Ciancabilla's *L'Aurora* in September 1899. Antonio Laner, the anarchist who met him aboard the ship to Italy and was later suspected of being his accomplice, claimed Bresci actually subscribed to *L'Aurora*, although he was never listed as such. Another shipboard companion, Nicola Quintavalle, who was Bresci's friend and barber in West Hoboken, also claimed that he was an antiorganizationist supporter of Ciancabilla.[70] In contrast, Paterson comrade Alberto Curolo dissented, testifying before U.S. investigators that Bresci was not in accord with Ciancabilla's ideas, a claim perhaps intended to divert suspicion away from the latter, whose support of violence was well known.[71] Ciancabilla himself, during an interview with a postal inspector after the assassination, insisted that he and Bresci were personal friends.[72] Finally, Pedro Esteve, who knew Bresci well, also provided testimony affirming that his ideas regarding political violence were more in accord with Ciancabilla's than with Malatesta's: "Bresci had faith in collective rather than individual action, because his great preoccupation was to prepare the people for revolution." However, he considered oral and written propaganda to be ineffective. "The more propaganda we make," Bresci allegedly said, "the fewer in number we are. . . . The people are tired of propaganda. Deeds, deeds, that is what we need.'" Esteve concluded that Bresci intended his deed as a means "to complicate the political situation in Italy," to the point of making revolution inevitable.[73]

But ideological commitment to direct action was not the defining characteristic of Bresci's *attentat*, which differed in significant respects from the deeds of his predecessors. Bresci was not driven by spontaneous impulse. Caserio, Acciarito, and Lucheni had leaped into action just a few days after conceiving the idea of committing an assassination. Lega and Angiolillo struck within weeks or months after the precipitating events had transpired. Bresci, in contrast, had resolved to exact vengeance upon King Umberto as early as 1895, after the onset of the Crispian reaction, a decision greatly strengthened by the *Fatti di Maggio* in 1898. During his trial, he explained that "It was after the states of siege in Sicily and Milan, illegally applied with a royal decree, that I thought of killing the king to avenge the victims. . . . The events in Milan, where they used cannons, made me cry with rage, and I thought of revenge. I thought of the king, because he not only signs the decrees, he rewarded the evil men who carried out the slaughter. I formulated a plan to return to Italy and began to save for it."[74]

Another significant difference between Bresci and his predecessors was the circumstances of their lives at the time they embarked upon their deadly missions. Lega, Caserio, Angiolillo, Lucheni had each experienced constant economic hardship, periodic police persecution (save for Lucheni), and unceasing anxiety about their personal survival, whether in Italy or in exile. They were dealing with dire circumstances and great emotional stress when they decided to act, almost as if they concluded they had nothing to lose and were resigned to their fate. Bresci, in contrast, lived a relatively normal life, economically comfortable and emotionally secure, in a stable environment with a loving wife and child. It was remarkable, under the circumstances of his life in 1900, that he was still bent on the revenge he had first conceived of exacting while languishing in *domicilio coatto* in 1895. Bresci certainly knew that his assassination of Umberto or a failed attempt constituted a suicide mission from which there was no return. Yet Bresci was prepared not only to sacrifice his own life but to risk the dire consequences that would surely befall his entire family, in the United States and Italy. Bresci's willingness to endanger so much was interpreted by his fellow anarchists as a sign of great courage and heroism. Ciancabilla went further in his belief that the impatient and rebellious spirit that drove him to act was rooted in his "anarchist consciousness."[75] A less partisan interpretation might suggest that Bresci acted out of fanatical and fatalistic commitment to exact revenge for the perceived injustices committed by King Umberto and the Italian government.

Concealing his true intentions, Bresci informed Sophie in February 1900 that he needed to return to Italy sometime soon in order to dispose of the house and land his recently deceased parents had bequeathed to him and his siblings. That same month he purchased a .38 caliber revolver, and on Sunday outings in the countryside with his family, Bresci engaged in target practice. As this was a common sport among gun-toting Americans, Bresci's new "hobby" did not arouse Sophie's suspicion, and within a few weeks Bresci had become an excellent marksman. On May 12 Bresci quit his job at Hamill and Booth and alerted a few comrades of his imminent departure. A French passenger line was offering a 50 percent discount to U.S. residents who planned to visit the Universal Exposition in Paris. To avail himself of the discount, Bresci purchased a ticket previously issued at the discount to another Italian. Using the excuse of her pregnancy and Maddalena's youth, Bresci did not invite his wife to accompany him to Italy, promising her they would visit together in the future. To finance his sea voyage ($31) and travel in France and Italy, Bresci took $162.40 from his accumulated savings; he even requested reimbursement of his $10 share in the Casa Editrice "L'Aurora." Bresci departed from New York harbor aboard the French steamship *Gascogne* on May 17, 1900. He made no attempt to disguise his identity, and his name was included in the ship's passenger list.[76]

On board the vessel were at least sixty-six other Italians who had availed themselves of the discount fare, including his friend Nicola Quintavalle along with Antonio Laner, and Emma Quazza. All three were Bresci's constant companions aboard ship.[77] Quintavalle, a thirty-five-year-old barber, originally from Elba, had been a friend of Pietro Gori; he fled Italy during the Crispian reaction and settled in West Hoboken, where he became a well-known figure among local comrades, noted for his ability to shave clients with either hand. Quintavalle had never been a member of the Gruppo Diritto all'Esistenza in Paterson; he was aligned with the *anti-organizzatori* and was well acquainted with Ciancabilla. More committed to sustaining the anarchist press, Quintavalle was a periodic contributor to *La Questione Sociale* and later to *L'Aurora*. Laner, another anarchist, was a forty-three-year-old baker originally from Trento, who had formerly lived in Turin; he had not known Bresci or Quintavalle before the voyage. Quazza, a nineteen-year-old weaver from Biella, had lived and worked in Paterson for four and a half years. Her father was a socialist, and she had belonged to Circolo Socialista Italiano in Paterson largely because of her engagement to Camillo Cianfarra, the former editor of *Il Proletario*. Her family had disapproved of the relationship, and she was now returning to her hometown in the company of her uncle and his family. Her plans were to visit her mother in Biella and then return to the United States. Aboard ship she made the acquaintance of Bresci who knew her former fiancé Cianfarra. She later recounted to Italian authorities that while Quintavalle was very forthcoming about his anarchist beliefs, Bresci did not identify himself as such and did not discuss politics with her. Neither of the men, she recalled, had expressed any proposals to commit violence against anyone. Subsequent rumors that she and Bresci had a shipboard romance were false.[78]

The voyage across the Atlantic took little more than ten days. Bresci's plans could have come to naught upon disembarkation at Le Havre if customs officials had discovered the revolver he had hidden on his person. Having surmounted that obstacle, Bresci and his companions traveled on to Paris, where he arranged for Quazza to stay at the Rue Lausanne home of Carlo Fodere, a Piedmontese whose French wife was the sister of the cook at the Bertoldi Hotel, who was married to the anarchist weaver Luigi Prina in Paterson.[79] The three men found lodgings elsewhere, at the Roussel boarding house on the Rue de Vanves. For eight days the group thoroughly enjoyed themselves, touring Paris and visiting the exposition. Bresci impressed Quazza with the freedom with which he spent money. Quintavalle was so captivated with Paris that he expressed the possibility of someday opening his own barbershop there. At one point, he and Laner tried unsuccessfully to locate Salvatore

Pallavicini, a comrade who formerly lived in Paterson and wrote many articles for *La Questione Sociale*, who was working at the Paris exposition as a translator. Once their Parisian sojourn ended, the group traveled together to Modane, where they departed for their respective connection points and final destinations. On route to his hometown, Bresci stopped off in Genoa, where he exchanged a $90 postal money order for 500 lira. He arrived in Coiano on June 5.[80]

Bresci resided for more than a month with his older brother Lorenzo, the latter's wife, and his sister Teresa's eight-year-old daughter, who was visiting. He spent most of his time with his family, exchanging accounts of recent developments in Coiano and Paterson, visiting former comrades from the Fabbricone, with whom he spoke positively about the United States, telling them how much more money they could earn in Paterson, and taking numerous photographs of family and friends. He also corresponded by letter with his three shipboard companions to arrange meetings before returning to the United States. To Quazza he wrote from Prato that he preferred Italy to the United States, but "I could not readapt to the miserable conditions in which we are forced to work in our homeland."[81]

Up to this point, Bresci's behavior gave no indication of his true purpose—save one. In the United States, Bresci had become accustomed to carrying his revolver with him, so he brazenly submitted an official request to do the same during his sojourn in Italy. The request was refused, but the local police chief did not take alarm even though Bresci was listed in local police records as a "dangerous anarchist." The police chief also failed to inform the interior ministry of Bresci's presence in Italy, as required; nor did he comply with another regulation: retaining Bresci's passport until his departure. Evidently convinced that Bresci had returned home only for a brief vacation, the police chief did not order any surveillance of this "dangerous anarchist," thereby failing to learn that almost every morning Bresci would go out into the countryside and continue to engage in target practice with his revolver.[82]

From Coiano, Bresci traveled with his young niece Maddalena to Castel San Pietro, near Bologna, to visit his sister Teresa on July 18. In Castel San Pietro, Bresci initiated an affair with Teresa Brugnoli, a worker in his brother-in-law's umbrella factory. From there, Bresci went to Bologna on the morning of July 20 in the company of his new lover, taking lodging at the Hotel Milano. On the afternoon of July 21, Bresci received a telegram from Luigi Granotti, an anarchist from Paterson who was visiting his hometown of Sagliano Micca near Biella. Granotti had migrated to the United States in May 1894, settling in Paterson together with his older brother Giuseppe. The Granotti brothers were very active members of the Gruppo Diritto all'Esistenza, Giuseppe a frequent financial supporter of *La Questione Sociale*, and Luigi, as the treasurer and administrator of the newspaper in 1899. He resigned this position as treasurer in January 1900 as a gesture of protest against the polemic being waged between Malatesta and Ciancabilla.[83] Luigi had departed for Italy on May 31, 1900, accompanying his mother, who planned to remain permanently in Sagliano Micca. The ostensible reason for the trip was the constant discord between Giuseppe's wife and his mother. Luigi may also have intended to marry a local woman. But the innocuous beginning of his visit back home turned ominous when he connected with Bresci two months later. The first telegram he sent to Bresci in Bologna read "I await you in Biella on Monday; if not, write me."[84] The telegram may have been an innocent exchange between two comrades, who several months earlier in Paterson may have agreed to rendezvous in Milan, as both of their visits home would coincide. Nevertheless, the seemingly harmless message aroused Brugnoli's concern when Bresci discarded the telegram after tearing in into little pieces. He assured her that nothing was amiss, but that he had to depart for Piacenza that same evening. That telegram was the first clue that led Italian authorities to conclude that Granotti was Bresci's chief accomplice.

During his three-day stay in Bologna, Bresci wrote a letter to his brother Lorenzo, stating that he would return to Coiano on or before July 28. According to Bresci's biographer, Giuseppe Galzerano, this letter and others to his wife, sister, and lover pose an intriguing question: was it possible that Bresci had not committed himself fully to the assassination he had contemplated since 1895?[85] If that were the case, however, why had he brought along his revolver and kept practicing his marksmanship? There is no satisfactory answer to these questions; however, Bresci was not a man given to hesitation or impulsiveness, so it is unlikely that he was reconsidering his plan. Moreover, Bresci said nothing in his subsequent interrogations to indicate that at some point he entertained doubts about carrying out his mission. In all likelihood, the reassuring content of his letters represented a calculated effort to maintain an air of normality and to avoid arousing anyone's suspicions.

After leaving Bologna, Bresci went to Piacenza for reasons unknown, perhaps to see the city and to develop some film with photographs he had previously taken. On July 23, Bresci sent Granotti a telegram, stating, "I wish to see you in Milan. Respond at Caffè Arisi, Piacenza." The next day Granotti replied, "Write to me in Milan, I will come find you." Before departing by train for Milan on the morning of July 24, Bresci notified his comrade that he would be renting a room at the Ramella boardinghouse on the Via San Pietro all'Orto, No. 4. Bresci arrived in Milan that afternoon and was joined the following day by Granotti, who found lodging elsewhere. Once in the Lombard capital, the two anarchists behaved as tourists for two days, visiting famous sites, eating meals together, and consuming large quantities of ice cream. That Granotti—identified by witnesses as "*il biondino*" or "the young blond one"—was seen in Bresci's company on several occasions during their Milan visit would solidify official belief that he was Bresci's primary accomplice. On July 27, they left Milan together and arrived by midday at Monza, where King Umberto was vacationing. Bresci rented a room on the Via Cairoli, No. 4, while Granotti found lodging elsewhere. Bresci later acknowledged that he and Granotti met again the following day, but Granotti's whereabouts on the fatal day of July 29 remains in doubt. Bresci maintained that on July 28 Granotti had extended an invitation to accompany him the next day to Biella and then on to his home in Sagliano Micca. Bresci declined the invitation, indicating he had some business to conduct in Monza. Granotti, he insisted under interrogation, had no idea what Bresci's business entailed, and Granotti departed Monza that day for home in Piedmont. Bresci's account was contradicted by witnesses at Granotti's lodgings who claimed that he returned on the night of July 29 in an agitated state and left Monza the following day.[86]

Having learned from newspapers that King Umberto planned to visit Monza to observe a contest of gymnasts in the Royal Park, Bresci reconnoitered the scene for two days, asking local coach drivers, vendors, and even the *carabinieri* specific questions about the king's habits, claiming he wished to see His Majesty close up. Having decided that the best time to strike would be at the conclusion of the festivities, Bresci began his preparations the night before, cleaning his revolver and cutting crosses into the lead bullets with a scissors to increase their lethality. He spent the day of the fatal encounter as if on a holiday. He arose at around 10:00 a.m. and spent almost two hours washing, shaving, and cleaning his nails. Fastidious as always about his appearance, Bresci dressed himself in a hazel jacket, a hat of the same color, a black necktie with a gold pin, a gold watch and chain, and a jewel ring. Leaving his *pensione* around noon, Bresci stopped first at a dairy bar and ate ice cream and a half-hour later sat down in an outdoor seat at the Caffè del Vapore and ordered lunch. The proprietor observed that his customer appeared melancholic and asked if anything was troubling him. Bresci responded, "Today will be a terrible day for me." He also spoke about his wife and child in a manner evidencing how much he missed them. To pass the time, Bresci invited a young man in the restaurant to join him at his table for a chat. He introduced himself as "Caserio," a choice suggesting preoccupation with his mission and awareness of the fate that most likely awaited him. As the two men conversed, Bresci appeared increasing nervous, especially when two *carabinieri* walked past. After paying the bill for himself and his lunch companion, Bresci bid the young man farewell, saying "Look at me carefully, because you will perhaps remember me for the rest of your life." He spent the remainder of the day walking around town and returning to the dairy bar four more times for ice cream. By evening, Bresci had entered the royal park, hoping to position himself along the road by which the king would enter, thereby giving himself a chance to escape. But the crowd was so dense that he was pushed toward the center of activities, within three meters of the spot where the king's carriage would park. The location was optimum for his purpose but afforded no possibility of escape. Undaunted, Bresci patiently awaited the moment when he would avenge the peasants and workers killed during the Fasci Siciliani and *Fatti di Maggio*.[87]

The onslaught of repression the anarchists in Italy expected the government to unleash in the wake of King Umberto's assassination never materialized.[88] Italy's experiment with reactionary politics had been defeated by a temporary alliance of left-wing elements, and with the acquiescence of the new prime minister, Giuseppe Saracco, and the new king, Vittorio Emanuele III, a new era in Italian politics was beginning, often described as "democracy in the making."[89] This is not to say that the anarchists remained unmolested in the days and weeks after Bresci's deed. Hundreds—literally anyone who knew or had contact with Bresci—were interrogated, arrested, and frequently detained in prison during the frantic campaign to discover Bresci's alleged accomplices.

It was axiomatic to the Italian government, judiciary, and police that Bresci had not acted alone. As with every *attentat*, the authorities assumed the existence of a plot. Typical of the conspiracy theories seriously entertained was that concocted by the police chief of Milan just one day after the assassination. He asserted that a plot to assassinate King Umberto had been hatched in London by the anarchist Comitato Rivoluzionario at the end of 1898. The committee supposedly assigned Ciancabilla the task of assassinating the king and provided him with 500 lire to pay for the trip to Italy and other expenses. Instead of fulfilling his mission, Ciancabilla supposedly absconded with the money and went to Paterson, where he assumed the editorship of *La Questione Sociale*. While the committee searched for a substitute, Malatesta escaped from *domicilio coatto*, and after returning to London and being informed of Ciancabilla's treachery, Malatesta was dispatched to Paterson to unmask the culprit and take over the publication of *La Questione Sociale*. During the ensuing conflict between the two anarchist notables, Ciancabilla shot Malatesta at a meeting in West Hoboken. The injury did not prevent Malatesta from organizing a revolutionary committee among the anarchists of Paterson, West Hoboken, and New York and then selecting Bresci and other local individuals to plan and execute the regicide.[90] This fanciful account—typical of others to follow—was replete with factual errors and misconceptions about how the anarchists operated, but the government's a priori assumption and continuing belief that an international conspiracy involving anarchists in London, Paterson, West Hoboken, and New York was responsible for Umberto's assassination continued to influence the judicial investigation and government action for the next two years.

In the frenzied atmosphere of panic that immediately followed the assassination, eleven individuals—not all of them anarchists—were designated as accomplices and held in custody, some for a few weeks, others for many months, sometimes in solitary confinement: Bresci's brother Lorenzo, Emma Quazza, Antonio Laner, Nicola Quintavalle, Vittorio Jaffei (an ex-customs guard), Carlo Colombo (a janitor), Egidio Galli (a cart maker), Achille Consolini (a livestock merchant), Renato Caprotti (an accountant), Domenico Menozzi (an innkeeper and former policeman), and Luigi Granotti. But after a year of unproductive investigation, the Court of Appeals of Milan announced on August 28, 1901, that insufficient evidence had been uncovered to proceed against ten of the suspects. Lorenzo Bresci had been arrested for no other reason than his familial relationship with the assassin. He emerged from prison with his mental health destroyed. Quazza, Laner, and Quintavalle were objects of suspicion because they lived in Paterson and West Hoboken, had been Bresci's shipboard companions, and had accompanied him to the Paris Exposition before going their separate ways in Italy. Although her relationship with the noted socialist Camillo Cianfarra had made her even more suspect, the court's investigation established that Quazza had not known Bresci in Paterson and that their shipboard and postarrival acquaintance had been innocent and devoid of political intent. Released from prison on August 18, Quazza returned to Paterson in November 1901. Laner as well had not known Bresci prior to their meeting aboard ship, and nothing suggesting any measure of complicity was ever discovered. He returned to Paterson immediately after the court dropped charges, and he conducted a lecture tour describing his experience as a suspect in the assassination. Suspicion lay more heavily upon Quintavalle, a well-respected militant in West Hoboken who had known Bresci (a regular customer in his barbershop) prior to their departure, had been acquainted with both Malatesta and Ciancabilla (he was selected to serve on the jury of honor convened, but never held, to adjudicate the conflict between them), and had discussed anarchism openly with Bresci aboard ship. But nothing linking him to the assassination was ever discovered. He remained in Italy rather than return to the United States and continued to have trouble with the authorities.[91]

Several of the others had been arrested for the flimsiest of reasons. Galli, prior to returning to Italy, had been photographed by Bresci in West Hoboken; he was released after two weeks. Consolini aroused suspicion because he had been overheard discussing the assassination. Caprotti, having spent some time in the United States, was arrested for having manifested "equivocal behavior" at Umberto's funeral and for uttering some "anarchist words." He was released after a few days. Manozzi was taken into custody because he had claimed to have possessed important information about the regicide before it happened. He was released after the authorities determined that he was mentally unbalanced. Jaffei, while in Switzerland, had written to Bresci in prison, predicting the forthcoming assassination of King Vittorio Emanuele III. Extradited to Italy, Jaffei was released after the authorities determined that he, too, was a mental case.[92]

Out of the original eleven, the only credible suspects were Carlo Colombo and Luigi Granotti. A shoemaker by trade and the janitor at the house where he lived, Colombo was described by Milan's police chief as "a noted and dangerous anarchist . . . [who] is one of the most active anarchists in Milan, very capable, if not of carrying out, certainly favorable to criminal enterprise." Colombo came under immediate suspicion because he was in frequent contact with anarchists in London and Paterson and was known as the "go-to" man for comrades visiting Milan. Moreover, Colombo resided and worked at Via San Pietro all'Orto, no. 16, just a stone's throw from the house at no. 4 on the same street where Bresci rented a room during his stay in Milan. The police chief did not believe the proximity was coincidental. Furthermore, because Bresci supposedly arrived at his rooming house without his suitcase, the police chief assumed he must have left it with Colombo when he first arrived in Milan. From that assumption, he concluded, contact between Bresci and militant activist Colombo could only have meant one thing: Colombo's complicity. Arrested on July 30, Colombo remained in prison under preventive detention until January 9, 1901, when the court ruled the evidence insufficient to prosecute him.[93]

If Bresci did indeed have an accomplice, the most likely candidate was Luigi Granotti, "*il biondino*," the fellow silk weaver whom he knew in Paterson and with whom he had communicated and met several times in Italy. The court's investigation accumulated the following physical evidence: (1) a stamp postmarked "Prato" found in Granotti's house in Sagliano Micca; (2) a copy of the July 15 issue of *La Stampa* (Turin), indicating the date of the king's arrival in Monza, which had been sent to Bresci from Sagliano Micca, in an envelope addressed in Granotti's handwriting; (3) the various telegrams they had exchanged; a register indicating Granotti's stay at the Brigada Inn in

Monza from July 27 to 30. Eyewitness testimony placed Granotti and Bresci together in Bologna (Bresci denied they had met there), Milan, and Monza. Highly compelling, in the eyes of the authorities, was the testimony provided by Granotti's cousin, Giacomo Bussetti of Sagliano Micca. He recounted that on the evening of July 30 Granotti returned home in a highly agitated state and announced his desire to depart the next day for the ski resort town of Gressoney, in the Aosta Valley, adjacent to the frontier with Switzerland. Granotti chose not to take the tram but to proceed to Gressoney on foot, which required hiring an Alpine guide. During their trip, Granotti confided to his cousin that he was fearful of arrest because of his friendship with Bresci. Now suspicious, especially after Granotti gave him his pistol for safekeeping, Bussetti concluded that his cousin was involved with the assassination as a backup man in the event that Bresci failed in his attempt. Arrested a few days later, Bussetti gave this information to the police, but upon his release he retracted his statements, claiming that his interrogators had threatened and manhandled him to obtain information associating Granotti with the crime. Soon thereafter Bussetti migrated to the United States.[94]

Granotti, meanwhile, had crossed the border into Switzerland and made his way to Paris, where Isidore Besso supposedly provided him with a passport and the means to reach Great Britain. From there, Granotti made his way back to the United States, where he disappeared into a clandestine existence with the help of comrades. Frustrated by the failure to apprehend him and determined to justify months of futile investigation, the Milan Court of Assizes tried Granotti in absentia on November 25, 1901, condemning him to *ergastolo* for his alleged role as Bresci's accomplice. Ironically, public outrage over King Umberto's assassination had dissipated to the point that the national press devoted only a few lines to Granotti's trial and conviction. The Italian government, however, remained obsessed with Granotti's capture, and the hunt for "*il biondino*" continued for decades, with consular reports from five continents periodically claiming sightings of him. Granotti continued to elude detection until his death in New York in 1949.[95]

# 7  U.S. Investigation and Death
of the *Giustiziere*

| | |
|---|---|
| Folli non siam nè tristi | We are neither crazy nor sad |
| nè bruti nè birbanti, | neither brutes nor criminals, |
| ma siam degli anarchisti | instead we are anarchists |
| pel bene militanti | fighters for good. |

—Attilio Panizza, *Canto dei Malfattori*, 1892

The hunt for Bresci's accomplices in Italy having yielded nothing more than the symbolic conviction of Luigi Granotti, Italian authorities were hopeful that the U.S. government could root out the culprits in the United States who presumably had plotted King Umberto's assassination in the first place. Until Bresci's assassination of King Umberto, local police in Paterson and federal authorities in Washington scarcely knew that the Italian anarchists of Paterson even existed.

Although the reasons that motivated Bresci to assassinate King Umberto could have prompted his deed regardless of where he worked and resided, there can be no doubt that the Italian anarchist community that thrived in Paterson at the turn of the century influenced his thinking and commitment to revolutionary action. Efforts to uncover a conspiracy responsible for the assassination were conducted by the Paterson police, the New Jersey State authorities, the Italian ambassador and consul general of New York, and several federal government agencies. Local police in Paterson had the unenviable task of investigating a murder-suicide case that the U.S. press seized upon as proof that the plot to assassinate King Umberto had indeed originated in Paterson. On July 18, Giuseppe Pessina, a foreman at the Weidman Silk Dying Company, who was widely hated for his brutal treatment of the workers, was shot and killed by Sperandio Cariboni, formerly employed at the same mill. Later that evening, Cariboni killed himself "rather than have my head cut off by these cannibal Americans." Cariboni's motive for killing Pessina, according to the anarchist Antonio Cravello, was a combination of revenge and desperation: Pessina owned seventy dollars to Cariboni for piano lessons the latter had given to his daughter, but the foreman not only refused to pay, he arranged to have Cariboni discharged from his job when he asked for his money.[1]

What cast a mysterious cloud over this simple murder-suicide was a bizarre letter allegedly written by Cariboni and found on his body. Addressed to "My Dear Friends and Comrades," the letter related "the horrible fate that has come to me—not of my own will, but compelled to act by the grand and brave society to which I belong, that is to say, the Anarchists." Supposedly, at an anarchist meeting in Milan on February 2, 1900, lots were drawn to determine who would assassinate King Umberto. "That lot fell to me, but I being in America, the society has left it to my full liberty to choose as a substitute whomsoever I wish." He indicated that he chose the "brute animal" Pessina. "There will be many . . . [who] will say I have done well and have done my part to free my country. *Vive 'Anarchie!*" Cautioning "companions and comrades," the letter stated, "when you are in a society, do your duty or resign, absolutely, because the societies are sacred. It is to say you must obey and follow orders, no matter the cost or what may happen." In closing, Cariboni signed himself "your pitiable friend and companion."[2]

Nothing about the letter made any sense. Cariboni was not an anarchist. No one had ever heard him refer to himself as such, nor had he ever attended an anarchist meeting or read an anarchist newspaper. His depiction of the anarchists in Milan drawing lots and giving orders reflected bourgeois fantasies about how anarchists operated but flew in the face of reality. And even if such a meeting had taken place, why would the anarchists have selected someone in faraway Paterson rather than closer at hand? And if Cariboni had the option to pick a substitute target, why would he choose Pessina, who was known to be hostile to radicals? The letter itself, written in Italian, had been found by the owner of the mortuary in charge of Cariboni's body, who on his own initiative allegedly had it translated into English. But when the anarchists in Paterson demanded to examine the letter to determine its authenticity, it had "disappeared." The anarchists concluded that the letter was either a forgery intended to damage the reputation of Italian workers or the product of a delusional mind.[3] The Paterson police did nothing to challenge their conclusion. Police investigators failed to form an opinion about the letter, nor did they find any connection between the assassination and the anarchists of Paterson. Police Chief Frederick Graul merely commented, "I don't know anything about any Anarchists in Paterson. They have not bothered us, and until they do we can do nothing."[4] In the end, despite the myriad inconsistencies that completely eliminated its evidentiary value, the

Cariboni letter continued to be regarded by the U.S. press and independent writers as proof of a plot involving the anarchists of Paterson. Ironically, suspicion in that regard was fostered by the anarchists themselves, who, out of concern for a fellow worker's family, collected funds for Cariboni's funeral.[5]

Italy's efforts to enlist the federal government in the investigation of the anarchists who allegedly plotted Umberto's assassination began within days of the event. "Confidential and personal" communications from Ambassador Baron Fava to the State Department were couched in terms of utmost urgency and secrecy. Fava supposedly learned from a "good source" that the anarchists of Paterson had held a meeting on August 8 at which they opened "a subscription for the defense of Bresci and to aid the assassination of the new king of Italy. The President of the meeting, Mr. Estena [Esteve] is reported to have declared that the new attempt would take place before the condemnation of the regicide." The ambassador expressed his confidence that the federal government would "exert itself" to take appropriate measures to prevent the plots from taking place. "I have no need to add that the first condition for attaining the end in view is that the utmost reserve should be maintained, especially toward the press."[6] That the anarchists would have discussed the assassination of Vittorio Emanuele III at an open meeting only days after the demise of his predecessor was typical of the sensationalist nonsense the Italian authorities continually propagated. Typical as well was the ambassador's desire for the investigation and suppression of the anarchists to be conducted secretly.

Meanwhile, the Italian Consulate General of New York had launched its own investigation with the assistance of the city's police force. Numerous Italians from Paterson and West Hoboken were summoned to the consulate and interrogated by Consul General Bianchi and Vice Consul Prato, often with the assistance of Sergeant Joseph Petrosino of the New York City police, whose later claim to fame was his murder at the hands of the Mafia in 1909, a few days after his arrival in Sicily to investigate their activities. Besides lending the consulate the services of Petrosino, the detective bureau under Captain George W. McClusky was entrusted with the task of investigating the Paterson anarchists and exposing the plot assumed to have originated there. The investigation resulted in a report submitted by McClusky that relied heavily on information furnished to the detective bureau by an Italian spy in the employ of the Italian consulate in New York. In fact, portions of McClusky's report were a verbatim translation of a report submitted by the spy to his superiors at the consulate. Not surprisingly, McClusky's report affirmed the predetermined conclusion that a plot to assassinate Umberto had been orchestrated by Malatesta during his sojourn in the United States.

Bresci supposedly became Malatesta's good friend after saving his life at the West Hoboken debate, serving thereafter as his bodyguard during propaganda tours (an impossibility, considering Bresci's need to work). Before his departure for London, Malatesta allegedly established an information committee (a mistranslation of "action committee" in the spy's report), and when Malatesta cabled the committee [no such telegram was ever sent] that "the moment had arrived to make a quick move," Bresci supposedly drew the lot designating the assassin or volunteered himself for the mission. After the Paterson anarchists allegedly collected money to finance the trip [never happened], "Brasci [sic], Quintavalla [sic], Sassi [Bresci's relative in Italy], and Larner [sic] started for Italy with mandate to kill Umberto." McClusky also asserted that the Paterson anarchists had "seriously discussed the idea of assassinating President McKinley, but cooler heads prevailed," because they "would thereby lose a nation that gave them hospitality . . . and inflame the minds of the American people" who, they feared, would rise en masse and either kill or drive all the anarchists out of the United States.[7]

Satisfied with the misinformation furnished by McClusky, the Italian ambassador, Baron Fava, forwarded the report to the U.S. secretary of state, declaring that it

> seems to place beyond doubt the notorious existence of a regularly organized association, with a recognized head, an executive committee, special organs of propaganda and more or less secret meetings at which criminal acts of violence against social order and human life were plotted and decided. The assassination of H. M. Umberto is the last criminal act of this society which continues to devise fresh offences with impunity.[8]

The intended purpose of transmitting McClusky's report to the State Department was to convince U.S. authorities to suppress the anarchists in Paterson: "It seems to me that the police report in point could, if communicated to the proper magistrate move the public agents to institute regular proceedings for the punishment of the members of the association."[9]

Besides the investigations of the Paterson and New York police departments, the Italian consulate in New York relied even more heavily upon the spies Italian authorities systematically infiltrated into immigrant communities wherever significant numbers of anarchists and other subversives resided, in the United States, Europe, and South America. Paterson was a logical target for such surveillance, because it was a major center of radical activity and a nexus for the transnational ebb and flow of prominent anarchist leaders and immigrants. At the time of Bresci's assassination of Umberto, several spies were operating in Paterson, New York, Barre (Vermont), and elsewhere.[10]

One of them in New York, an ex-anarchist named Giuseppe Ruggiu, who had ceased his activities in Paterson for fear of physical harm if exposed, was rehired temporarily for the purpose of obtaining new information from his former contacts in Paterson. After conducting his investigation for a few days in Paterson, allegedly interviewing Esteve, Widmar, and Guabello, the spy Ruggiu furnished a report to Sergeant Petrosino—the report that provided the information in McClusky's account. He also sent a report to the Ministry of the Interior in Italy and to the New York consulate. Ruggiu's report provided a general history of the anarchist community in Paterson and a detailed account of Bresci's activities. The Bresci he portrayed was a far more active militant than the man usually described by his comrades, supposedly never missing a meeting, always discussing ideas with others in his circle, and helping with the distribution of *La Questione Sociale*. Ever the spy, Ruggiu concluded his report with a request to the consulate to resume his activities as a full-time agent.[11]

In a surprising coda to Ruggiu's efforts, the consul general wrote to the Foreign Ministry and the Milan Court of Appeals on October 5, recommending that they attribute "little or no value to Ruggiu's declarations." The consul general had come to question the spy's reliability, doubting that he had even gone to Paterson to conduct an investigation, much less that he had interviewed Esteve, Widmar, and Guabello. He concluded that the spy's information was too general in nature to be useful. All told, the consulate's investigation continued for six months but found no trace of a plot.[12]

Still determined to expose the culpability of the Paterson anarchists, the Italian government instructed Ambassador Fava to prevail upon the State Department to enlist the assistance of state authorities in New Jersey. Governor Foster McGowan Voorhees intervened as requested, and the supreme court of New Jersey appointed James M. Trimble, a prominent local attorney, to serve as a commissioner of the court and investigate the presumed plot. Starting in October 1900, Trimble's investigation consisted of interviews with more than a score of Italians from Paterson and West Hoboken, both anarchists and nonradicals. Among the former were Beniamino Mazzotta, Pedro Esteve, Ernestina Cravello, Alberto Guabello, Antonio Taggiasco, Alberto Curolo, Luigi Granotti's brother Giuseppe, and others. Every anarchist summoned to testify refused to swear on the bible but promised to tell the truth.[13]

Although the interviews yielded considerable information and insight about anarchist views on violence and the assassination, they were essentially worthless as a means to uncover the alleged plot. Did Trimble and the New Jersey authorities seriously believe the anarchists of Paterson and West Hoboken would expose themselves to criminal prosecution or deportation by admitting the existence of a conspiracy to undertake the assassination of King Umberto? This obvious impediment to determining the truth never seems to have dawned on Trimble and his associates. In the event, each anarchist interviewed (and nonradicals as well) denied the existence of a plot. Their denials did not constitute a cover-up; they reflected a reality of anarchist life invariably lost upon Italian and U.S. authorities inflexibly committed to the belief that anarchist *attentats* were always the result of a conspiracy. Asked about a possible connection between Bresci and Ciancabilla (Trimble seemed to think Ciancabilla a more likely mastermind behind the assassination than Malatesta), Antonio Taggiasco, one of the *anti-organizzatori* in West Hoboken, provided Trimble with the key to understanding why Italian anarchists did not engage in group conspiracies: "I believe Bresci acted independently. He had no need of a teacher. I have never heard anyone speak about a plot. Besides, plots never succeed because there are always some spies."[14] As described earlier, ever since the late 1870s, Italian anarchists of every persuasion, but especially the *anti-organizzatori*, believed that any substantial group of militants would inevitably be infiltrated by police spies. This belief was not a function of irrational fear or paranoia but the result of painful experience, both in Italy and the United States, where several spies were exposed in this period. Fear of exposure and persecution explained why group activity involving political violence had become rare in the 1880s and 1890s, save for the failed insurrectionary attempts usually undertaken by Malatesta.[15] Thus the likelihood of a group as large as the Gruppo Diritto all'Esistenza having organized a plot to assassinate King Umberto was nil. Such a collective enterprise could not have been kept secret. And nothing discovered by Trimble suggested otherwise.

Trimble's queries about Bresci evoked the same response from everyone to whom the question was put—Bresci by nature and behavior was an improbable assassin by any measure. The decision to assassinate King Umberto was his alone. He gave no indication of his intentions to anyone. Nor did Bresci have a special relationship with Ciancabilla, as Trimble seemed to suspect, much less with Malatesta, as consulate spies and New York police affirmed. For answers to the crucial question of Bresci's relationship with the alleged accomplice Luigi Granotti, Trimble interrogated the latter's brother, Giuseppe. During questioning, Giuseppe confirmed that Luigi had accompanied his mother back to Italy because of her illness as well as her inability to get along with his wife. Giuseppe stated that he had never seen Luigi and Bresci together in Paterson—"Bresci did not speak with anyone." Nor had Luigi mentioned any plan to meet Bresci in Italy. He first learned about the charges against Luigi from a friend who had just returned to Italy. The latter also indicated that the incriminating account of Luigi's movements furnished by his cousin Giacomo Busetti had been obtained through torture.[16]

To his credit, Trimble was the only investigator who sought not only to determine whether a plot in Paterson had been responsible for Umberto's assassination, but to understand why such violent deeds occurred and what the anarchists thought about them. Trimble's challenging questions evoked very candid answers that revealed the attitudes toward violence and *attentats* held by working-class, rank-and-file anarchists rather than those of the movement's intellectuals, which so often dominated the debates in the movement's press. Alberto Guabello, a key figure in the Paterson anarchist community, informed Trimble that "no anarchist is a partisan of violence." They have assassinated heads of state "because they are persecuted."[17] Alberto Curolo insisted that "anarchist theories do not teach [individuals] to strike down kings, emperors, etc." Bresci, Angiolillo, Caserio, and the other individuals killed "because of the reaction that raged against them."[18] Questioned about whether anarchists approved all *attentats*, Beniamino Mazzotta, the editor of *Il Movimento* and a prominent militant in Paterson who had assumed responsibility for educating Bresci's children, explained that approval or disapproval depended upon the facts of the case. "No anarchist is discontent when a potentate falls, but as a party we cannot give official sanction." Some *attentats*, like Lucheni's assassination of Empress Elizabeth, "have no logic."[19] Trimble also wished to know whether the anarchists considered Umberto's assassination useful to their cause. Antonio Taggiasco answered, "As a man, no; as a king, yes."[20] By distinguishing between Umberto the man and Umberto the king—between a human being and an abstract symbol of authority—Taggiasco demonstrated that this approach to regicide was common to many anarchists rather than unique to Bresci.

In October 1900, Trimble's report was transmitted to the Italian consul general but no copy was retained by the New Jersey authorities. Doubtless it was not well received in Italy. Like the previous investigations conducted by the Italian consulate in New York and the New York Police Department, Trimble's efforts had failed to establish the existence of a plot in Paterson or even to provide incriminating evidence for the eventual trial *in absentia* of Bresci's presumed accomplice, Luigi Granotti. The last hope in this regard was the investigation by U.S. authorities already underway.

In a letter of August 31, 1900, marked "personal, confidential, and unofficial," Italian ambassador Fava reminded U.S. Attorney General J. W. Griggs of an earlier request about "what measures the Federal would be willing to take against the Italian anarchists who make their residence in the United States." What Ambassador Fava and the Italian government desired was "the investigation of anarchist plots directed against the Kingdom of Italy in the past and planned for the future, and that all legal steps be taken for the punishment of the conspirators and for the prevention of their criminal purposes." Italian authorities additionally hoped to achieve "the extradition of all members of the Society that plotted in America the murder of King Humbert, if the trial and the investigations which are now conducted by the Italian authorities showed evidence of the existence of such a society."[21] Anticipating a positive outcome, Baron Fava presented supporting documentation from two prestigious law firms the embassy had already hired for the purpose of determining legal grounds for the extradition of the plotters.[22]

To obtain this objective, the U.S. government would have to be convinced that Umberto's assassination was a common, rather than political, crime. The extradition treaty between the two nations did not provide for political offenses. But the Italians were not deterred by the inconvenient fact that the political nature of Bresci's deed was beyond cavil. Although the Italian authorities' desire to manipulate the U.S. officials for their own purposes was utterly transparent, federal authorities conducted a remarkably extensive investigation of the alleged plot, one that has never been explored previously by historians. No less than four agencies of government were committed to the search: the Secret Service; the Justice Department; the Post Office Department; and the U.S. Marshals Service.

While prior to Umberto's assassination the Paterson police may not have been concerned about the anarchists in their midst, the Secret Service infiltrated an Italian-born agent into what it considered the principal anarchist association in October 1898. He maintained an active membership for only three months but thereafter remained in contact with the "moving spirits" of the group by means of correspondence. Although no longer employed by the Secret Service at the time of the assassination, the agent was rehired temporarily to investigate the possibility of a plot orchestrated in Paterson. The report he submitted to the Secret Service, containing only a few details subject to challenge, provided more accurate information about the anarchists of Paterson than any other investigative source. The agent claimed that Bresci was a member of the individualist Gruppo Pensiero e Azione, which believed in individual action. Its own members supposedly considered Bresci "an eccentric" and "mentally unsound." There was never any meeting at which lots were drawn for the "honor" of assassinating Umberto; nor was there any collection of funds to pay for the passage of Bresci and his alleged accomplices. This belief may have derived from the anarchists' collection of money for Cariboni's funeral. The agent's report also rejected the widespread belief that a cable was received announcing the assassination. Moreover, "there was none of the suppressed excitement which would surely have manifested had they been waiting consummation of a plot in which they were directly interested." The Gruppo Diritto all'Esistenza, he reported, had assumed the responsibility for providing financial support for Bresci's widow ($200 to date) and with her approval had entrusted the care of her two children to members of the group. During the course of his investigation, the agent gave particular attention to the attitude of the anarchists toward President McKinley, now a source of concern to the Secret Service. He determined that

> occasionally some "Individualist" under the influence of liquor would denounce the President as quite deserving of removal as any European ruler, but such expressions always developed decided opposition on the ground that any assault on the President would react disastrously against the Anarchists and Italians generally.

Finally, apparently having read McCluskey's report, the agent noted that "a great deal of alleged information has been supplied to the New York police authorities, most of which is absolutely without foundation."[23]

Besides the information derived from his anarchist contacts, summarized in his report of November 2, 1900, the Secret Service agent in Paterson managed somehow to obtain a list of Pedro Esteve's correspondents—512 of them, scattered throughout the country, in some of the remotest sites, including the territories of New Mexico and Alaska. The task of locating and gathering information about these anarchists was delegated to the Justice Department. Only in cities hosting large Italian immigrant populations and significant numbers of anarchists were local U.S. attorneys capable of gathering information: notably, Boston, Providence, New Haven, Hartford, Barre, and Pittsburgh.[24] Curiously, the attorney general of New York—of all places—had no person connected with his office capable of undertaking the task. He requested the authority to hire a private detective ("at a limited outlay") or a postal inspector in his district, but the absence of subsequent reports from the New York district attorney would suggest that his request was not granted.[25] Even in New Jersey, the district attorney could not adequately concentrate on Paterson—ostensibly the focal point of the federal investigation—because the Secret Service agent who had compiled the most informative report (cited above) had withdrawn from government service for personal reasons.[26] The great majority of state attorneys general were also stymied because they did not have staff members who knew Italian and had no discretionary funds available to hire Italian-speaking investigators. Probably more relieved than frustrated, the U.S. attorneys whose hands were thus tied invariably recommended that Italian speakers in the Secret Service be delegated to assist them. But the Secret Service was likewise bereft of Italian speakers. What reports the Secret Service Division did manage to accumulate, according to the acting secretary of the treasury, "do not indicate that these correspondents are a source of serious menace."[27]

The secretary of the treasury suggested to the district attorney for the Southern District of New York that better results might be obtained if the investigation were to include the Post Office Department. Inevitably, the issue of turf arose. The acting postmaster general indicated that "it is not considered advisable to detail Inspectors for service under the direction of United States District Attorneys." However, in view of the desired objective, "the Inspectors of the various divisions will be instructed to cooperate with the District Attorneys in this matter."[28] In point of fact, the postal inspectors and letter carriers actually were in the best position to obtain information about the suspected anarchists. The sanctity of the mails was an easy obstacle to overcome when it came to anarchists. In an aide-memoir of August 29, 1900, Ambassador Fava literally begged the State Department to intercept and read letters sent to Luigi Granotti's brother Giuseppe in Paterson. The acting secretary of state sent copies of Fava's aide-memoir to the governor of New Jersey and the postmaster general, noting that "such a step appears to be within the province of the federal Government as it can be ordered by the Postmaster General with the President's authority."[29] In the weeks that followed, instead of the incriminating information Fava anticipated, violation of Giuseppe Granotti's mail yielded a letter from his nephew Gaspare Ferraris in Philadelphia, requesting fifty portraits of Bresci, fifty lapel buttons of Bresci, and a complaint about some books that had not been paid for by the purchasers.[30] Such startling revelations could hardly assist Italy's prosecution of "Il Biondino."

By the time investigations concluded at the end of the year, not a trace of a plot had been discovered by federal agents. Save for a few individuals characterized as possessing a "bad" or "hard" reputation, the anarchists on Esteve's correspondence list were discovered to be ordinary, hardworking, law-abiding Italian immigrants who represented a threat to nobody. They were distinguishable from their conationals only by the ideas they professed and the newspapers they read. Only Giuseppe Ciancabilla aroused suspicion because of his former ties to the assassin. "I am convinced," Postal Inspector Frank A. O'Brien of Pittsburgh reported, "of the intimate relations between Crancabilla [*sic*] and Bresci and the West Hoboken anarchists. It would seem that Crancabilla [*sic*] is a leader among this class of Anarchists and is in his migrations casting the seed which can bring forth naught but evil fruit."[31] A national search was hardly needed to reach that conclusion about Ciancabilla.

What, in the final analysis, was this fruitless investigation all about? Did federal authorities really consider it possible that—as in one case that was by no means unique—an anarchist living alone in a cabin on Douglas Island in the wilds of Alaska could have been a party to or had knowledge of a conspiracy to assassinate the king of Italy? Was this extraordinary waste of time and resources conducted merely to placate the Italian government, or was it indicative of the sincere U.S. belief in the existence of plot and growing paranoia about anarchists, and thus a portent of future repression? The Justice Department files do not answer these questions.

Despite the presumptions that guided their respective efforts, the investigations conducted in Italy and the United States failed to demonstrate the existence of a plot to assassinate King Umberto, the convictions of Bresci and Granotti notwithstanding. Nor have historians, journalists, or independent scholars provided answers to the mystery that satisfy critical analysis, much less furnish a definitive interpretation that resolves all debate about the assassination, its execution, or its origination.[32]

After temporary confinement in San Vittore prison in Milano, Bresci was transferred to the fortress prison of Portolongone on the island of Elba. News of Bresci's arrival quickly circulated among the prisoners, who regarded him as a hero and defied their jailors with cries of "Viva Bresci!" Unrest among the inmates increased when they learned that like a previous guest of the Crown, the failed regicide Giovanni Passanante, Bresci had been entombed in a subterranean cell below the water level in the prison tower located in the harbor of the nearby town of Portoferraio—aptly known as the "Torre di Passanante"—the use of which had been prohibited by the prison reforms legislated a few years earlier. Fearing that protests would result if news of the irregular treatment afforded Bresci reached the press, prison authorities decided to transfer him to the island prison of Santo Stefano on January 23, 1901.

Santo Stefano was selected because it was remote from prying eyes and located on a tiny island (1.2 square miles) near the penal colony of Ventotene in the Tyrrhenian Sea, and hopefully far enough from the mainland to discourage any attempt by the anarchists to liberate Bresci, a ridiculous fear seriously entertained by the Italian government. Built in 1794–95, Santo Stefano had justly gained its reputation as an inhospitable facility where thousands of serious felons and political prisoners such as Luigi Settembrini were incarcerated by the Bourbons throughout the Risorgimento. Italy under the Savoy Monarchy continued its special use for *ergastolani*, most notably the other failed regicide Pietro Acciarito, who had been transferred to an insane asylum before Bresci's arrival. The prison itself was constructed in a horseshoe shape, with three tiers of single-window cells looking down and inward upon the guards' watchtower, denying the condemned any vision of the sea and reminding them of their wretched fate.[33]

A special cell, formerly occupied by Acciarito, had been renovated in preparation for the arrival of prisoner 515; it was completely isolated in the highest tier of the prison, with two adjacent rooms from which guards would keep Bresci under surveillance twenty-four hours a day. Larger (three square meters) and cleaner than the veritable dungeon at Portoferraio, Bresci's cell contained a wooden bed and horsehair mattress that folded against the wall, a stool affixed to the floor, a wooden basin, a bucket to accommodate physical waste, and an iron chain secured to the wall should it become necessary to restrain the prisoner. The few personal items to which he was entitled included a hair brush, a comb, a handkerchief, a napkin, a pair of socks, and a sweater. Despite the strong cold winds that buffeted the island, he was furnished with a sheet and blanket only at night. Daily rations consisted of a bowl of thin soup with pasta and beans (half of which he would save for the evening) and 600 grams of brown bread. Sunday meals included soup with a small piece of meat. On four special occasions—Christmas, Easter, the Sunday celebration of the Constitution, and the king's birthday—prisoners were feted with soup with dry pasta and beef. A few prisoners like Bresci, who had been sent twenty dollars by his wife (around 60 lira), were allowed to purchase supplementary items like wine and cheese at the prison commissary.[34]

Worse than the dietary privation and Spartan quarters was the physical and psychological isolation to which Bresci was subjected. Confined twenty-three hours a day in his cell, his sole opportunity for unconfined movement was an hour's exercise in the narrow corridor that surrounded his cell complex. As his cell and the corridor were located apart from other quarters, Bresci had no contact with fellow prisoners, and his guards were strictly forbidden to reply if he attempted to speak with them. The hours he spent in his cell were virtually devoid of activity or indirect contact with the outside world. Bresci was prohibited from having visitors. Nor was he permitted to receive letters—not even from his wife—newspapers, or books. The prison chaplain attempted to give him a Bible, and a guard offered a book on the lives of the saints. He rejected both. His only literary material was a French dictionary and a manual of prison regulations. For self-entertainment Bresci devised a game wherein he tied his napkin into a knot and kicked it against the wall like a soccer ball. Isolation and inactivity such as Bresci and other *ergastolani* endured often resulted in psychological breakdown, as was the case with the preceding regicides, Passanante and Acciarito. Yet by all accounts Bresci survived with his mental facilities intact and exhibited remarkably good spirits, considering the adverse circumstances of his daily existence. His psychological equilibrium was attributed by prison officials to his belief that his incarceration would be brief, that he was soon to be liberated by the revolution.[35]

At 4:00 p.m., May 22, 1901, the director of Santo Stefano informed the Interior Ministry by telegram that Bresci had committed suicide by hanging himself with a towel tied to the bars of his cell window. The veracity of this assertion was doubted from the outset. How did Bresci acquire a towel, an item forbidden the prisoners, and how was a towel long enough to be used for such a purpose? Eight days later the official version changed: Bresci had lengthened the towel by knotting it together with the collar of his jacket, a jacket said to have been found intact on the day of his suicide. His acquisition of a towel and a jacket was never revealed. And how, moreover, had he contrived and executed his suicide when he was supposed to be under 24-hour surveillance by two guards in three-hour shifts? The lapse in security observation was attributed to happenstance: one of the guards was asleep; the other had left his post for three minutes to answer nature's call. How Bresci managed to knot a towel, suspend himself, and suffocate all within a few minutes was also never explained. Why, if he intended to kill himself, had Bresci ordered and left uneaten the wine and cheese he had purchased from the commissary that morning, and why had he set aside half of his soup to consume later, as was his habit? And why did he end his life before his pending appeal before the Court of Cassation was decided?

Before these questions were raised by the Italian press and other skeptics, Alessandro Doria, the prison inspector of Acciarito fame, arrived at Santo Stefano on orders from Interior Minister Giovanni Giolitti—supposedly very late on the night of May 22. Two days later Inspector Doria presided over the autopsy performed by three physicians from the mainland. The physicians confirmed that Bresci had indeed died of strangulation, but asserted that his body showed evidence of greater putrefaction than would have been expected of someone dead less than forty-eight hours. Was it possible that Bresci's demise had occurred a few days earlier? The autopsy findings of the three physicians brought the actual date of his death into question, but the issue was never pursued by the authorities. Bresci was buried in the prison's small cemetery on May 26, together with his few belongings and nearly one hundred letters written to him by his wife—letters he had never been allowed to read.[36]

Suspicion in regard to the date of Bresci's "suicide" revolves around the date when Inspector Doria arrived at Santo Stefano, officially May 22, the same date as the prisoner's death. Among Giolitti's confidential papers on deposit at the Archivio Centrale dello Stato in Rome (ACS) are two folders with inscriptions indicating inclusion of the following reports, the titles inscribed thus: "Relazione del Direttore di polizia Doria circa l'ergastolo di Santo Stefano-Ventotene e la detenzione del regicida Bresci Gaetano. 18 maggio 1901; Notificazione del suicidio del Bresci. 22 maggio 1901." The folders, however, are empty. Archivists at the ACS indicated that the folders had originally arrived empty and expressed their belief that the reports had been removed because they contained incriminating evidence about Giolitti. Another student of the case, the journalist Arrigo Petacco, tracked down Santo Stefano's prison register in search of information about Bresci's incarceration and death. The registry, which contained details about each prisoner, lacked only a single page—that pertaining to prisoner 515, Bresci. The page had been torn out.[37]

What could these missing documents have revealed? The first report cited in the ACS inventory indicates that Inspector Doria arrived at Santo Stefano on May 18, four days before Bresci's death, not May 22, the date given to the press. Why the discrepancy? The presence of Inspector Doria at Santo Stefano on May 18 and the more advanced state of the body's decay suggest that death had occurred earlier than May 22. The missing page from the prison registry likewise lends credence to the suspicion raised by the missing ACS file—that Bresci did not commit suicide, that he was murdered by Inspector Doria's minions at the order of Giolitti.[38]

More famous as Italy's perennial prime minister between 1903 and 1915, Giolitti asserted in his memoirs of 1928 that Umberto's assassination had been the "effect on an unbalanced brain of the reactionary politics followed in the preceding years." His memoirs are silent, however, about the manner of Bresci's death and the role he may well have played in the regicide's demise.[39] The untold story involved Giolitti, Maria Sofia, the former queen of Naples, and Errico Malatesta. Italy's most feared revolutionary, Malatesta had once again aroused government concern after his escape from Lampedusa and resettlement in London. In June 1899, Malatesta had written a pamphlet entitled *Contro la monarchia*, which was smuggled into Italy with a false cover that read "*Aritmetica elementare.*" The pamphlet urged the anarchists, socialists, and republicans to unite in common cause and overthrow the Savoy Monarchy as a first step toward revolution. Once the pamphlet was intercepted, alarm bells went off at the Ministry of the

Interior. Further credence to an accord between subversive elements was provided by the subprefect of La Spezia, who claimed that such an alliance was being established by the quarrymen of Carrara under the influence of Malatesta.[40] In London, meanwhile, the spies "Calvo," "Secret Agent 113," and "Virgilio" intensified their snooping activities but reported nothing of significance at this juncture.[41] Fear subsided when Malatesta departed for the United States, but concerns were rekindled when he returned to London in April 1900. For almost a year Rome remained uncertain of Malatesta's intentions.

Alarm at the Ministry of the Interior sounded anew on March 23, 1901, when the Italian ambassador to France, Count Giuseppe Tornielli, informed Giolitti that Malatesta had visited the ex-Queen of Naples, Maria Sofia, at her villa in Neuilly outside Paris.[42] Fear of Maria Sofia's alleged schemes to subvert the House of Savoy had become a veritable obsession of the interior minister, who seriously entertained the belief that her tentacles extended even into the Vatican. The alleged machinations of the nefarious ex-Queen were periodically conjured up by the inventive reports of spies like "Dante" and "Virgilio" (the former anarchists Enrico Insabato and Ennio Belelli) in the pay of the Italian ambassador Tornielli. They portrayed Maria Sofia's villa in Neuilly as a veritable den of conspirators, including such alleged *habitués* as the Italian-French anarchist Charles Malato and even Malatesta. Even before this latest alert, Giolitti had believed that Maria Sofia had arranged with Malatesta to recruit Bresci for the assassination of King Umberto, even asserting to the prefect of Turin, Alessandro Guiccioli, that the government had proof of the plot.[43] By the early months of 1901, Giolitti became extremely fearful that Maria Sofia and Malatesta were now plotting to liberate Bresci as a means of destabilizing the monarchy and perhaps assassinate the new king, Vittorio Emanuele III, as well.[44]

Strangely enough, links between Malatesta and the ex-queen actually did exist, although he probably never visited her, or if he had, the number of times could only have been a few.[45] Despite Lucheni's assassination of her sister, Empress Elizabeth of Austria-Hungary, Maria Sofia was sympathetic toward the anarchists, if only because of their mutual hatred of the House of Savoy, and she proved willing to help finance Malatesta's revolutionary endeavor of 1901. Malatesta, for his part, was willing to accept the funds despite the improbable source. This was confirmed in a letter of May 18, 1901, which Malatesta had written to an unknown source in Paris and that was intercepted and sent to the Ministry of the Interior. Although he used only first names, the authorities had no trouble determining the identity of the assumed participants: Angelo Insogna, the socialist Oddino Morgari,

Charles Malato, and a few other anarchists, and *"la Signora"*—Maria Sofia! Malatesta had stated unequivocally "that *Lady* has been in contact with us and has furnished us with [financial] means."[46] It was apparent, therefore, that Malatesta was contemplating a revolutionary enterprise of some sort. Malatesta's letter did not reach Giolitti's desk until July 7, 1901, and only subsequently had the spy "Virgilio" determined that Malatesta had hoped to conduct a coup de main in southern Italy but could not obtain the necessary funds.[47]

Back in March the target of Malatesta's intended endeavor still remained unknown. At the time, Tornielli's report of Malatesta's presence at Neuilly was incorrect, but the ambassador was intelligent enough to assure Giolitti that the anarchists, whatever their intentions, would never serve the interests of the Bourbons.[48] This assurance did not assuage Giolitti's renewed paranoia about the machinations of the ex-queen. What incited his latest suspicion was the arrival in Italy that March of the ex-queen's agent, Angelo Insogna, to whom Giolitti assigned extraordinary importance. In reality, Insogna was merely a former Neapolitan journalist and consummate opportunist who had written a favorable biography of Maria Sofia's late husband, King Francesco II of Naples. On that basis, he had insinuated himself into Maria Sofia's entourage at Neuilly and gained her confidence. But Giolitti believed Insogna had gone to the United States at the beginning of 1900, during the "preparation" of the regicide, and had now come to Italy furnished with instructions from Malatesta to convene with local anarchists and make preparations for a coup de main. Giolitti's alarm was further heightened by a report from General Ugo Brusati, the new king's aide-de-camp, suggesting that Insogna's visit might include a visit to the Vatican.[49] When Insogna reached Naples, Giolitti ordered the local prefect to keep him under constant surveillance and intercept his correspondence. Once Insogna arrived in Rome, Giolitti had him arrested but could not detain him because the suspected conspirator had done nothing criminal and a search of his belongings had failed to uncover any incriminating links with Malatesta. Giolitti was unwilling to take any chances, however, and had Insogna taken to the French border and expelled.[50]

But Giolitti remained convinced that a plot to liberate Bresci was still afoot. He stationed troops on Santo Stefano as a deterrent to any rescue attempt. The anarchists' coup de main never materialized, as any rational observer could have foretold, and on May 18, 1901, Italy learned that Bresci was dead, officially by his own hand. The unanswered question was whether Giolitti decided to preclude an escape attempt by having Bresci murdered. The plausible theory holds that Bresci's elimination was entrusted to Inspector

Doria, who by some remarkable coincidence was promoted two months later to the position of general director of Italian prisons, at more than double his previous salary.[51] His benefactor Giolitti, according to some, even when informed of Bresci's death, could not escape his morbid obsession, admitting to colleagues in Parliament that during the night of May 18, he dreamed the regicide had escaped from Santo Stefano.[52]

In years that followed, several accounts of Bresci's death were offered by former prisoners who were serving sentences at Santo Stefano at the time of his alleged suicide. One version asserted that Bresci was strangled by guards; another claimed he was killed by guards who subjected him to the *Santantonio,* that is, a sheet or blanket was thrown over him and his body beaten with clubs.[53] These assertions, to be sure, were anecdotal, and as such unverifiable. But together with the documented accounts of Giolitti's obsessive fear of a conspiracy to liberate Bresci, Inspector Doria's probable arrival at Santo Stefano prior to the regicide's death, and the advanced state of decomposition of Bresci's body, there is enough evidence to cast serious doubt that King Umberto's assassin died by suicide.

Among Italian anarchists, Bresci has always ranked as the quintessential *giustiziere,* the noble and heroic avenger whose motives were pure and selfless, and whose victim qualified as a tyrant fully deserving the act of retribution he received. Even before his mysterious death, Bresci was enthroned at the highest level in the pantheon of anarchist martyrs, beside fellow avenger Michele Angiolillo. A later example of hagiographic excess was the single commemorative issue published by the anarchists of New York: *Umberto e Bresci: 1900–29 Luglio-1903,* whose front-page illustration depicts a high school on one side juxtaposed with a church in crumbling ruin on the other, symbols of enlightenment versus ignorance and obscurantism. Flying together through the air above in triumph are Bresci and Lady Liberty, she holding a shining torch, he bearing a flag emblazoned with the words *"Libertà e Giustizia."* Presumably Bresci was en route to the celestial pantheon of anarchist heroes and martyrs.[54]

# Conclusion

## Terrorists or *Giustizieri*?

The bombings and assassinations committed by anarchists in France, Spain, and Italy certainly qualify the fin de siècle as one of the most violent periods in the history of international anarchism. Historical interpretation of these deeds all too often continued to be negatively influenced by the lingering residue of misinformation, misinterpretation, and outright fiction derived from nineteenth-century authorities, government pronouncements, and journalistic accounts. This observation applies to anarchists in general and the perpetrators of *attentats* in particular, and among the latter none have suffered more distortive description, pseudo-scientific analysis, and sensationalist demonization than the Italians.

Not surprisingly, Italy's political rulers at the time fervently embraced Lombroso's theories because they provided "scientific" validation to government efforts to divest the anarchists of their legal status as political subversives and to criminalize their activities. The "born criminal" and the "*malfattore*" became one and the same. Furthermore, acceptance of Lombroso's theories about anarchists and "born criminals" enabled government officials to deflect attention away from the conditions of political oppression and economic poverty that plagued Italy, particularly in the tumultuous years of 1893–94 and 1897–98—conditions, as this book argues, that contributed directly to anarchist violence. Assassinations and bombings, according to the consensus generated by officialdom, social scientists, and the bourgeois press, were the work of outlaws and madmen extraneous to Italy's intractable problems. Thus, in July 1894, after his own escape from an assassin's pistol and President Carnot's death from Caserio's blade, Prime Minister Crispi described the anarchists as a "cult of madmen" in a report to the Chamber of Deputies,[1] and when haranguing his colleagues to pass repressive legislation against this "new enemy of society," he insisted that they were "outside of ordinary law," so "whatever provisions you enact against them will always be legitimate."[2]

Portraying anarchists as a "cult of madmen" not only divested the assassinations of political intent and importance but, as we have seen, also raised the specter of a "conspiracy." The possibility that an *attentat* was committed by a single individual was almost inconceivable to Italian authorities—assuming the government officials who asserted the existence of anarchist conspiracies actually believed what they were saying. Thus, in 1898 the chief prosecutor attached to the Court of Appeals of Parma informed the minister of justice that "the assassins of President Carnot, Empress Elizabeth of Austria, as well as the assassin who failed to kill King Umberto of Italy, did not act alone or from personal impulse, but from part of a campaign by evil doers who really intend to murder all the Monarchs of Europe."[3] That reports of international conspiracies were often based on nothing more than rumors did not deter their being considered. Even invented conspiracies facilitated government repression, especially to buttress false claims of national peril—*la patria in pericolo*. Prime Minister Crispi in 1894 went so far as to claim that the anarchists and the socialist leaders of the *Fasci dei Lavoratori* were in league with France, Russia, and the Vatican to wrest Sicily away from Italy, according to the provisions of the nonexistent "Treaty of Bisacquino."[4] Although Crispi's paranoiac ranting was transparently absurd, even more rational minds like Giovanni Giolitti gave unquestioning credence to the notion that anarchists were involved in an international conspiracy threatening Italy's monarchy, an egregious miscalculation that, as we have seen, most likely resulted in the murder of King Umberto's assassin Gaetano Bresci in prison. The likely elimination of Bresci resulted directly not only from the almost axiomatic belief that assassinations were the result of conspiracies and plots, but that such criminal endeavors were invariably orchestrated by Italy's most feared revolutionary, Errico Malatesta. Knowledge that Malatesta had spent time in Paterson, New Jersey, whence Bresci departed, was proof positive for the yellow press that "whenever Errico Malatesta appears or disappears a ruler is killed or an attempt is made to kill one."[5]

That the Italian political ruling class, the daily press, otherwise reputable academics, and the bourgeoisie in general could seriously accept as gospel truth the farrago of lies and misconceptions propagated about anarchist plots, chosen assassins, and Malatesta the "mastermind" must be attributed to a remarkable ignorance of anarchist theory and practice. Nothing would have been more antithetical to anarchist principles than the idea of Malatesta or any other preeminent figure functioning as a veritable dictator, making decisions for the entire movement, ordering individuals to conduct missions of death. Even if such an authoritarian figure were deleted from the equation, any plot comprising presumed equals would still require some measure of hierarchical leadership, organization, and uniformity of opinion and purpose—characteristics anarchists rejected on principle and probably could not have attained even had they so desired, given the diversity of opinion about such tactics. The very idea of drawing lots to choose an assassin—the standard imagery fostered by government assertions and sensationalist accounts in the press—would have been regarded as an infringement upon individual liberty and free initiative. Moreover, after years of experience with spies infiltrating the closest circles and groups, Italian anarchists would have feared that secret decisions to assassinate a monarch or high-ranking official would inevitably reach the ears of the government. Avoiding such a threat had become automatic by the 1890s. Detection or even suspicion of a plot to assassinate an important personage would have condemned any group of anarchists to imprisonment or *domicilio coatto*. Thus, the likelihood that any of the assassinations committed by Italians in the 1890s resulted from a genuine conspiracy was minimal at best. A few comrades might have been privy to the intentions of Lega, Angiolillo, and Bresci and perhaps rendered moral encouragement or some minimal form of material assistance. Yet when various anarchists were tried for their alleged complicity, incriminating evidence was nonexistent or so dubious as to result in acquittal. The only alleged accomplice convicted as an accomplice—in absentia, notwithstanding a lack of credible evidence—was, as we have seen, Bresci's comrade Luigi Granotti.

Once the barrier of pseudo-scientific theories and imaginary conspiracies is penetrated, a very different picture emerges of anarchist violence in general and of the *attentatori* in particular—or more specifically that of the assassins. Anarchists were but an expression of a long-established tradition of tyrannicide in Italian history. Unambiguously, they would and did learn to commit and justify deeds of violence from the cultural environment created by the Italian bourgeoisie. During the decades after the Risorgimento, all levels of the ruling elite and bourgeoisie revered and glorified the legendary figures who had committed every manner of violence in the cause of national liberation and unity. Even within the exalted sphere of Italian science, especially positivist criminology, the tendency to defend acts of violence carried out by bourgeois revolutionaries during the Risorgimento was prevalent. But, of course, while political violence committed during the Risorgimento or even in classical antiquity was considered noble and morally justified, comparable deeds perpetrated by the anarchists were excoriated as reprehensible and criminal, the work not of political subversives like Mazzini and

Pisacane but of antisocial miscreants and madmen. At the first international congress of criminologists held in Rome in 1885, Cesare Lombroso, Enrico Ferri, and Roberto Laschi concurred in their differentiation between "political violence" committed by bourgeois nationalists and "criminal violence" perpetrated by subversives. Paraphrasing Ferri's comments at the congress, Daniel Pick wrote, "It was methodologically possible and socially essential . . . to delineate good idealist revolutionaries and sick rebels—degenerates. Thus the good struggle for the independence of the Italian nation could be distinguished from the regressive outbreaks (peasant riots, anarchist attacks and so on), which had occurred *in* unified Italy."[6] In sum, class prejudice and selective morality enabled Italy's political elites and bourgeoisie, on the one hand, to justify Milano, Orsini, and Oberdan as heroes and martyrs and, on the other, to brand Caserio, Angiolillo, Lucheni, and Bresci as degenerates and criminals. This hypocritical double standard on political violence was pervasive and irrepressible in Italian middle-class society and government circles, a perspective that contributed decisively to the misunderstanding and harsh treatment of the anarchists throughout the nineteenth century and beyond.

In fact, as we have seen, the anarchists' resort to "propaganda of the deed" against the liberal state was entirely consistent with Italian revolutionary tradition, their ideas and tactics about political violence inherited directly from the radical democrats who spearheaded the fight for national liberation and unity throughout the Risorgimento, especially Carlo Pisacane, Giuseppe Mazzini, Giuseppe Garibaldi, and others less known outside Italy. The ideology and tactics of political violence were transmitted directly from radical democracy to anarchism by the revolutionaries whom Bakunin recruited during his 1864–67 sojourn in Italy: Giuseppe Fanelli, Saverio Friscia, Carlo Gambuzzi, Alberto Tucci, Attanasio Dramis, Raffaele Mileti, Pier Vincenzo De Luca, and others. All were former disciples of Mazzini, and several had seen action in the battles of the Risorgimento. Similarly, the ideas and practices previously formulated and undertaken by radical democrats were then passed on to a second generation of Italian anarchist leaders: Malatesta, Carlo Cafiero, Andrea Costa, Emilio Covelli, Francesco Saverio Merlino, and their principal associates. The relationship between the Risorgimento with anarchist ideals and practices does not mean that Bakunin had no influence in this regard. On the contrary, Bakunin's ideas about violence and revolution profoundly influenced the younger generation of anarchists, but it must be noted that his legacy on political violence was strikingly similar to that of Mazzini and Pisacane, a point lost on most of the Russian's biographers.

Ignorance of the nexus between democratic and anarchist violence in Italy is invariably accompanied by failure to investigate, much less understand, the extent to which the motivation for the *attentats* resulted from political and social circumstances at home and abroad. Instead, the standard interpretations ascribe the principal cause of anarchist bombings and assassinations to a combination of anarchist ideology with unique psychological characteristics and personal circumstances.

As we have seen, *attentatori* were neither madmen nor criminals. Ranging in age from twenty-one (Caserio) to thirty-one (Bresci), on average *attentatori* were in their midtwenties when they committed their deeds. Overall, they could be described as quite ordinary members of the Italian working class: artisans like Lega, a cabinetmaker; Caserio, a baker; and Acciarito, a blacksmith. Bresci was a skilled silk weaver and the only one employed in modern industry, namely textile factories in Prato and Paterson. Lucheni was unusual in that he had served willingly as a soldier and subsequently as a manservant to his former commander—occupations anarchists would generally have disdained. Only Angiolillo came from the petite bourgeoisie, trained as a printer like his father. He was also the only assassin who was relatively well educated, having graduated from a technical high school (*scuola tecnica*) in his hometown. Bresci had frequented a professional school for specialized weavers. Of the others, none had been formally educated beyond the third grade, if even that, a level normative for Italian artisans and workers at a time when woeful economic circumstances often relegated public education to the status of an unattainable luxury. The geographical origins of the assassins differed appreciably, without any discernible pattern. Several grew up in small towns adjacent to or near major and middle-sized towns: Caserio (Milan/Lombardy) and Acciarito (Rome/Lazio); Lega (Lugo/Romagna), Lucheni (Parma/Emilia), and Bresci (Prato/Tuscany). Angiolillo was the only southerner, hailing from Foggia in Puglia. None had been exposed to radical ideas or activities within their immediate families. Their association with the anarchist movement ranged from deep involvement (Lega, Caserio, Angiolillo, and Bresci) to almost none at all (Acciarito and Lucheni).

Although this study delved into the individual lives and personalities of the *attentatori*, our approach rejects any notion of Italian anarchist violence as solely or primarily a function of individual psychology. Interpretations based on psychology cannot account for the behavior of the *attentatori*. Empirical evidence pertaining to their personalities is minimal and generally derived at second or third hand. Moreover, any psychoanalytical approach to Italian assassins would inevitably be superficial and based on a priori assumptions and conjectures. Even if such a procedure were scientifically legitimate, four assassins and two failed perpetrators constitutes a sample far too small to yield valid generalizations and conclusions. Simply put, there is no psychological profile that fits each of the Italian anarchist assassins and failed aspirers, no one-size-fits-all explanation of their behavior, although to claim that emotional factors played no role in the behavior of the *attentatori* would be absurd, of course.

What remains elusive, if not ultimately unfathomable, is what turbulent process occurred inside the minds of the assassins and failed perpetrators, what propelled them to strike out with violence, especially since none had exhibited violent behavior before. The investigator can probe only minimally into the psyche of these men, and conclusions must be considered tentative in the absence of more definitive information than that which is presently available. In the final analysis, the most that can be said about this group is that their motivation derived from a complex mix of multiple causes and catalysts: class origin, economic privation and unemployment, government repression, the travails of migration or exile, and in a few cases some degree of emotional instability. Delving into the individual experiences of each *attentatore* reveals that, in most cases, the common denominator was government repression of the movement and police persecution of the individual. The frequency, pervasiveness, and intensity of state violence in the 1890s—in France and Spain as well as Italy—enabled the Italian anarchists to sanction attacks against members of royalty and government deemed personally responsible for the misdeeds committed directly by them or under their orders. In fact, in four of the six cases, a reciprocal relationship existed between official repression and retaliatory violence, the one generating the other and vice versa. Specifically, for Paolo Lega, his activities as an anarchist militant caused him to be hounded relentlessly by the police in Italy and Switzerland. His self-proclaimed motive for attacking Prime Minister Crispi in June 1894 was to exact revenge for his own suffering and that of the Sicilian victims of Crispi's harsh suppression of the Fasci Siciliani. Sante Caserio's emotional makeup was highly sensitive and fragile, and his profound empathy for the poor and the oppressed caused him considerable distress. Caserio's assassination of Sadi Carnot, however, was an act of revenge for the execution of the French anarchist Auguste Vaillant, whose bomb had killed no one. Acciarito was a man of limited intelligence, whose frustrations and despondency due to chronic poverty and unemployment caused him to lash out against the king after brief consideration. In contrast, Angiolillo became politically active as a republican while still a student. His activities as an anarchist resulted in imprisonment and exile. Willing to avenge the brutal torture and execution of Spanish anarchists in the dungeons of Montjuich, Angiolillo exhibited characteristic composure and resignation when he fatally shot Cánovas del Castillo, apologizing for the deed to his new widow but noting that she had been married to a beast. Lucheni, another wretch like Acciarito, assassinated Empress Elizabeth with emotionless efficiency for no reason save that of her eminence. Finally, Bresci was a polar opposite of young Caserio. Notoriously taciturn and emotionally self-contained, Bresci was an active militant in the movement in Prato and Paterson. Although gainfully employed in the silk mills of Paterson, and married with a young daughter and another child on the way, Bresci was stone-cold in his determination to avenge his own suffering and that of the peasants and workers brutally victimized by the government and army in 1894 and in 1898. He specifically targeted Umberto I for punishment because he had signed the decree imposing martial law and then bestowed Italy's highest military decoration on the general who ordered grapeshot to be used against defenseless demonstrators in Milan during the *Fatti di Maggio*. Bresci continued to manifest his sangfroid at every stage of his interrogations and trial. Even when sentenced to *ergastolo*, Bresci maintained an air of disdainful indifference toward his accusers and his own fate, a stance that generated great pride and inspiration among the anarchists.

One of the very few contemporary scholars who understood that anarchist violence was essentially retaliatory violence precipitated by government repression was the liberal historian Guglielmo Ferrero, who, ironically, was also the son-in-law of Cesare Lombroso. Writing in the midst of the Crispian reaction of 1894, Ferrero observed that governments "believed they could sever the seven heads of the anarchist hydra with the guillotine, but instead of succumbing to the blows of the law and infamy, anarchism not only acquired renewed vigor but greatly increased its type of heroes." This "purification of anarchism" was "one of the least observed aspects but the most important [cause] of the terrible deeds of our time. It is the direct consequence of persecution." He further observed that

> after persecution, the passage of exceptional laws, the repeated executions, the legend of the anarchist martyr was created. That was sufficient to drive even the honest fanatics of the party onto the path of *attentats*. They were not stirred by other causes, but when they began to see comrades imprisoned by the hundreds, their newspapers confiscated, and the heads of friends tumble into the basket of the guillotine, they must have felt excited by altruistic sentiments and political solidarity that are alive in all extreme parties and honest fanatics.[7]

Ferrero was particularly critical of Prime Minister Crispi, characterizing violence committed by the anarchists directly as retribution to his authoritarian rule. Ferrero contrasted, for example, the relatively benign policies and practices toward the anarchists that characterized the premiership of Agostino Depretis (1881–87) with the draconian methods employed by Crispi—differences that accounted for the lack of assassination attempts against Depretis and two against Crispi. Ferrero astutely observed that "It is a historical law of absolute inevitability that violence excites violence. Crispi among all Italian statesmen is the one who demonstrates greatest pleasure in resolving issues by force. By this means he provokes in his enemies the attraction of the use of force, and bewitches them with the unconscious temptation of his example."[8] Rather than the repressive legislation instigated by Crispi and passed by legislators who "must have lost their sense of social reality," Ferrero proposed as a remedy for *attentats* the establishment of an effective police force to keep tabs on extremists and the extension of greater political liberty to the anarchists, which would have encouraged them to channel their ideas and frustrations into nonviolent avenues of expression.[9] But Ferrero's was a voice in the wilderness. There was as much of a chance of Crispi's adopting such policies as of Mt. Etna ceasing its eruptions.

Therefore, an essential commonality linking most of the assassins was the conceptualization of their deeds as a form of political violence that did not constitute assassination under the societal definition of murder. The *giustiziere*, in the lexicon of Italian anarchists, was the avenging executioner who exacted retributive justice for the victims of state violence and oppression. All six of the *attentatori* struck out against those monarchs and chiefs of state deemed responsible, directly or indirectly, for crimes perpetrated against themselves, the people, or the anarchist movement. What made the Italian anarchist *giustiziere* perhaps unique or certainly rare in the annals of political assassination was the clear distinction they made between the office and the individual, that is to say, the official position of their target as opposed to the person of flesh and blood who occupied it. As Paolo Lega explained at his trial, "I decided to strike a man [Francesco Crispi] who is responsible for so many evils, not as a man but rather as the most important personage of the State."[10] Pietro Gori maintained that Caserio "had no personal resentment against Sadi Carnot; but Carnot was the political representative of the French bourgeoisie, on whose behalf he signed the death decrees for those guillotined in Paris."[11] Similarly, when interrogators asked Bresci why he had killed Umberto, he answered, "I did not kill Umberto, I killed the King."[12] Despite the futility and negative consequences of most assassinations, the anarchists could not withhold respect and reverence for *giustizieri*, men who rightly or wrongly sacrificed their lives in the fight for liberty and justice. Enshrined as heroes and martyrs in the pantheon of revolutionaries, the lives and deeds of the *giustizieri* were commemorated in newspaper articles, pamphlets, and songs for decades after their bones had turned to dust, reverential paeans that continue to appear in present-day Italy.

The Italian anarchists' conception of the *giustiziere* resembled historical notions of the tyrannicide, defined as one who kills a despot for the common good. Therefore, as noted earlier, in the case of Italy the term "propaganda of the deed" becomes problematic when employed as a synonym for terrorism intended as wholesale violence against innocent people for the purpose of creating an atmosphere of fear and insecurity to destabilize government and ordered society. Although this is the rubric under which Italian anarchist *attentats* are typically subsumed, as we have seen, indiscriminate violence was not characteristic of the *attentats* perpetrated by the Italian anarchists during the fin de siècle.

Unfortunately, analysis of the bombings in this period and even earlier is hindered by the anonymity of the deeds. Save for the most famous Italian anarchist bomber of the period, Paolo Schicchi, who acknowledged his responsibility after capture, the perpetrators did not leave their calling cards. This did not prevent the authorities from blaming the anarchists in virtually every instance, despite recurrent acquittals for lack of evidence.

But even if, hypothetically, all the bombings in Italy in the 1890s were attributable to the anarchists, the essential characteristic of these bombings—overlooked by virtually all studies—is that innocent victims were never the intended target, not even the members of the bourgeoisie. Antibourgeois rhetoric notwithstanding, Italian anarchist explosives in the nineteenth century were directed against the state and its symbolic personifications rather than middle-class elements. Unlike the Spanish anarchist Santiago Salvador, who targeted Barcelona's bourgeoisie with his bombing of the Liceu Theater, or the French anarchist Émile Henry, who threw a bomb amid the petit-bourgeois patrons of the Café Terminus at the Gare Saint-Lazare, the Italians directed their ire against the stone edifices of government buildings or against police stations, military barracks, and an occasional church. Nor did their bombs contain metal fragments (shrapnel) of the kind designed to cause human lethality. Only a handful of innocent people near the bombsites were killed or injured in the course of the entire post-Risorgimento, and only the worst fanatics sanctioned such unintended results. But whether their devices impacted hard stone or tender flesh, Italian anarchist bombers were never so naive, as often portrayed, that they seriously believed their deeds could undermine government or destabilize bourgeoisie society through terror. Even had they not read Kropotkin, they intuitively agreed with the Anarchist Prince that "Institutions rooted in centuries of history are not destroyed by a few pounds of explosives."[13] Committed during periods of heightened repression, anarchist bombings of government structures were gestures of protest and resistance against the state.

To be sure, there were elements among the Italian anarchists—notably the *individualisti*—who would have and did endorse throwing bombs into bourgeois cafés. These fanatics generally agreed with the French anarchist Léon-Jules Léauthier, who famously declared after his failed attempt to assassinate the Serbian minister M. Georgewitch in 1893 that "I would not be striking an innocent if I struck the first bourgeois who came by."[14] Prevailing more among exiles, whose views often tended to be more extreme, than anarchists at home, this sentiment was expressed by Giuseppe Ciancabilla, the leading intellectual among the *individualisti* in the 1890s, who echoed Léauthier and Émile Henry when he argued there were "no innocents among the bourgeoisie."[15] Yet, in spite of the extremists' belief in the collective guilt of the bourgeoisie, anarchist violence against ordinary, nonpolitical individuals of whatever class was virtually unheard of in Italy. Perhaps attributable to revolutionary tradition of the Risorgimento, when revolutionaries of bourgeois origin directed their struggles against authoritarian governments, the degree of animus exhibited against the bourgeoisie by the anarchists in France and Spain was never equaled in nineteenth-century Italy, at least not in the form of gratuitous physical attacks. The few instances of attacks against individuals (excluding political leaders and monarchs) involved political motivation carried to extremes, as in the case of Vittorio Pini and Luigi Parmeggiani (described in chapter 2) or the murder of the journalist Giuseppe Bandi in Livorno, carried out by fringe elements of an anarchist group, following his denigration of Sante Caserio.[16]

Some credit for this lack of antibourgeois aggression must also be attributed to the teachings of Bakunin, who insisted that the revolution "will be a war, not against particular men, but primarily against the anti-social institutions upon which their power and privileges depend,"[17] and later to his disciple Malatesta, who emphasized on numerous occasions that "the struggle against the state has greater practical importance than the struggle against the bourgeoisie . . . ," because "once the government is defeated, the strength of the conscientious proletariat will suffice to settle accounts with the bosses."[18] Consequently, the bourgeoisie, even in times of great social tension, could walk the streets of Italy without fear of being struck down by an anarchist—as long as they avoided proximity to government buildings.

Assassination of royal personages and political leaders (the main focus of this book) was a far more complex phenomenon than bombing government buildings and a few churches. By virtue of targeting only high personages considered guilty of crimes, the assassinations and failed attempts were acts of tyrannicide, a form of political violence that enjoyed a long and honored tradition in Italy. In the end, the motivations and purpose behind the deeds of Acciarito, Lucheni, Lega, Caserio, Angiolillo, and Bresci do not conform to contemporary definitions of terrorism, with its emphasis on the slaughter of innocents.

A distinction between tyrannicide and terrorism in relation to the latter was advanced by the noted Italian historian and prominent antifascist Gaetano Salvemini. Salvemini argued that terrorism is a violent act committed against unknown people, without distinguishing between the innocent and the guilty. The Italian anarchist *attentatori*, as Salvemini correctly observed, never targeted political personages or figures of social eminence considered innocent of crimes against the people or the anarchists. With the sole exception of Lucheni's assassination of Empress Elizabeth of Austria, the other anarchists described in this book—Lega, Caserio, Acciarito, Angiolillo, and Bresci—attacked only those exalted figures believed to have blood on their hands. According to Salvemini, therefore, these assassins had committed tyrannicide rather than terrorism, because in the minds of the anarchists their targets had caused, in their official capacity, the oppression, suffering, and deaths of hundreds of innocent people.

A counterargument would hold that the victims struck down by the Italian anarchists hardly qualified as genuine tyrants. But whom the anarchists considered a tyrant must be understood through a working-class perspective. King Umberto was lauded by the middle and upper classes as *"il re buono"* (the good king), whereas for the anarchists and much of the working class he was *"il re mitraglia"* (the grapeshot king), whose crimes merited death. The same argument could be made for the assassinations of President Carnot of France and Prime Minister Cánovas del Castillo of Spain.

Analysis of the assassinations should also take into account that anarchism was a sociopolitical movement of international dimension, with shared ideals and objectives linking anarchists everywhere. Ties with other national movements were particularly strong in the case of the Italians because of the transnational and diasporic nature of the Italian movement, with political exiles and workers living permanently or temporarily in France, Switzerland, England, Belgium, Spain, Egypt, and Malta, as well as Argentina, Brazil, and the United States. Indeed, during periods of intense government repression in Italy, such as the Crispian reaction of 1894–96 and the Pelloux reaction of 1898–99, the vitality and continuity of Italian anarchism was sustained by leaders and militants abroad. Consequently, a major event affecting an anarchist militant or a movement in another country almost always reverberated among Italians, generating coverage in newspapers, expressions of solidarity, debates, fund raising, and in some cases calls for revenge. This interconnection of movements accounted for Caserio's assassination of President Sadi Carnot of France, Angiolillo's dispatching of Prime Minister Cánovas del Castillo in Spain, Lucheni's murder of Empress Elizabeth in Switzerland, and even Bresci's decision to return to Italy to assassinate Umberto I.

Properly viewed in the context of Italy's grinding poverty and authoritarian methods of dealing with popular unrest and dissent, along with the economic and political pressures that fostered mass migration and the cosmopolitan nature of Italian anarchism, the *attentats* of the 1890s collectively represented desperate acts of protest and rebellion against a political system and social order based on inequality, exploitation, and oppression. The *attentats* sounded a clarion reminder to the ruling political class and the bourgeoisie: "As ye sow, so shall ye reap." This call was finally heard when Bresci assassinated King Umberto, a deed that underscored the maladies afflicting Italian society and helped change the course of the nation's political history. And with Bresci's deed, the so-called heroic period of Italian anarchism came to an end, opening the door for the movement to develop greater ideological complexity and energetic militancy that endured until World War I—a period in which "propaganda of the deed" played virtually no role in Italy.[19]

# Notes

## Preface

1. Nunzio Pernicone, *Carlo Tresca: Portrait of a Rebel* (New York: Palgrave, 2005), vii.

## Introduction

1. *New York Evening Journal*, July 31, 1900.

2. Ibid.

3. *Freedom* (London), September–October 1900.

4. Francesco Saverio Nitti, "Italian Anarchists," *North American Review*, 167 (November 1898): 599.

5. Cesare Lombroso, "Anarchist Crimes and Their Causes," *The Independent* 50 (December 8, 1898): 1674.

6. See Cesare Lombroso, *Gli anarchici* (Turin: Fratelli Bocca, 1894). See also Emilia Musumeci, *Cesare Lombroso e le neuroscienze: un parricidio mancato* (Milan: Franco Angeli, 2012); Delia Frigessi, *Cesare Lombroso* (Turin: Einaudi, 2003); Silvano Montaldo and Paolo Tappero, *Cesare Lombroso cento anni dopo* (Turin: UTET, 2009); Massimo Centini, *Il re è morto, viva il re: attentati, regicidio e anarchica* (Turin: ANANKE, 2009); Daniel Pick, "The Faces of Anarchy: Lombroso and the Politics of Criminal Science in Post-unification Italy," *History Workshop* (1986): 60–86.

7. Lombroso, "Anarchist Crimes," 1670.

8. Pick, "Faces of Anarchy," 78.

9. *New York Times*, July 31, 1900.

10. Richard Hostetter, *The Italian Socialist Movement; Origins, 1860–1882* (Princeton, NJ: Van Nostrand, 1958); T. R. Ravindranathan, *Bakunin and the Italians* (Kingston, ON: McGill-Queen's University Press, 1988). To achieve narrative and interpretive continuity and thoroughness, several chapters revisit issues and developments treated more extensively in Nunzio Pernicone, *The Italian Anarchists, 1864–1892* (Princeton, NJ: Princeton University Press, 1993).

11. James Joll, *The Anarchists* (New York: Grosset & Dunlap, 1964); Barbara W. Tuchman, *The Proud Tower: A Portrait of the World before the War, 1890–1914* (New York: Bantam, 1967), 72.

12. Tuchman, *The Proud Tower*, 72–73.

13. George Woodcock, *Anarchism: A History of Libertarian Ideas and Movements* (Cleveland: World, 1962); Daniel Guérin, *L'anarchisme: de la doctrine à l'action* (Paris: Gallimard, 1965); Peter Marshall, *Demanding the Impossible: A History of Anarchism* (London: HarperCollins, 1992); D. Novak, "Anarchism and Individual Terrorism," *Canadian Journal of Economics and Political Science/Revue canadienne d'économique et de science politique* 20, no. 2 (May 1954): 176–84; Walther L. Bernecker, "The Strategies of 'Direct Action' and Violence in Spanish Anarchism," in Wolfgang J. Mommsen and Gerhardt Hirschfeld, eds., *Social Protest, Violence and Terror in Nineteenth and Twentieth Century Europe*, 88–111 (London: Macmillan, 1982); Andrew R. Carlson, "Anarchism and Individual Terror in the German Empire, 1870–1890," in Mommsen and Hirschfeld, 175–200; and Ulrich Linse, "'Propaganda by Deed' and 'Direct Action': Two Concepts of Anarchist Violence," in Mommsen and Hirschfeld, 201–29.

14. Carl Levy, "Social Histories of Anarchism," *Journal for the Study of Anarchism* 4, no. 2 (Fall 2010): 1–44.

15. Pier Carlo Masini, *Storia degli anarchici italiani: da Bakunin a Malatesta (1862–1892)* (Milan: Rizzoli, 1969); Massini, *Storia degli anarchici italiani nell'epoca degli attentati* (Milan: Rizzoli, 1981); Gino Cerrito, *Dall'internazionalismo alla settimana rossa: per una storia dell'anarchismo in Italia (1881–1914)* (Florence: Crescita Politica, 1977); Maurizio Antonioli and Pier Carlo Masini, *Il sol dell'avvenire: l'anarchismo in Italia dalle origini alla prima guerra mondiale (1871–1918)* (Pisa: Franco Serantini, 1999); Adriana Dadà, *L'anarchismo in Italia: fra movimento e partito. Storia e documenti dell'anarchismo italiano* (Milan: Teti, 1984); Gianpietro Berti, *Errico Malatesta e il movimento anarchico italiano e internazionale, 1872–1932* (Milan: Franco Angeli, 2003); Davide Turcato, *Making Sense of Anarchism: Errico Malatesta's Experiments with Revolution, 1889–1900* (New York: Palgrave, 2012).

16. Ettore Sernicoli, *L'anarchia e gli anarchici: studio storico e politico* (Milan: Treves, 1894); Ettore Zoccoli, *L'anarchia: gli agitatori, le idee, i fatti: saggio di una revisione sistematica e critica e di una valutazione etica* (Turin: Bocca, 1907).

17. Giuseppe Galzerano, *Gaetano Bresci—Vita, attentato, processo, carcere e morte dell'anarchico che "giustiziò" Umberto I* (Casalvelino Scalo: Galzerano, 2001), *Giovanni Passanante—La vita, l'attentato, il processo, la condanna a morte, la grazia "regale" e gli anni di galera del cuoco lucano che nel 1878 ruppe l'incantesimo monarchico* (Casalvelino Scalo: Galzerano, 2004), and *Paolo Lega: Vita, viaggio, "complotto" e morte dell'anarchico romagnolo che attentò' alla vita del primo ministro Francesco Crispi* (Casalvelino Scalo: Galzerano, 2014); Arrigo Petacco, *L'anarchico che venne dall'America* (Milan: A. Mondadori, 1974); Massimo Ortalli, *Gaetano Bresci, tessitore, anarchico e uccisore di re*, 2nd ed. (Rome: Nova Delphi, 2011); Roberto Gremmo, *Sante Caserio: Vita, tragedia e mito di un anarchico lombardo* (Biella: ELF, 1994).

18. Erika Diemoz, *A morte il tiranno: anarchia e violenza da Crispi a Mussolini* (Turin: Einaudi, 2011).

19. Aldo Romano, *Storia del movimento socialista in Italia*, vol. 2: *L'egemonia borghese e la rivolta libertaria 1871–1882* (Milan: Bocca, 1954); Franco Della Peruta, *Democrazia e*

*socialismo nel Risorgimento* (Rome: Editori Riuniti, 1965); Enzo Santarelli, *Il socialismo anarchico in Italia* (Milan: Feltrinelli, 1959); Gastone Manacorda, *Il movimento operaio italiano attraverso i suoi congressi: dalle origini alla formazione del Partito socialista (1853–1892)* (Rome: Editori Riuniti, 1963).

20. Nello Rosselli, *Mazzini e Bakunin: dodici anni di movimento operaio in Italia (1860–1872)* (Turin: Bocca, 1927); Rosselli, *Carlo Pisacane nel Risorgimento italiano* (Turin: Bocca, 1932); Leo Valiani, *Storia del movimento socialista*, 2 vols. (Florence: La Nuova Italia, 1951); Elio Conti, *Le origini del socialismo a Firenze: 1860–1880* (Rome: Rinascita, 1950).

## Chapter 1. *The Risorgimento and the Origins of Anarchist Violence*

1. Quoted in Arthur Lehning, "Bakunin e gli storici," in *Bakunin cent'anni dopo: atti di convegno internazionale di studi Bakuninani* (Milan: Antistato, 1977), 375.

2. Errico Malatesta to Armando Borghi, Rome, March 2, 1932, in Armando Borghi, *Mezzo secolo di anarchia, 1898–1945* (Naples: Scientifiche italiane, 1954), 267.

3. Francesco Saverio Nitti, "Italian Anarchists," *North American Review* 167 (November 1898): 598–99.

4. Luigi Salvatorelli, *The Risorgimento: Thought and Action* (New York: Harper, 1970).

5. Quoted in Walter Laqueur, *Terrorism* (Boston: Little, Brown, 1977), 23.

6. Ibid.

7. *Scritti editi ed inediti di Giuseppe Mazzini* (Imola: Paolo Galeati, 1910), 9: 71.

8. Selection from Bianco's *Manuale* in Walter Laqueur, ed., *Voices of Terror: Manifestos, Writings and Manuals of Al Qaeda, Hamas and Other Terrorists from around the World and throughout the Ages* (New York: Reed Press, 2004), 258, 262.

9. Giovanni Belardelli, *Mazzini* (Bologna: Mulino, 2010), 36, 54.

10. *Scritti editi ed inediti di Giuseppe Mazzini*, 2: 52–54.

11. Ibid., 3: 214–17.

12. Quoted in Gaetano Salvemini, *Mazzini* (New York: Collier, 1962), 62.

13. *Scritti editi ed inediti di Giuseppe Mazzini*, 77: 162–83; Belardelli, *Mazzini*, 56–60.

14. Nunzio Pernicone, *Italian Anarchism, 1864–1892* (Princeton, NJ: Princeton University Press, 1993), 11–13. For a comprehensive study, see Nello Rosselli, *Carlo Pisacane nel Risorgimento italiano* (Turin: Fratelli Bocca, 1932).

15. Carlo Pisacane, *La rivoluzione*, ed. Augusto Illuminati (Bologna: Sampietro, 1967), 206.

16. Alessandro Luzio, *Carlo Alberto e Giuseppe Mazzini* (Turin: Fratelli Bocca, 1923), 341.

17. *Scritti editi ed inediti di Giuseppe Mazzini*, 2: 210.

18. Giuseppe Mazzini, *Opere*, 9: 136, quoted in "La teoria del pugnale secondo il Mazzini e il Garibaldi," *Civiltà cattolica*, Ser. 18, vol 4, fasc. 1231 (September 23, 1901): 14.

19. Ibid., 14–15.

20. *Scritti editi ed inediti di Giuseppe Mazzini*, 77: 168.

21. Ibid., 77: 167–72. Also Luzio, *Carlo Alberto e Giuseppe Mazzini*, 337–55, and Belardelli, *Mazzini*, 56–57.

22. Giuseppe Garibaldi to Felice Pjat, March 6, 1880, quoted in Federazione Anarchica Italiana, *Michele Angiolillo: Il suo eroico atto a ciò di lui si scrisse* (Foggia: Gruppo Anarchico "Michele Angiolillo," n.d.), 33.

23. Ibid. On the political cult of Garibaldi among nineteenth-century revolutionary and radical leaders, see Lucy Riall, *Garibaldi: Invention of a Hero* (New Haven, CT: Yale University Press, 2007), and Marco Severini, ed., *Garibaldi Eroe Moderno* (Rome: Aracne, 2007).

24. Luigi Villari, *Gli eredi di Bruto: un secolo di attentati politici* (Rocca San Casciano: F. Capelli, 1952), 59–60.

25. Quoted in Michael St. John Packe, *Orsini: The Story of a Conspirator* (Boston: Little, Brown, 1957), 273.

26. See also Adrien Dansette, *L'attentat d'Orsini* (Paris: Éditions mondiales, 1972).

27. See Pernicone, *Italian Anarchism*, 15–20, 38–41, 48, 87.

28. Quoted in Christopher Seton-Watson, *Italy from Liberalism to Fascism* (London: Methuen, 1967), 115.

29. Ibid.

30. Borghi, *Mezzo secolo di anarchia, 1898–1945*, 43.

31. Nitti, "Italian Anarchists," 599, 608.

32. Guglielmo Ferrero, "Gli ultimi attentati anarchici e la loro repressione," *Riforma Sociale* 1 (1894): 993–94.

33. On the memory of the "democratic" nature of the Risorgimento at the end of the nineteenth and the early twentieth century, see Fulvio Conti, *L'Italia dei democratici. sinistra risorgimentale, massoneria e associazionismo fra Otto e Novecento* (Milan: Franco Angeli, 2000).

34. Max Nomad, *Apostles of Revolution* (Boston: Little, Brown, 1939), ch. 3; Fritz Brupbacher, *Michael Bakunin, der Satan der Revolte* (Zurich: Neuer Deutscher Verlag, 1929); Eugene Pyziur, *The Doctrine of Anarchism of Michael A. Bakunin* (Milwaukee, WI: Marquette University Press, 1955), 3; and James Joll, *The Anarchists* (New York: Grosset & Dunlap, 1964), 84, 87.

35. Aileen Kelly, *Mikhail Bakunin: A Study in the Psychology and Politics of Utopianism* (New Haven, CT: Yale University Press, 1987), 75.

36. Max Nettlau, *Michael Bakunin: Eine Biographie*, 3 vols. (London: n.p., 1896–1900); Arthur Lehning, ed., *Michel Bakounine et ses relations avec Sergej Necaev* (Leiden, Netherlands: Brill, 1971); E. H. Carr, *Michael Bakunin* (New York: Vintage, 1961); Mark Leier, *Bakunin: The Creative Passion* (New York: St. Martin's, 2006).

37. Carr, *Bakunin*, 178–88; Paul Avrich, *The Russian Anarchists* (Princeton, NJ: Princeton University Press, 1967), 22–23.

38. See Richard Hostetter, *The Italian Socialist Movement*, vol. 1, *Origins, 1860–1882* (Princeton, NJ: Van Nostrand, 1958), 70–139, 186–214; Aldo Romano, *Storia del movimento socialista in Italia*, vol. 1, *L'unificazione nazionale e il problema sociale (1861–1870)* (Milan-Rome: Fratelli Bocca, 1954), 120–64.

39. Errico Malatesta, Preface to Max Nettlau, *Bakunin e l'internazionale in Italia dal 1864 al 1872* (Geneva: Risveglio, 1928), xxi–xxiii; Andrea Costa, *Bagliori di socialismo: ricordi storici* (Florence: Nerbini, 1900), 7–8; Hostetter, *Italian Socialist Movement*; Aldo Romano, *Storia del movimento socialista in Italia*, 3 vols. (Milan: Fratelli Bocca, 1954–56).

40. Leier, *Bakunin*, 212, 216–17; Michel Dragomanov, *Correspondance de Michel Bakounine: lettres à Herzen et à Ogareff (1860–1874)* (Paris: Perrin, 1896): 85; Pyziur, *Anarchism of Michael A. Bakunin*, 107–9.

41. Gerald Brenan, *The Spanish Labyrinth: An Account of the Social and Political Background of the Spanish Civil War* (Cambridge: Cambridge University Press, 1960), 163n1.

42. Letter to Herzen, June 23, 1867, quoted in Brenan, *Spanish Labyrinth*.

43. For examples of Bakunin's views on the anticipated stages of revolutionary violence, see his treatise "Revolutionary Catechism," published in 1866, as well as "The Program of the International Revolutionary Brotherhood," published in 1869, both in Sam Dolgoff, *Bakunin on Anarchy* (New York: Vintage, 1971), 76–97 and 148–59.

44. Errico Malatesta, "Un peu de théorie," *L'En Dehors* (Paris), August 17, 1892.

45. Barbara W. Tuchman, *The Proud Tower: A Portrait of the World before the War, 1890–1914* (New York: Bantam, 1967), 81.

46. Peter Kropotkin, *Words of a Rebel* (New York: Black Rose, 1992), 207–8.

47. "La propaganda a fatti" *L'Associazione* (Nice), October 16, 1889.

48. "A proposito di uno sciopero," *L'Associazione* (Nice), September 6, 1889; Malatesta to Luigi Fabbri, July 11, 1931, in Fabbri, *Malatesta: L'uomo e il pensiero* (Naples: RL, 1951), 8; Malatesta, [*Aritmetica elementare*], *Contro la monarchia* (n.p., n.p., n.d). Published in London in June 1899, the pamphlet bore the title "Elementary Arithmetic" to avert its confiscation by the censors.

49. Caroline Cahm, *Kropotkin and the Rise of Revolutionary Anarchism, 1872–1886* (Cambridge: Cambridge University Press, 1989), 154–58; Peter Marshall, *Demanding the Impossible: A History of Anarchism* (Oakland: PM Press, 2010), 316.

50. Errico Malatesta, "Pietro Kropotkin—Ricordi e critiche di un vecchio amico," *Studi Sociali* (Montevideo), April 15, 1931; Max Nettlau, *Die erste Blutezeit der Anarchie: 1886–1894* (Vaduz, Liechtenstein: Topos, 1981), 157–58; Gino Cerrito, "Il movimento anarchico dalle sue origini al 1914: problemi e orientamenti storiografici," *Rassegna Storica Toscana* 16, no. 1 (January–June 1968): 122.

51. Errico Malatesta, Preface to Nettlau, *Bakunin e l'internazionale*, xxvii.

52. Nello Rosselli, *Mazzini e Bakunin: dodici anni di movimento operaio in Italia (1860–1872)* (Turin: Bocca, 1927), 229–36; Aldo Romano, *Storia del movimento socialista in Italia*, 3: 94–96, 197–201; Elio Conti, *Le origini del socialismo a Firenze* (Rome: Rinascita, 1950), 128–31, 169–72.

53. Andrea Costa, "Annotazioni autobiografico per servire alle 'Memorie della mia vita,'" *Movimento Operaio* 4, no. 2 (March–April 1952): 322. Also cited in Hostetter, *Italian Socialist Movement*, 330.

54. Conti, *Le origini del socialismo a Firenze*, 173–74, 178–83; Costa, *Bagliori di socialismo*, 18–20; James Guillaume, *L'internationale: documents et souvenirs (1864–1878)*, 4 vols. (Paris: Georges Bellais et al., 1905–1910), 3: 204–6; Hostetter, *Italian Socialist Movement*, 340; Carr, *Bakunin*, 483–96; Franco Della Peruta, "L'internazionale a Roma dal 1872 al 1877," *Movimento Operaio* 4, no. 1 (January–February 1952): 24–28.

55. For the trials proceedings, see Pernicone, *Italian Anarchism*, 95–98; Hostetter, *Italian Socialist Movement*, 344–52; Romano, *Storia del movimento socialista in Italia*, 3: 174–81.

56. Jacque Freymond, ed., *La première internationale: recueil de documents*, 4 vols. (Geneva: E. Droz, 1962–71), 4: 487.

57. Pernicone, *Italian Anarchism*, 108–10; Pier Carlo Masini, ed., *La federazione italiana dell'associazione internazionale dei lavoratori* (Milan: Avanti!, 1963), 135–41.

58. Freymond, *Première internationale*, 4: 487–90.

59. *Bulletin de la Fédération jurassienne* (Sonvillier, Switzerland), December 3, 1876.

60. Pernicone, *Italian Anarchism*, 119.

61. Ceccarelli to Amilcare Cipriani, March or April 1881, reproduced in Franco Della Peruta, *Democrazia e socialismo nel risorgimento: saggi e ricerche* (Rome: Editori Riuniti, 1965), 390.

62. Ibid., 390–91.

63. The insurrection is treated at length by Franco Della Peruta, "La banda del Matese e il fallimento della teoria della moderna '*jacquerie*' in Italia," *Movimento Operaio* 6 (1956): 337–80; Piero Carlo Masini, *Gli internazionalisti: la banda del Matese, 1876–1878* (Milan: Avanti!, 1958); Leone Gasparini, *La "banda del Matese": la guerriglia nell'Italia post-unitaria* (Casalvelino Scalo: Galzerano, 1983); Pernicone, *Italian Anarchism*, 118–28. For an invaluable collection of documentary material, see Bruno Tomasiello, *La banda del Matese, 1876–1878* (Casalvelino Scalo: Galzerano, 2009).

## Chapter 2. Malfattori: *Government Repression and Anarchist Violence*

1. Margherita to Colonel Osio, August 2, 1899, quoted in Robert Katz, *The Fall of the House of Savoy* (New York: Macmillan, 1971), 41.

2. Ibid., 88.

3. Nunzio Pernicone, *Italian Anarchism, 1864–1892* (Princenton, NJ: Princeton University Press, 1993), 147–48.

4. Aldo Romano, *Storia del movimento socialista in Italia*, vol. 3, *La scapigliatura romantica e la liquidazione teorica dell'anarchismo (1872–1880)* (Milan: Fratelli Bocca, 1954), 306–8; Richard Hostetter, *The Italian Socialist Movement* (Princeton, NJ: Van Nostrand, 1958), 393–94, 400–405.

5. Aldo De Jaco, ed., *Gli anarchici* (Rome: Editori Riuniti, 1971), 544.

6. For details of the *attentat* and the events immediately preceding, see Giuseppe Galzerano, *Giovanni Passannante* (Casalvelino Scalo: Galzerano, 1997), 11–95. Also Giuseppe Porcaro, *Processo a un anarchico a Napoli nel 1878* (Naples: Del Delfino, 1975), 58.

7. Galzerano, *Passannante*, 364–65; Pier Carlo Masini, *Storia degli anarchici italiani da Bakunin a Malatesta (1862–1892)* (Milan: Rizzoli, 1969), 151–52.

8. Some writers insist on calling him an anarchist despite all evidence to the contrary. See Porcaro, *Processo a un anarchico*; Arrigo Petacco, "I terroristi fanno tremare i re," *Storia illustrata* (October 1973): 57–70. Although corroboration is completely lacking, Luigi Galleani claimed that an old friend and comrade from Naples told him that Passannante had joined the Avvocata section of the International while in Naples. See Mentana [pseudonym of Luigi Galleani], *Faccia a faccia col nemico* (Boston: Gruppo Autonomo, 1914), 21–22.

9. Masini, *Storia degli anarchici italiani*, 152.

10. Paola Feri, "Il movimento anarchico in Italia dopo la svolta di Andrea Costa, pt. 1," *Trimestre* 11, nos. 1–3 (January–September 1978): 7–8; Elio Conti, *Le origini del socialismo a Firenze: 1860–1880* (Roma: Rinascita, 1950), 213–14; Hostetter, *Italian Socialist Movement*, 403–4; Masini, *Storia degli anarchici italiani*, 152–53; Francesco Pezzi, *Un errore giudiziario ovvero un po' di luce sul processo della bomba di Via Nazionale* (Florence: Birindelli, 1882), 89–93.

11. For a detailed list, see Galzerano, *Passanante*, 213–42.

12. Francesco Saverio Merlino, *L'Italie telle qu'elle est* (Paris: Albert Savine, 1890), 173; Galzerano, *Passanante*, 450–52.

13. Galzerano, *Passanante*, 479–84.

14. Ibid., 489–98; and Porcaro, *Processo a un anarchico*, 113–26.

15. Galzerrano, *Passanante*, 527, 544; Merlino, *L'Italie telle qu'elle est*, 173; and Porcaro, *Processo a un anarchico*, 146–55.

16. Galzerano, *Passanante*, 569.

17. Merlino, *L'Italie telle qu'elle est*, 168–70.

18. Ibid., 168–70; Galzerano, *Passanante*, 627–74; Porcaro, *Processo a un anarchico*, 157–83.

19. For the trial's proceedings, see Stefano Merli, ed., *Autodifese di militanti operaii e democratici italiani davanati ai tribunali* (Milan: Avanti!, 1958), 22–27; Pernicone, *Italian Anarchists*, 95–98; Hostetter, *Italian Socialist Movement*, 344–52; Romano, *Storia del movimento socialista in Italia*, 3: 174–81.

20. Eugenio Forni, *L'internazionale e lo stato: studi sociali*, 420–24; Bruno Tomasiello, *La banda del Matese, 1876–1878* (Casalvelino Scalo: Galzerano, 2009), 15–19.

21. Pernicone, *Italian Anarchists*, 104.

22. Malatesta, "Anche questa!—A proposita di massoneria," *Umanità nova* (Milan), October 7, 1920, in Errico Malatesta, *Scritti*, ed. Luigi Fabbri (Geneva: Risveglio, 1934–36), 3: 183.

23. Forni, *L'internazionale e lo stato*, 420–24; Tomasiello, *La banda del Matese*, 15–19.

24. Conti, *Socialismo a Firenze*, 198; Romano, *Storia del movimento socialista in Italia*, 3: 297–99; Hostetter, *Italian Socialist Movement*, 385–86, 388.

25. For an overview of the evolution of state repression in Italy at the end of the nineteenth century, see Susanna Di Corato Tarchetti, *Anarchici, governo, magistrati in Italia, 1876–1892* (Rome: Carocci, 2010); John A. Davis, *Conflict and Control: Law and Order in Nineteenth-Century Italy* (Atlanta Highlands, NJ: Humanities Press International, 1988), 211–342.

26. Lorenzo Cenni, ed., *Le celebre autodifese (stenografate) pronunciate da un meccanico e da un contadino, Francesco Natta e Giuseppe Scarletti (Corte d'Assise di Firenze 1875–1879)* (Florence: A. Vallecchi, 1909), 15.

27. *La Legge, XX (1880),* quoted in Romano Canosa and Amedeo Santosuosso, *Magistrati, anarchici e socialisti alla fine dell'ottocento in Italia* (Milan: Feltrinelli, 1981), 28–29.

28. For a comprehensive account of these measures, see Davis, *Conflict and Control*, 223–50.

29. Quoted by Deputy Ercole in *Atti parlamentari: discusioni della Camera dei Deputati* (hereafter cited as *AP*), meeting of December 13, 1876 (session of 1876–77), 1: 257–58. See also Vittorio Lollini, *L'ammonizione e il domicilio coatto* (Bologna: Fratelli Treves, 1882), 16.

30. Merlino, *L'Italie telle qu'elle est*, 196–97.

31. *Il codice penale*, pt. 3: 61–63; Lollini, *L'ammonizione*, 15–147; Pasquale Villari, *Scritti sulla questione sociale in Italia* (Florence: G. C. Sansoni, 1902), 178–83; Richard B. Jensen, "Italy's Peculiar Institution: Internal Police Exile, 1861–1914," in June K. Burton, ed., *Essays in European History: Selected from the Annual Meeting of the Southern Historical Associa-*

*tion, 1986–1987*, 99–114 (Lanham, MD: University Press of America, 1989). For personal recollections of *domicilio coatto*, see Amedeo Boschi, *Ricordi di domicilio coatto* (Turin: Seme Anarchico, 1954); Ettore Croce, *A domicilio coatto* (Lipari: Pasquale Conti, 1899); Adamo Mancini, *Memorie di un anarchico* (Imola: Paolo Galeati, 1914), 24–36. For brief treatments of *ammonizione* and *domicilio coatto*, see Davis, *Conflict and Control*, 217–26.

32. Jensen, "Italy's Peculiar Institution," 108.

33. See founding documents, *La federazione italiana dell'associazione internazionale dei lavoratori: atti ufficiali, 1871–1880*, ed. Pier Carlo Masini (Milan: Avanti!, 1963), 1–46.

34. "Il comitato italiano per la rivoluzione sociale al rappresentanti del Congresso generale dell'associazione internazionale dei lavoratori in Brusselle, September 1874," in founding documents, *Federazione italiana*, 101.

35. Ibid.

36. For the details of Costa's defection and transformation, see Hostetter, *Italian Socialist Movement*, 312–25; Manuel G. Gonzales, *Andrea Costa and the Rise of Socialism in the Romagna* (Washington, DC: University Press of America, 1980), 146–62; Gino Cerrito, *Andrea Costa nel socialismo italiano* (Rome: Goliardica, 1982), 177–86, 197–209.

37. Malatesta, "I nostri propositi-II: l'organizzazione," *L'Associazione* (London), December 7, 1889.

38. *Dizionario biografico degli anarchici italiani*, curated by Maurizio Antonioli, Gianpietro Berti, Santi Fedele, and Pasquale Iuso (Pisa: Franco Serantini, 2003), 1: 284.

39. *Le Révolté* (Geneva), December 25, 1880.

40. Ibid.

41. Letter of June 27, 1881, in *Il grido del popolo*, July 4, 1881.

42. Ibid.

43. *Il grido del popolo*, April 24, 1881.

44. *I malfattori* (Geneva), May 21, 28, 1881.

45. See Franco Venturi, *Roots of Revolution: A History of the Populist and Socialist Movements in Nineteenth Century Russia* (New York: Grosset & Dunlap, 1966), 411–12; Astrid von Borcke, "Violence and Terror in Russian Revolutionary Populism: The *Narodnaya Volya*," in *Social Protest and Terror in Nineteenth- and Twentieth-Century Europe*, ed. Wolfgang J. Mommensen and Gerhard Hirshfeld (New York: St. Martin's Press, 1982), 48–62.

46. On this critical point, see also Masini, *Storia degli anarchici italiani*, 226–27.

47. *Il grido del popolo*, April 24, 1881.

48. Letter of July 13, 1881, in *Il grido del popolo*, August 3, 1881.

49. The proceedings of the London Congress were published in *Le Révolté* (Geneva), July 23, August 6, 20, September 3, 1881. For secondary accounts, see Max Nettlau, *Anarchisten und Socialrevolutionare: Die Entwicklung des Anarchismus in den Jahren 1880–1886* (Berlin: Asy, 1931), 177–23; G. M. Stekloff, *History of the First International* (London: Martin Lawrence, 1928), 349–62.

50. For biographical sketches of Covelli, see Antonio Lucarelli, *Carlo Cafiero: Saggio di una storia documentata del socialismo* (Trani: Vecchi, 1947), 103–10; *Dizionario biografico degli anarchici italiani*, 1: 462–63.

51. Quoted in Masini, *Storia degli anarchici italiani*, 167n21.

52. *I malfattori*, May 28, 1881. See Masini's account of Covelli's ideology of the *malfattori* in his *Storia degli anarchici italiani*, 166–68.

53. "Coi malfattori!" (unsigned), *I malfattori*, June 23, 1881. Credit for distinguishing between the unsigned articles of Covelli and Cafiero is due to Pier Carlo Masini, *Cafiero* (Milan: Rizzoli, 1974), 420n9.

54. *I malfattori*, June 23, 1881.

55. Archivio Centrale dello Stato (Rome; hereafter cited as ACS), *Ministero del Interno. Gabinetto. Rapporti Semestrali dei Prefetti (1882–1890)*, busto 12, fascicolo 49. For the republican bombs, see prefect of Pisa to Ministry of the Interior, October 12, 1887, in *Rapporti Semestrali dei Prefetti (1882–1890)*.

56. Circular in ACS, Ministero di Grazia e Giustizia. Direzione Generale Affari Penali. Miscellanea, busto 83, fascicolo 248.

57. Police chief to prefect of Florence, April 7, 1884, in Archivio di Stato di Firenze, Questura della Provincia di Firenze (1864—1919), busto 15, fascicolo 5.

58. *Humanitas* (Naples), February 6, 1887.

59. *Humanitas*, March 8, 1887.

60. Pier Fausto Buccellato and Marina Iaccio, *Gli anarchici nell'Italia meridionale: la stampa, 1869–1893* (Rome: Bulzoni, 1982), 322–28, 330–32.

61. Caroline Cahm, *Kropotkin and the Rise of Revolutionary Anarchism, 1872–1886* (Cambridge: Cambridge University Press, 1989), 200–203.

62. Nettlau, *Die erste Blutezeit der Anarchie*, 212–35; Marie Fleming, *The Anarchist Way to Socialism: Elisée Reclus and Nineteenth-Century European Anarchism* (London: Croom Helm, 1979), 195–98; Masini, *Storia degli anarchici italiani*, 229.

63. *Le Révolte* (Paris), quoted in Jean Maitron, *Histoire du mouvement anarchiste en France 1880–1914* (Paris: SUDEL 1951), 169.

64. For Duval, see Maitron, *Histoire du mouvement anarchiste*, 167–77. Galleani translated Duval's autobiography in 1917, but government repression and financial difficulties prevented publication of a complete version until 1929. See Clement Duval, *Memorie autobiografiche* (Newark, NJ: L'adunata dei refrattari, 1929). Hundreds of copies were printed and, after World War II, the *L'adunata* group wanted to send them to Italy for propaganda purposes, but the mailing costs for a heavy volume of 1,044 pages were prohibitive. Meanwhile, before his death in 1935, Duval lived in the home of Raffaele Schiavina (alias Max Sartin), the editor of *L'adunata dei refrattari* in New York.

65. *Il Paria* (Ancona), January 30, 1887.

66. *L'Associazione* (Nice), October 15, 27, 30, 1889; January 23, 1890. Also *Dizionario biografico degli anarchici italiani*, 2: 297–99, 354–55; Masini, *Storia degli anarchici italiani*, 229–33.

67. Sernicoli, *L'anarchia e gli anarchici*, 1: 286, 294.

68. Ibid., 285–97; *Dizionario biografico degli anarchici italiani*, 2: 354–55.

69. *Il ciclone* (Paris), September 4, 1887.

70. Ibid.

71. The warning came from "a perfectly reliable source" and was conveyed to the Italian ambassador in Berlin by the king of Portugal. See Archivio Centrale dello Stato (Rome), *Carteggi di personalità*, Archivio Francesco Crispi (Palermo), scat. 67, fascicoli 452 and 458. See also Francesco Crispi, *The Memoirs of Francesco Crispi*, ed. Thomas Palamenghi-Crispi (London: Hodder and Stoughton, 1912), 3: 321–26.

72. Sernicoli, *L'anarchia e gli anarchici*, 1: 285–90; *Dizionario biografico degli anarchici italiani*, 2: 354–55.

73. Sernicoli, *L'anarchia e gli anarchici*, 1: 285–90; *Dizionario biografico degli anarchici italiani*, 354–55.

74. Unsigned secret letter to the minister of the interior from a self-described friend of General Luigi Pelloux, in ACS, Ministero del Interno. Direzione generale pubblica sicurezza. Ufficio Riservato (1879–1912); "Complotto e attentato Acciarito," busto 3, fascicolo 7.

75. Masini, *Storia degli anarchici italiani*, 229–33; Maitron, *Histoire du mouvement anarchiste*, 170–72; Luigi Galleani, *Aneliti e singulti* (Newark, NJ: Biblioteca de l'Adunata dei Refrattari, 1935), 94–96; *Dizionario biografia degli anarchici italiani*, 2: 297–99, 354–55.

76. *La Rivendicazione* (Forlì), November 10, 1888, December 14, 1888; April 6, 20, 1889. "Vittorio Pini," *L'Associazione* (London), December 7, 1889; letter to *L'Associazione* (London), December 21, 1889; see also issue of January 23, 1890.

77. Masini, *Storia degli anarchici italiani*, 229, 233; Osvaldo Bayer, *Anarchism and Violence: Severino Di Giovanni in Argentina, 1923–1931* (London: Elephant, 1985); Reminiscences of Bartolomeo Provo, in Paul Avrich, ed., *Anarchist Voices: An Oral History of Anarchism in America* (Princeton, NJ: Princeton University Press, 1995), 118–19.

## Chapter 3. Bombings, Insurrections, and Cosmopolitanism: Paolo Lega and Sante Caserio

1. George Esenwein, *Anarchist Ideology and the Working-Class Movement in Spain, 1868–1898* (Berkeley: University of California Press, 1989), 187–88.

2. Ibid., 84–92, 174–79; Richard Bach Jensen, *The Battle against Anarchist Terrorism: An International History, 1878–1934* (New York: Cambridge University Press, 2015), 34; Murray Bookchin, *The Spanish Anarchists: The Heroic Years, 1868–1936* (New York: Harper & Row, 1977), 106–8, 118–19.

3. Jean Maitron, *Histoire du mouvement anarchiste en France, 1880–1914* (Paris: Société universitaire d'éditions et de librairie, 1951), 195–201; Henri Varennes, *De Ravachol à Caserio: Notes et documents* (Paris: Garnier frères, n.d.), 5–62; John Merriman, *The Dynamite Club: How a Bombing in Fin-de-Siècle Paris Ignited the Age of Modern Terror* (Boston: Houghton Mifflin Harcourt, 2009), 72–73, 81–85.

4. Quoted in George Woodcock, *Anarchism: A History of Libertarian Ideas and Movements* (Cleveland: World, 1962), 310–11.

5. Maitron, *Histoire du mouvement anarchiste en France*, 209–10; Henri Varennes, *De Ravachol à Caserio* (Paris: Garnier, 1895), 78–94.

6. Quoted in Varennes, *De Ravachol à Caserio*, 169–70.

7. Ibid., 165–75; Maitron, *Histoire du mouvement anarchiste en France*, 211.

8. Maitron, *Histoire du mouvement anarchiste en France*, 212–19; Varennes, *De Ravachol à Caserio*, 98–128.

9. Charles Malato, "Some Anarchist Portraits," *Fortnightly Review*, n.s., 56 (September 1, 1894): 327–33, Maitron, *Histoire du mouvement anarchiste en France*, 219–27; Merriman, *Dynamite Club*, passim, 59ff.

10. Malato, "Some Anarchist Portraits," 319.

11. Ibid., 331.

12. Quoted in Varennes, *De Ravachol à Caserio*, 217.

13. Ibid., 238.

14. Quoted in Varennes, *De Ravachol à Caserio*, 238, 240–41.

15. Ibid., 210–45; Maitron, *Histoire du mouvement anarchiste en France*, 219–27; Merriman, *Dynamite Club*, 99–135, 146–201.

16. Ettore Sernicoli, *L'anarchia e gli anarchici: studio storico e politico* (Milan: Treves, 1894), 1: 325–26.

17. Ibid., 325–26.

18. Ibid., 339–40.

19. Ibid., 340–41.

20. Ibid., 363–66; Pier Carlo Masini, *Storia degli anarchici italiani nell'epoca degli attentati* (Milan: Rizzoli, 1981), 35–36.

21. *L'Ordine* (Turin), March 25, 1893.

22. Prefect of Piacenza to Ministry of the Interior, February 27, 1894, in Archivio Centrale dello Stato (hereafter cited as ACS), Archivio Francesco Crispi (Roma), busta 33, fascicolo 599, sottofascicolo 1.

23. Interview with Charles Malato, "Anarchici e bombe," in *La Sera* (April 13, 1893), a bourgeois daily published in Milan. Reproduced in *L'Ordine* (Turin), April 29, 1893.

24. Ibid.

25. Masini, *Storia degli anarchici italiani*, 199.

26. Malato, "Anarchici e bombe."

27. *Le Révolté* (Geneva), August 6, 1881.

28. *La federazione italiana dell'Associazione internazionale dei lavoratori: atti uficiali, 1871–1880* (Milan: Avanti!, 1963), 114.

29. *Pensiero e volontà* (Rome), September 1, 1924, as given in Vernon Richards, ed., *Errico Malatesta: His Life and Ideas* (London: Freedom Press, 1965), 62.

30. For details of Malatesta's return and settling in Nice, see Davide Turcato, *Making Sense of Anarchism: Errico Malatesta's Experiments with Revolution, 1889–1900* (London: Palgrave Macmillan, 2012), 36–40. His call for anarchist organization was a constant theme. See "I nostri propositi-II: l'organizzazione," *L'Associazione* (London), December 7, 1889.

31. "A proposito di uno sciopero," "Propaganda a fatti," "I nostri propositi-II: l'organizzazione," *L'Associazione* (Nice), September 6 [actually October 6], October 16, December 7, 1889.

32. See the *Appello*, a four-page flyer Malatesta issued in September 1889, and his articles "Programma" and "L'indomani della rivoluzione" in *L'Associazione* (Nice), September 6 [actually October 6], October 16, 1889.

33. *Il congresso di Capolago: ai socialisti ed al popolo d'Italia* (Castrocaro: Barboni e Paganelli, 1891); *La Rivendicazione* (Forlì), January 3, 10, 1891; *Il Proletario* (Marsala), February 6, 1892; Francesco Saverio Merlino, "Socialisme et anarchisme: le congrès socialiste italien de Capolago (Suisse)," *Société Nouvelle* 7, Pt. 1 (1891): 347–55; By a Comrade Who Was Present, "The Capolago Congress" [unsigned but written by Malatesta] in *Freedom* (London), March 1891; Max Nettlau, *Die erste Blutezeit der Anarchie: 1886–1894* (Vaduz, Liechtenstein: Topos, 1981), 166–67; Luis [Luigi] Fabbri, "Crepusculo en Capolago," *La protesta: suplemento semanal* (Buenos Aires, Argentina), December 27, 1926.

34. Luigi Galleani, *Figure e figure* (Newark, NJ: Biblioteca de L'Adunata dei Refrattari, 1930), 182; Malatesta to Merlino, February 29, 1891, in ACS, Min. Int., Casellario Politico Centrale (hereafter cited as CPC), Malatesta: busta 286, fascicolo 31568, sottofascicolo 1.

35. Malatesta to Merlino, February 29, 1891, in ACS, Min. Int., CPC, Malatesta: busta 286, fascicolo 31568, sottofascicolo 1.

36. Giampietro Berti, *Francesco Saverio Merlino: Dall'anarchismo socialista al socialismo liberale, 1856–1930* (Milan: FrancoAngeli, 1993), 127–29.

37. Cipriani to Merlino, February 19, 1891; Malatesta to Merlino, February 29, 1891, in ACS; *Il proletario* (Marsala), April 23, 1891; Salvatore F. Romano, *Storia dei fasci siciliani* (Bari: Laterza, 1959), 26, 385–86.

38. President of Prussian police to minister of state and interior minister, March 10, 1891, in ACS, Min. Int., CPC, busta 286, fascicolo 31568, sottofascicolo. 1.

39. *La Rivendicazione* (Forlì), April 11, 1891. See also Rome police chief to king's prosecutor, May 14, 1891, in ACS, Min. Int., *Ufficio Riservato*, busta 2; Antonio Labriola to Friedrich Engels, March 30, 1891, in Antonio Labriola, *Lettere a Engels* (Rome: Rinascita, 1949), 13; Davide Turcato, *Making Sense of Anarchism: Errico Malatesta's Experiments with Revolution, 1889–1900* (New York: Palgrave, 2012), 81–86.

40. Quoted in Rome police chief to king's prosecutor, May 14, 1891, in ACS, Min. Int., UR, busta 2.

41. Ibid.; *Il Proletario* (Marsala), May 7, 1891; *La Rivendicazione* (Forlì), May 9 and 23, 1891; *La Campana* (Macerata), May 27, 1891; Turcato, *Malatesta*, 85; Luis [Luigi] Fabbri, *Vida y pensamiento de Malatesta* (Barcelona: Tierra y Libertad, 1938), 97; Luciano Cafagna, "Anarchismo e socialismo a Roma negli anni della 'febbre edilizia' e della crisi, 1881–1891," *Quaderni di Movimento Operaio (Milan: Feltrinelli, 1953),* 729–88; "Itinerario di Malatesta nel viaggio del 1891," ACS, Min. Int., CPC, Malatesta: busta 286, fascicolo 31568, sottofascicolo 1.

42. Labriola, *Lettere a Engels*, 128.

43. Giovanni Giolitti, *Memorie della mia vita*, 3rd ed. (Monza: Garzanti, 1945), 90.

44. The definitive study on the *fasci* is Romano, *Storia dei fasci siciliani*. Also essential are the articles by Romano, Massimo Ganci, Francesco Renda, Gino Cerrito, Salvatore Costanza, Ignazio Nigrelli, and Luigi Cortesi in *Movimento operaio* 6 (November–December 1954). For brief studies, see Renda, *Fasci siciliani*; Marsilio, *I fasci siciliani*.

45. Giolitti, *Memorie della mia vita*, 86–88; *Quarant'anni di politica italiana. Dalle carte di Giovanni Giolitti*, ed. Piero D'Angiolini (Milan: Feltrinelli, 1962) 1: 184; Romano, *Storia dei fasci siciliani*, 376.

46. Romano, *Storia dei fasci siciliani*, 313–38; Marsilio, *Fasci siciliani*, 40–44; Ganci, "Il movimento dei fasci nella provincia di Palermo," *Movimento operaio* 6 (November–December 1954): 870–71.

47. For excellent social histories of the Lunigiana, see Renato Mori, *La lotta sociale in Lunigiana, 1859–1904* (Florence: Monnier, 1958); Antonio Bernieri, *Cento anni di storia sociale a Carrara, 1815–1921* (Milan: Feltrinelli, 1961).

48. As cited in Mori, *La lotta sociale in Lunigiana*, 126–27.

49. Ibid., 177–82; Ugo Fedeli, "Il movimento anarchico a Carrara," *Volontà* 6, nos. 2–3 (January 15, 1952): 112–16; 6, no. 12 (January 31, 1953): 690–92; 7, nos. 1–2 (March 1, 1953): 65–78.

50. Ugo Fedeli, "Anni del di reazione"; "Carrara alla vigilia degli avvenimenti del 1894"; "Carrara 1894 (Come si svolsero i fatti: I)"; and "Come si svolser i fatti: II," in *L'Adunata dei Refrattari*, December 22, 1951; January 1 and 19, February 2 and 9, 1952.

51. *La Questione Sociale* (Paterson, NJ), September 30, 1899.

52. Francesco Crispi, *Politica interna* (Milan: Treves, 1924), 329.

53. Quoted in Erika Diemoz, *A morte il tiranno: anarchia e violenza da Crispi a Mussolini* (Turin: Giulio Einaudi, 2011), 6.

54. Ibid., 361–63.

55. The *gerente responsabile* was the editor of anarchist newspapers who took responsibility for articles deemed offensive by the censors, which could result in fines or jail time.

56. Prefect of Genoa to Ministry of the Interior, June 19, 1893, in ACS, *Carteggi di personalità: Francesco Crispi,* Archivio di Stato di Palermo, scatola 104, fascicolo 804: "Documentazione relative all'attentato di Paolo Lega a S. E. Crispi (June 16, 1894." [Hereafter cited as ACS, Archivio Crispi (Palermo).]

57. Prefect of Ravenna to Ministry of the Interior, June 17, 1894; prefect of Genoa to Ministry of the Interior, June 19, 1894, both in ACS, Archivio Crispi (Palermo).

58. Prefect of Genoa to Ministry of the Interior, June 19, 1893; prefect of Ravenna to Ministry of the Interior, June 17, 1894, in ACS, Archivio Crispi (Palermo). See also Maurizio Antonioli, Giampietro Berti, Santi Fedele, and Pasquale Iuso eds., *Dizionario biografico degli anarchici italiani,* vol. 2 (Pisa: BFS, 2003), 25–26; Masini, *Storia degli anarchici italiani,* 36–37.

59. Prefect of Ravenna to Ministry of the Interior, June 17, 1894, in ACS, Archivio Crispi (Palermo), scatola 104, fascicolo. 804.

60. Police chief of Bologna to Ministry of the Interior, August 27, 1894, in ACS, Archivio Crispi (Palermo), scatola 104, fascicolo 804.

61. Police chief of Rome to Ministry of the Interior, June 17, 1894, in ACS, Archivio Crispi (Palermo), scatola 104, fascicolo 804.

62. Quoted in Ettore Sernicoli, *I delinquenti dell'anarchia: nuovo studio storico e politico, 1894–1899* (Rome: Enrico Voghera, 1899), 82.

63. *Il secolo* (Milan), July 20–21, 1894, quoted in Masini, *Storia degli anarchici italiani,* 37.

64. Sernicoli, *I delinquenti dell'anarchia,* 77.

65. Police chief of Rome to king's prosecutor, August 14, 1894, in ACS, Archivio Crispi (Palermo), scatola 104, fascicolo 804.

66. Ibid.

67. The letter is reproduced in Diemoz, *A morte il tiranno,* 109–10.

68. *Dizionario biografico degli anarchi italiani,* 2: 26, 418; Nunzio Dell'Erba, *Giornali e gruppi anarchici in Italia, 1892–1900* (Milan: Franco Angeli, 1983), 25–26, 83–84, 418.

69. *Dizionario biografico degli anarchici italiani,* 2: 28, 418; Dell'Erba, *Giornali e gruppi anarchici,* 83–84. For a good cursory account of Lega's *attentat,* see Diemoz, *A morte il tiranno,* 83–90.

70. J. C. Longoni, *Four Patients of Dr. Deibler* (London: Lawrence & Wishart, 1970), 206–12; Varennes, *De Ravachol à Caserio,* 250–51; Maitron, *Histoire du mouvement anarchiste en France,* 228–30; Roberto Gemmo, *Sante Caserio: Vita, tragedia e mito di un anarchico lombardo* (Biella: ELF, 1994), 44–45; Max Frantel, *Caserio* (Paris: Émile-Paul Frères, 1934), 10–14, 85–90.

71. Longoni, *Four Patients of Dr. Diebler*, 206–12; Gemmo, *Sante Caserio*, 32–37.

72. Pietro Gori, "Sante Caserio," *Torch*, June 18, 1895.

73. Ibid.

74. Masini, *Storia degli anarchici italiani*, 40–43; *Dizionario biografico degli anarchici italiani*, 1: 333–35.

75. Filippo Turati, "Il loro duello. L'uccisione di Carnot," *Critica Sociale* (Milan), July 1, 1894.

76. Gori, "Sante Caserio."

77. Gori interview with *La Sera* (Milan), July 1894, in Pietro Gori, *Opere*, vol. 10, *Pagine di vagabondaggio* (Milan: Binazzi, 1912), 64.

78. Gori interview with *La Tribuna* (Rome), August 2, 1894, in *Opere*, 10: 59.

79. Gori, "Sante Caserio."

80. Ibid.

81. Caserio to a comrade, Lausanne, undated, *La Questione Sociale*, September 5, 1903. Guglielmo Ferrero dates the letter as July 13, 1893. Caserio described his life in exile in seven letters, which were obtained by Pietro Gori and entrusted to the historian Guglielmo Ferrero for study and publication. They were published in *Le Figaro* (Paris), *La Tribuna* (Rome), *Il Pensiero* (Chieti), and later in *La Questione Sociale*.

82. Varennes, *Ravachol à Caserio*, 252; Caserio's letters of July 3, 1893, May 13, 1894, and June 5, 1894, to comrades in Italy, in *La Questione Sociale*, September 5 and 12, 1903. Five of them are reproduced (some incomplete) in English translation in Longoni, *Four Patients of Dr. Diebler*, 192–97.

83. Letter of October 18, 1893, *La Questione Sociale*, September 12, 1903; Longoni, *Four Patients of Dr. Diebler*, 195.

84. Letter of May 15, 1893, in *La Questione Sociale*, September 12, 1903; Longoni, *Four Patients of Dr. Diebler*, 195. Longoni provides an incorrect date for this letter.

85. *Dizionario biografico degli anarchici italiani*, 333.

86. *La Questione Sociale*, September 12, 1903.

87. Ibid.

88. Letter of May 15, 1893, in *La Questione Sociale*, September 12, 1903.

89. Varennes, *De Ravachol à Caserio*, 261–63; *Dizionario biografico degli anarchici italiani*, 333.

90. Varennes, *De Ravachol à Caserio*, 247. Varennes is the standard account of the court proceedings. Longoni provides what is essentially a translation of Varennes (without acknowledgment) but includes a few passages and some information not found in the latter. A third version, the most complete of the three, is published in Luigi Galleani, *Faccia a faccia col nemico: cronache giudiziarie dell'anarchismo militante* (East Boston, MA: Gruppo Autonomo, 1914).

91. Longoni, *Four Patients of Dr. Diebler*, 213.

92. Ibid., 212–13.

93. Varennes, *De Ravachol à Caserio*, 268.

94. Ibid., 269.

95. Ibid., 267–70.

96. Ibid., 247, 260.

97. Galleani, *Faccia a faccia col nemico*. 471.

98. Varennes, *De Ravachol à Caserio*, 260, 266–67; Longoni, *Four Patients of Dr. Diebler*, 219.

99. Galleani, *Faccia a faccia col nemico*, 461.

100. Ibid., 468.

101. Ibid., 468–69.

102. Longoni, *Four Patients of Dr. Diebler*, 218.

103. Varennes, *De Ravachol à Caserio*, 260.

104. Ibid., 260–61.

105. Ibid., 271.

106. Masini, *Storia degli anarchici italiani*, 50. See Supplement to *Freedom* (London), October 1894.

107. Supplement to *Freedom* (London), October 1894.

108. Ibid., 271; Longoni, *Four Patients of Dr. Diebler*, 228–32.

109. Galleani, *Faccia a faccia col nemico*, 485; Longoni, *Four Patients of Dr. Diebler*, 232.

110. Gori, "Sante Caserio."

111. Gori's "Sante Caserio," sung to the tune of a popular Tuscan song, "Suona la mezzanotte," is reproduced in every anarchist songbook. See, for example, *Note ribelli: inni e canti rivoluzionari* (Bern: Biblioteca di Studi Sociali, 1902), 11–12; and *I canti della rivoluzione* (La Spezia: Cromo-Tipografia "La Sociale," 1920), 46–47.

## Chapter 4. Crispi and the "Exceptional Laws"

1. Domenico Farini, *Diario di fine secolo* (Rome: Bardi, 1961–62), 1: 455.

2. Quoted in Raffaele Majetti, *L'anarchia e le leggi che la reprimono in Italia* (Caserta: Domenico Fabiano, 1894), 41.

3. Report to the Senate, in Majetti, *L'anarchia*, 47.

4. Quoted in Cilibrizzi, *Storia parlamentare politica e diplomatica d'Italia*, 2: 526; Ente per la Storia del Socialismo e del Movimento Operaio Italiano, *Biografia del socialismo e del movimento operaio*, 2 vols. in 6 tomes (Rome: E.S.M.O.I, 1956–68), 1: 239.

5. Ente per la Storia del Socialismo, *Biografia del socialismo e del movimento operaio*, 2: 524–29.

6. Francesco Crispi, *Discorsi parlamentari*, vol. 3 (Rome: Camera dei Deputati, 1915), 807.

7. Ibid., 3: 808.

8. Ibid.

9. Minister of the interior to undersecretary of state, July 29, 1894, in Archivio Centrale dello Stato (hereafter cited as ACS), Archivio Crispi (Roma), fascicolo 647, sottofascicolo 1.

10. The three laws, together with legal commentary and the regulations for the laws' administration, are reproduced in Majetti, *L'anarchia*, 84. See also Ettore Sernicoli, *L'anarchia e gli anarchici* (Milan: Fratelli Treves, 1894), 2: 263–64.

11. "Documenti relative all'esplosione di una bomba in Piazza Montecitorio a Roma," in ACS, Archivio Crispi (Roma), busta 33, fascicolo 599, sottofascicolo. 1 and 2. [The Crispi Roma documents sometimes indicate busta as well as fascicolo numbers.]

12. Majetti, *L'anarchia*, 84–87; Pier Carlo Masini, *Storia degli anarchici italiani nell'epoca degli attentati* (Milan: Rizzoli, 1981), 35–36.

13. Crispi, *Discorsi parlamentari*, 3: 803.

14. Ibid.

15. Ibid., 3: 803–6.

16. "Domicilio Coatto," ACS, Archivio Crispi (Rome), fascicolo 657, sottofascicolo. 7; Majetti, *L'anarchia*, 265–66; Sernicoli, *L'anarchia e gli anarchici*, 118–20.

17. Alfredo Angiolini, *Socialismo a socialisti in Italia* (Florence: Nerbini, 1921), 282–84; Roberto Michels, *Storia critica del movimento socialista italiano fino al 1911* (Florence: La Voce, 1926), 167–68; Rinaldo Rigola, *Storia del movimento operaio italiano* (Milan: Domus, 1947), 140–41.

18. Amedeo Boschi, *Ricordi del domicilio coatto* (Turin: Seme Anarchico, 1954), 18.

19. "Documenti relativi alla legislazione sul domicilio coatto," in Boschi, *Ricordi del domicilio coatto*.

20. "Ispezione delle colonie dei coatti di Sicilia e Provincie Napolitane," in Boschi, *Ricordi del domicilio coatto*.

21. "Ispezione delle colonie."

22. Minister of the interior report of July 6, 1895, in Boschi, *Ricordi del domicilio coatto*. Also Zagaglia (pseudonym of L. De Fazio), *I coatti politici in Italia la repressione nell'Italia Umbertina* (Casalvelino Scalo: Galzerano, 1987), 26. Originally published in 1895, first in the daily newspaper *L'Asino* and then in book form, the journalist De Fazio exposed the dreadful living conditions of the *coatti* in Porto Ercole.

23. "Domicilio Coatto. Legge 19 luglio 1894, No. 316," in ACS, Archivio Crispi (Roma), fascicolo 647, sottofascicolo. 4.

24. "Domicilio Coatto. Denuncie e assegnazioni in base alla Legge 19 luglio 1894," No. 316, in ACS, Archivio Crispi (Roma), fascicolo 647, sottofascicolo 4.

25. "Elenco numerico per professionae degli individui assegnati a domicilio coatto in base alla leggi 19 luglio 1894, No. 316 e già destinati nelle Colonie," in ACS, Archivio Crispi (Roma), fascicolo 647, sottofascicolo 4.

26. Gianpietro Berti, *Errico Malatesta e il movimento anarchico italiano e internazionale, 1872–1932* (Milan: Franco Angeli, 2003), 222–23.

27. "Ispezione delle colonie dei coatti di Sicilia e Provincie Napoletane," ACS, Archivio Crispi (Roma), fascicolo 657, sottofascicolo 3.

28. Masini, *Storia degli anarchici*, 63–65; Adamo Mancini, *Memorie di un anarchico* (Imola: Paolo Galeati), 30.

29. Zagaglia, *I coatti politici in Italia*, 23–42.

30. Ettore Croce, *A domicilio coatto* (Casalvelino Scalo: Galzerano, 2000), 59.

31. Croce, *A domicilio coatto*, 26–27.

32. Croce, *A domicilio coatto*, 41–45.

33. Croce, *A domicilio coatto*, 31–32, 37, 52–56. See also Nunzio Dell'Erba, *Giornali e gruppi anarchici in Italia, 1892–1900* (Milan: Franco Angeli, 1983), 77–78.

34. Director of Tremiti to Ministry of the Interior, June 6, 1895, in ACS, Archivio Crispi (Roma), fascicolo 647, sottofascicolo 2.

35. Director of Tremiti to Ministry of the Interior, January 16, 1896; director of public security to director of Tremiti, January 1, 1896; director of Tremiti to Ministry of the Interior, March 2, 1896; director of public security to prefect of Foggia, July 2, 1896, in

ACS, Archivio Crispi (Roma), fascicolo 647, sottofascicolo 2. Also Mancini, *Memorie di un anarchico*, 31.

36. "Prospetti relativi all'attuazione della legge sui provvedimenti di pubblica sicurezza (19 luglio 1894, N. 316); nomina e lavori della commissione incaricata di studiare la riforma del domicilio coatto (11 aprile–2 dicembre 1895)," in ACS, Archivio Crispi (Roma), fascicolo 657.

37. Tancredi Canonico to Crispi, October 6, 1895, in ACS, Archivio Crispi (Roma), fascicolo 657, sottofascicolo 2.

38. Ibid.

39. Crispi to King Umberto (undated but contemporary with Cononico's report), in ACS, Archivio Crispi (Roma), fascicolo 657, sottofascicolo 1.

40. Ernesto Ragionieri, *Il movimento socialista in Italia, 1850–1922* (Milan: Teti, 1976), 48–49; Alessandro Galante Garrone, *I radicali in Italia, 1849–1925* (Milan: Garzanti, 1973), 320–24.

41. The statement is reproduced in Armando Borghi, *Errico Malatesta in 60 anni di lotte anarchiche* (New York: Sociali, 1933), 64–65.

42. Mancini, *Memorie di un anarchico*, 30.

43. Giorgio Candeloro, *Storia dell'Italia moderna: lo sviluppo del capitalism e del movimento operaio* (Milan: Feltrinelli, 1970), 6: 446–55; Christopher Seton-Watson, *Italy from Liberalism to Fascism, 1870–1925* (London: Meuthen, 1967), 171–75, 181–83. Umberto Levra, *Il colpo di stato della borghesia: la crisi politica di fine secolo in Italia, 1896–1900* (Milan: Feltrinelli, 1975), 17–18; Richard B. Jensen, "Italy's Peculiar Institution: Internal Police Exile, 1861–1914," in June K. Burton, ed., *Essays in European History: Selected from the Annual Meeting of the Southern Historical Association,1986–1987* (Lanham, MD: University Press of America, 1989), 102–8.

44. Seton-Watson, *Italy from Liberalism to Fascism*, 138–41, 176–83.

45. Ibid., 181–83.

## Chapter 5. Anarchist Assassins: Acciarito, Angiolillo, and Lucheni

1. The principal sources for the study of Acciarito's *attentat* are the following: Archivio Centrale dello Stato (Rome; hereafter cited as ACS), Ministero dell'Interno, Direzione Generale di Pubblica Sicurezza, Ufficio Riservato (1879–1912) (hereafter cited as Min. Int. UR), busta 3, fascicolo 7: "Complotto e attentato Acciarito a S. M. il Re"; and "Sentenza nella causa ad istanza del Pubblico Ministero a carico di Doria Alessandro e Canevelli Giuseppe, 3 agosto 1908 (Roma), Sezione 5 del Tribunale Civile e Penale di Roma," in ACS, Ministero di Grazia e Giustizia, Direzione Generale Affari Penali. Miscellanea, busta 115, fascicolo 219: "Attentati al Re—false testimonianze in processo collegato con l'attentato Acciarito in Teramo—atti fino al 1910" (cited hereafter as "Sentenza"). The "Sentenza" is a lengthy summary of the trial proceedings rather than a transcript. See also Marcello Santoloni and Nicola Marcucci, *Gli ingranaggi del potere: il caso dell'anarchico Acciarito attentatore di Umberto I* (Rome: Ianua, 1981); Aldo De Jaco, ed., *Gli anarchici: Cronaca inedita dell'Unità d'Italia* (Rome: Editori Riuniti, 1971); Ugoberto Alfassio Grimaldi, *Il re "buono"* (Milan: Feltrinelli, 1970); Alessandro Coletti, *Anarchici e questori* (Padua: Marsilio, 1971).

2. Prime Minister Rudinì to Giovanni Alfazio, April 26, 1897, in ACS, Min. Int. UR, busta 3, fascicolo 7: "Complotto e attentato Acciarito a S. M. il Re."

3. Galeazzi described his predicament in a report to the Astengo Committee: Inspector of Public Security Leopoldo Galeazzi to prefect of Roma, May 1, 1897, in ACS, Min. Int. UR, busta 3, fascicolo 7.

4. Antonio Labriola to Friedrich Engels, March 30, 1891, in Antonio Labriola, *Lettere a Engels* (Rome: Rinascita, 1949), 13; Nunzio Pernicone, *Italian Anarchism, 1864–1892* (Princeton, NJ: Princeton University Press, 1993), 261–70; Luciano Cafagna, "Anarchismo e socialismo a Roma degli anni della 'febbre edilizia' e della crisi 1882–1891," *Movimento Operaio* 4, no. 5 (September–October 1952): 729–88.

5. *Avanti!* (Rome), June 27, 1899.

6. Santoloni and Marcucci, *Gli ingranaggi del potere*, 39–50; lieutenant colonel of the Royal Carabinieri in Rome to minister of the interior, April 23, 1897, in De Jaco, *Gli anarchici*, 581–84; Acciarito's courtroom statement from *Avanti!*, May 29, 1897.

7. Police chief of Rome to prefect of Rome, April 24, 1897, in ACS, Min. Int. UR, busta 3, fascicolo 7.

8. Coletti, *Anarchici e questori*, 51; Grimaldi, *Il re "buono,"* 386–87.

9. Coletti, *Anarchici e questori*, 51; Grimaldi, *Il re "buono,"* 386–87.

10. See the previous chapter.

11. *Il Messagero* (Rome), April 23, 1897.

12. Ibid.

13. The signatures were published in *L'Agitazione* (Ancona), April 11, 1897.

14. Police chief of Rome to prefect of Rome, June 13, 1897; police chief of Rome to general prosecutor of the Court of Appeals (Rome), June 18, 1897, ACS, Min. Int. UR, busta 3, fascicolo 7. See also Santoloni and Marcucci, *Gli ingrannagi del potere*, 150–52.

15. *L'Agitatore* (Ancona), April 25, 1897. [*L'Agitatore* was a single issue published by Malatesta's *L'Agitazione*.]

16. *L'Avvenire Sociale* (Messina), May 1, 1897.

17. *L'Agitazione* (Ancona), May 22, 1897.

18. Farini, *Diario di fine secolo*, 2: 1174.

19. *Il Corriere della Sera* (Milan), April 24–25, 1897.

20. *L'Agitazione* (Ancona), April 25, May 22, 1897.

21. Sernicolo, *I delinquenti dell'anarchia*, 255; Santolini and Marcucci, *Gli ingranaggi del potere*, 30–38; Levra, *Il colpo di stato della borghesia*, 22–23; Farini, *Diario di fine secolo*, 2: 1185, 1189.

22. Quoted in *Avanti!* (Rome), May 29, 1897.

23. Ibid.

24. Farini, *Diario di fine secolo*, 2: 1174.

25. Police chief of Rome to chief prosecutor of the Court of Appeals, June 18, 1897, in ACS, Min. Int. UR, busta 3, fascicolo 7.

26. Report of July 24, 1897, in ACS, Min. Int. UR, busta 3, fascicolo 7.

27. Consul general of Geneva to the minister of the interior, April 29, 1897, in ACS, Min. Int. UR, busta 3, fascicolo 7: "Complotto e attentato a R. M. il Re."

28. Police chief of Rome to prefect of Rome, June 13, 1897, in ibid. Also [no author] "Un fedele combattente dell'umanità: Ernesto Diotallevi," *Il pensiero, rivista di studi sociali e cultura* (Rome: Gruppo Il Pensiero, 1952), 20.

29. Prefect of Rome to minister of the interior, December 17, 1897, in ACS, Min. Int., UR, busta 3, fascicolo 7.

30. *Il Corriere della Sera*, quoted in *L'Avvenire Sociale* (Messina), September 17, 1897.

31. At the Rome/Teramo trial of his "accomplices," Acciarito gave vivid accounts of his existence in Santo Stefano. See *Avanti!*, June 28, 1899; March 30, 1900.

32. Police chief of Rome to president of the Indictment Section of the Rome Court of Appeals, October 6, 1897, ACS, Min. Int. UR, busta 3, fascicolo 7.

33. Quoted in "Sentenza," 6.

34. Beltrani-Scalia to the director of Santo Stefano, Nicola, July 14, 1897. Fully quoted in *Il Corriere della Sera*, July 14, 1908; partially quoted in "Sentenza," 99.

35. "Sentenza," 94–95; *Il Corriere della Sera*, July 10, 1908.

36. "Sentenza," 64–66, 86–97; *Il Corriere della Sera*, July 3, 10, 11, 14, 1908.

37. "Sentenza," 7–14, 99–100, 109; *Avanti!*, June 20, 28, 1898; *Il Corriere della Sera*, July 5, 1898.

38. These details were revealed at the Rome/Teramo trial of Acciarito's "accomplice" in 1899. Particularly relevant was Acciarito's testimony at the trial. See *Avanti!*, June 20, 27, 28, 29, 1899; March 29, 30, 31, April 1, 1900; *Il Corriere della Sera*, June 26, 27, July 1, 1908. The 1908 investigation erred greatly (as part of the whitewashing) by attributing Angelelli's initiatives to the prisoner Petito. See "Sentenza," 7–14.

39. "Sentenza," 98–133; *Il Corriere della Sera*, June 27, 1908.

40. "Sentenza," 10; *Il Corriere della Sera*, July 4, 1908.

41. "Sentenza," 104.

42. "Sentenza," 13–14; *Avanti!*, June 27, 1899; *Il Corriere della Sera*, June 27, 1908.

43. Quoted in "Sentenza," 20–21.

44. "Sentenza," 21–22, 24–25, 28–34, 57; *Avanti!*, June 20, 1899; *Il Corriere della Sera*, July 3, 1908; *L'Avvenire d'Italia*, July 11, 14, 1908.

45. "Sentenza," 15–18, 20, 24–25; *Avanti!*, June 29, 1899; *Il Corriere della Sera*, June 26, 27; July 1, 2, 9, 10, 12, 14, 1908.

46. Quoted in *Avanti!*, June 28, 1899.

47. "Sentenza," 24–25.

48. Quoted in *Avanti!*, June 27, 1899.

49. *Avanti!*, March 30, 1900.

50. "Sentenza," 28–34, 57; *Avanti!*, June 20, 1899; *Il Corriere della Sera*, July 14, 1908.

51. "Sentenza," 37–39; *Avanti!*, March 29, 1900; *Il Corriere della Sera*, July 4, 24, 1908.

52. *Avanti!*, June 24, 25, 1899.

53. *Avanti*, June 27, 1899.

54. Ibid.

55. Ibid.

56. Ibid.; Santolini and Marcucci, *Gli ingranaggi del potere*, 160–61.

57. Quoted in Santolini and Marcucci, *Gli ingrannagi del potere*, 161.

58. "Sentenza," 70–71, 85, 127–33; *Il Corriere della Sera*, June 28; July 2, 3, 4, 5, 8, 11, 1908.

59. *Avanti!*, June 28; July 1, 2, 3, 4, 1899; Santolini and Marcucci, *Gli ingrannagi del potere*, 164–67.

60. Quoted in *Avanti!*, July 3, 1899.

61. Ibid.

62. Santoloni and Marcucci, *Gli ingrannagi del potere*, 173–74.

63. Ibid., 174.

64. *Avanti!*, April 5, 1900.

65. Ibid.; *Ernesto Diotallevi*, 24–25; Santolini and Marcucci, *Gli ingranaggi del potere*, 174–86.

66. *Avanti!*, 29, 1900.

67. Pier Carlo Masini, *Storia degli anarchici italiani nell'epoca degli attentati* (Milan: Rizzoli, 1981), 113–14.

68. George Esenwein, *Anarchist Ideology and the Working-Class Movement in Spain, 1868–1898* (Berkeley: University of California Press, 1989), 191–92.

69. Many letters written by prisoners are reproduced in I. Bó y Singla, *Montjuich notas y recuerdos históricos* (Barcelona: Publicaciones de la Escuela Moderna, 1917), 108–32. At the time, descriptions of the tortures were published by the famous journalist Henri Rochefort in his newspaper *L'Intransigeant* of Paris. Portions are reproduced in Federazione Anarchica Italiana, *Michele Angiolillo: Il suo eroico atto e ciò che di lui si scrisse* (Foggia: Gruppo Anarchico "Michele Angiolillo," n.d.), 13–14.

70. Esenwein, *Anarchist Ideology*, 194.

71. Federazione Anarchica Italiana, *Michele Angiolillo*, 12.

72. *La Scintilla: numero unico* (Messina), August 16–17, 1897.

73. For an account by someone who was present, see Rudolf Rocker, *En la borrasca* (Buenos Aires, Argentina: Americalee, 1949), 59–60. See also *Intransigeant*, May 14, 1897; Federazione Anarchica Italiana, *Michele Angiolillo*, 12–13; Francesco Tamburini, "Michele Angiolillo e l'assassinio di Cánovas del Castillo," *Spagna Contemporanea* 9 (1996): 100, 114; Esenwein, *Anarchist Ideology*, 194–96. Other newspapers that published accounts included *Il resto del Carlino* (Bologna); *Revue blanche* (Paris); *L'Agitazione* (Ancona).

74. Esenwein, *Anarchist Ideology*, 193–97; Murray Bookchin, *The Spanish Anarchists: The Heroic Years, 1868–1936* (New York: Harper and Row, 1977), 121–22; Tamburini, "Michele Angiolillo," 107–8; Rocker, *En la borrasca*, 58–59.

75. Quoted in *Freedom* (London), September 1897.

76. Reproduced in Federazione Anarchica Italiana, *Michele Angiolillo*, 44–45.

77. D'Angio's article in *La Tribuna* (Rome), August 12, 1897; *La Questione Sociale* (Paterson), September 15, 1897. D'Angio's account and the unsigned article in *La Questione Sociale* differ in many details.

78. For the letter, see Federazione Anarchica Italiana, *Michele Angiolillo*, 7–9.

79. Ibid., 9; D'Angiò in *Tribuna* (Rome), August 12, 1897; *La Questione Sociale* (Paterson), September 15, 1897.

80. Tamburini, "Michele Angiolillo," 105–7; police chief of Florence to delegate of Public Security, Pontassieve, July 3, 1896, in Archivio di Stato di Firenze, *Questura della Provincia di Firenze: Atti Polizia*, fascio 49, fascicolo 1. The Italian authorities mistakenly believed Angiolillo had departed for Nice in July.

81. Letters to his parents: September 25, 1896 (Marseilles), October 21, 1896 (Marseilles), November 20, 1896 (Liège), December 8, 1896 (Brussels). Also *La Questione Sociale* (Paterson), September 15, 1897; *Freedom* (London), September 1897.

82. *La Questione Sociale* (Paterson), September 15, 1897; *Freedom* (London), September 1897; Tamburini, "Michele Angiolillo," 107–8; Rocker, *En la borrasca*, 62.

83. Rocker, *En la borrasca*, 63.

84. Esenwein, *Anarchist Ideology*, 197–98; Tamburini, "Michele Angiolillo," 108–9; Rocker, *En la borrasca*, 62–64.

85. Francesco Tamburini, "L'indipendenza di Cuba nella coscienza dell' 'estrema sinistra' Italiana (1895–1898)," *Spagna contemporanea, 7* (1995): 39–80.

86. Tamburini, "Michele Angiolillo," 111–16.

87. *La Questione Sociale* (Paterson), September 15, 1897; *Freedom* (London), September 1897; Ettore Sernicoli, *I delinquenti dell'anarchia: nuovo studio storico e politico, 1894–1899* (Rome: Enrico Voghera, 1899), 153–54; Tamburini, "Michele Angiolillo," 118–20.

88. As quoted in *Freedom* (London), September 1897. Sernicoli, *I delinquenti dell'anarchia*, 154, provides a different version of Acciarito's remarks: "Madame, I am not evil as you believe. . . . I have done my duty. I am calm. I have avenged the comrades of Barcelona."

89. For details of the assassination, see Sernicoli, *I delinquenti dell'anarchia*, 153–54.

90. *L'Agitazione* (Ancona), September 2, 1897; also Federazione Anarchica Italiana, *Michele Angiolillo*, 16–17.

91. *L'Agitazione* (Ancona), September 2, 1897; also Federazione Anarchica Italiana, *Michele Angiolillo*, 16–17.

92. *Freedom* (London), September 1897; *La Questione Sociale* (Paterson), September 15, 1897; Federazione Anarchica Italiana, *Michele Angiolillo*, 17–18.

93. Lucheni's name has traditionally been given as "Luccheni," but the former is the spelling he used.

94. For the life of Empress Elizabeth, see Count Egon Corti, *Elizabeth, Empress of Austria* (New Haven, CT: Yale University Press, 1936); Brigitte Hamann, *The Reluctant Empress: A Biography of Empress Elisabeth of Austria* (New York: Knopf, 1986); Andrew Sinclair, *Death by Fame: A Life of Elisabeth, Empress of Austria* (New York: St. Martin's, 1998).

95. Sernicoli, *I delinquenti dell'anarchia*, 98–101; Hamann, *The Reluctant Empress*, 368–69.

96. *Revue des revues*, November 1, 1898.

97. Luigi Lucheni, *Mémoires de l'assassin de Sissi: histoire d'un enfant abandonné à la fin du XIXe siècle racontée par lui-même*, ed. Santo Cappon (Paris: Cherche Midi, 1998), 105–71. This book contains Lucheni's memoirs, which cover only his boyhood years, with other text by Cappon. The former will be cited as Lucheni, *Mémoires;* the latter as Cappon, *Lucheni mémoires.* Cappon's father was a collector of old documents, his son claimed to have found the manuscript in his father's archive.

98. *Dizionario biografico degli anarchici italiani,* 2: 40; Sernicoli, *I delinquenti dell'anarchia*, 103–4; Corti, *Elizabeth*, 463–64; Cappon, *Lucheni mémoires*, 15–16.

99. *Dizionario biografico degli anarchici italiani*, 2: 40; Sernicoli, *I delinquenti dell'anarchia*, 106; Corti, *Elizabeth*, 464–65; Cappon, *Lucheni mémoires*, 16–20.

100. Quoted in Cappon, *Lucheni mémoires*, 24.

101. Sernicoli, *I delinquenti dell'anarchia*, 108; Corti, *Elizabeth*, 466; Cappon, *Lucheni mémoires*, 22–23.

102. Sernicoli, *I delinquenti dell'anarchia*, 109; Corti, *Elizabeth*, 466; Cappon, *Lucheni mémoires*, 24–29.

103. Quoted in Cappon, *Lucheni mémoires*, 33. Se also Sernicoli, *I delinquenti dell'anarchia*, 102, 104, 108–9; Corti, *Elizabeth*, 482–83.

104. Quoted in Cappon, *Lucheni mémoires*, 34.

105. Quoted in Corti, *Elizabeth*, 483–84.

106. Ibid., 484.

107. Ibid.

108. Quoted in Senicoli, *I delinquenti dell'anarchia*, 110.

109. Quoted in Masini, *Storia degli anarchici italiani*, 118; "anarchist formerly considered very dangerous."

110. The entire letter is reproduced in ibid., 246–47.

111. Corti, *Elizabeth*, 486.

112. Ibid., 116–18.

113. Sernicoli, *I delinquenti dell'anarchia*, 112–22.

114. Ibid., 120.

115. Cappon, *Lucheni mémoires*, 70–72.

116. Quoted in ibid., 220.

117. Ibid., 88, 92.

118. Ibid., 77.

119. Ibid.

120. Quoted in ibid., 55.

121. Masini, *Storia degli anarchici italiani*, 117.

122. Cappon, *Lucheni mémoires*, 180–82, 187–93.

## Chapter 6. Fatti di Maggio *and Gaetano Bresci*

1. Maurice F. Neufeld, *Italy: School for Awakening Countries: The Italian Labor Movement in Its Political, Social, and Economic Setting from 1800 to 1960*, Cornell International Industrial and Labor Reports, No. 5 (Ithaca, NY: Cornell University, New York State School of Industrial and Labor Relations, 1961), 219.

2. Giorgio Candeloro, *Storia dell'Italia moderna: la crisi di fine secolo e l'età giolittiana* (Milan: Feltrinelli, 1974), 7: 51–52.

3. Napoleone Colajanni, *L'Italia nel 1898: tumulti e reazione* (Milan: Lombarda, 1898), 28–29.

4. Colajanni, *L'Italia nel 1898*, 28–35; Levra, *Il colpo di stato della borghesia: la crisi politica di fine secolo in Italia 1896–1900* (Milan: Feltrinelli, 1975), 38–45.

5. Colajanni, *L'Italia nel 1898*, 25–30; Levra, *Il colpo di stato della borghesia*, 41–45, 94–102; Roberto Michels, *Storia critica del movimento socialista italiano dagli inizi al 1911* (Florence: La Voce, 1926), 199–201; Raffaele Colapietra, *Il novantotto: la crisi politica di fine secolo, 1896–1900* (Milan: Avanti!, 1959), 75–80; Alfredo Angiolini, *Socialismo e socialisti in Italia* (Firenze: Nerbini, 1920), 1: 333–45.

6. Levra, *Il colpo di stato della borghesia*, 100–105.

7. Colajanni, *L'Italia nel 1898*, 37–59; Colapietra, *Il novantotto*, 81–83; Michels, *Storia critica del movimento socialista italiano*, 201–5.

8. Colajanni, *L'Italia nel 1898*, 79, 81; Michels, *Storia critica del movimento socialista italiano*, 204–5.

9. Domenico Farini, *Diario di fine secolo (1891–1895)* (Rome: Bardi, 1962), 2: 1308.

10. Ibid., 1346–47.

11. Quoted in full in Colajanni, *L'Italia nel 1898*, 95, and Angiolini, *Socialismo e socialisti in Italia*, 363.

12. Farini, *Diario di fine secolo*, 2: 1294.

13. Colajanni, *L'Italia nel 1898*, 104–19; Candeloro, *Storia dell'Italia moderna*, 7: 59–61.

14. Farini, *Diario di fine secolo*, 2: 1166.

15. Ibid., 2: 1174–75; Levra, *Il colpo di stato della borghesia*, 16–17.

16. Luigi Fabbri, *Malatesta: L'uomo e il pensiero* (Naples: RL, 1951), 7–8.

17. *Il processo Malatesta e compagni innanzi al Tribunale Penale di Ancona* (Castellamare Adriatico: C. Di Sciullo, 1908), 3–8; Enzo Santarelli, "L'azione di Errico Malatesta e i moti del 1898 ad Ancona," *Movimento operaio* 6 (1954): 248, 262–63, 267.

18. *Il processo Malatesta*, 9–94; Santarelli, "L'azione di Errico Malatesta," 265–66.

19. Ettore Croce, *A domicilio coatto: appunti di un relegato politico* (Lipari: Pasquale Conti, 1899), 59.

20. For personal recollections of life in *domicilio coatto*, see Croce, *A domicilio coatto*, and Pietro Calcagno, *Verso l'esilio: memorie di un anarchico confinato in Valsesia alla fine dell'ottocento* (Milan: Contemporanea, 1976). Originally published in 1905.

21. See *Pro Coatti* (Genoa), October 1–December 31, 1899.

22. Ugoberto Alfassio Grimaldi, *Il re "buono"* (Milan: Feltrinelli, 1970), 432–40.

23. Ibid., 445–46.

24. Ibid., 446–47; Robert Katz, *The Fall of the House of Savoy* (New York: Macmillan, 1971), 148–49.

25. *Paterson Daily Press*, August 3, 1900.

26. For biographical information here and below, see Giuseppe Galzerano, *Gaetano Bresci: Vita, attentato, processo, carcere e morte dell'anarchico che 'giustizio' Umberto I*, 2nd ed. (Casalvelino Scalo: Galzerano, 2001), 111–28; Arrigo Petacco, *L'anarchico che venne dall'America: storia di Gaetano Bresci e del complotto per uccidere Umberto I*, 2nd ed. (Milan: Arnoldo Mondadori, 2000), 13–29; Roberto Gremmo, *Gli anarchici che uccisero Umberto I: Gaetano Bresci, il 'Biondino,' e i tessitori biellesi di Paterson* (Biella: Storia Ribelle, 2000), 27–31; *Dizionario biografico degli anarchici italiani*, 1: 252–55.

27. Municipal Police Report, "Prato," reproduced in Petacco, *L'anarchico che venne dall'America*, 249–50.

28. James D. Osborne, "Italian Immigrants and the Working Class in Paterson: The Strike of 1913," in Paul A. Stellhorn, ed., *New Jersey's Ethnic Heritage* (Trenton: New Jersey Historical Commission, 1978), 14, 16, 22–24.

29. Rinaldo Rigola, *Rinaldo Rigola e il movimento operaio del Biellese* (Bari: Laterza, 1930), 96–99.

30. *New York Tribune*, July 31, 1900. William Gallo, son of Fermino Gallo, a local militant, placed the figure at three to four hundred in Paul Avrich, *Anarchist Voices* (Princeton, NJ: Princeton University Press, 1995), 154. See also Luigi Vittorio Ferraris, "L'assassinio di Umberto I e gli anarchici di Paterson," *Rassegna storica del risorgimento* 55, No. 1 (January–May 1968), 52; George W. Carey, "*La Questione Sociale*, an Anarchist Newspaper in Paterson, N.J. (1895–1908)," in Lydio F. Tomasi, ed., *Italian Americans: New Perspectives in Italian Immigration and Ethnicity* (New York: Center for Migration Studies, 1985), 291.

31. Mario De Ciampis, "Storia del movimento socialista rivolutionario italiano," *La Parola del Popolo* 9, No. 37 (December 1958–January 1959), 136–38; Elizabetta Vezzosi,

*Il socialismo indifferente: immigrati italiani e Socialist Party negli stati uniti del primo novecento* (Rome: Edizioni Lavoro, 1991), 27–29.

32. *La Questione Sociale*, September 15, 1897. For further information on Roda's work, see Jennifer Guglielmo, *Living the Revolution: Italian Women's Resistance and Radicalism in New York City, 1880–1945* (Chapel Hill: University of North Carolina Press, 2010), 139–40, 155–59.

33. *La Questione Sociale*, June 30, October 15, December 15, 1897; July 30, November 26, 1898; March 18, July 29, 1899; February 17, 1900. See also *L'Era Nuova*, July 17, 1915.

34. Giampietro Berti, *Francesco Saverio Merlino: Dall'anarchismo socialista al socialismo liberale, 1865–1930* (Milan: Franco Angeli, 1993), 192–201.

35. Davide Turcato, "Italian Anarchism as a Transnational Movement, 1885–1916," *International Review of Social History* 52 (2007): 421–24; Carey, "La Questione Sociale," 289–93; Carlo Molaschi, *Pietro Gori* (Milan: Il Pensiero, 1959), 15.

36. Turcato, "Italian Anarchism," 423–24.

37. Ugo Fedeli, *Giuseppe Ciancabilla* (Cesena: L'Antistato, 1965), 28–29.

38. *La Questione Sociale*, January 28, 1899.

39. *La Questione Sociale*, January 21, 1899.

40. Fedeli, *Giuseppe Ciancabilla*, 28–29, 38, 42–53.

41. *La Questione Sociale*, December 10, 17, 1898; January 26, 31, February 4, 1899. For a counterargument, see, for example, the letter by Salvatore Pallavicini in *La Questione Sociale*, December 17, 1898.

42. *La Questione Sociale*, June 30, October 30, December 15, 1897; December 17, 1898.

43. *L'Era Nuova* (Paterson), July 17, 1915.

44. *L'Era Nuova*, July 17, 1915.

45. Luis [Luigi] Fabbri, *Vida y pensamiento de Malatesta* (Barcelona: Tierra y Libertad, 1938), 107–8.

46. Ibid., 108–9; *La Questione Sociale*, August 5, 19, 26; September 2, 1899; Davide Turcato, "The Hidden History of the Anarchist Atlantic: Errico Malatesta in America, 1899–1900," paper delivered at the European Social Science History Conference, Ghent 2010; Max Nettlau, *Errico Malatesta: Vita e pensieri* (New York: Il Martello, 1922), 255–56.

47. *New York Sun*, July 31, 1900; *Paterson Daily Press*, July 30, 1900. Also Max Nomad, *Rebels and Renegades* (New York: Macmillan, 1932), 30.

48. *La Questione Sociale*, October 28, 1899.

49. Fabbri, *Vida y pensamiento de Malatesta*, 109; Nettlau, *Errico Malatesta*, 256; Turcato, "The Hidden History of the Anarchist Atlantic," 4–10; Fedeli, *Giuseppe Ciancabilla*, 65; *Dizionario biografico*, 395.

50. Petacco, *L'anarchico che venne dall'America*, 27.

51. Galzerano, *Bresci*, 297.

52. Report of attorney James M. Trimble, 7, in Archivio di State di Milano, Procedimento penale contro Bresci ed altri, cartella 2 (cited hereafter as Trimble Report). The Trimble Report—no copy of which is available in the United States—was furnished to Nunzio Pernicone by Giuseppe Galzerano.

53. Galzerano, *Bresci*, 116–17, 655–61; Petacco, *L'anarchico che venne dall'America*, 27–31.

54. *Paterson Daily Press*, July 31, 1900.

55. Ibid.

56. *L'Aurora* (Yogohany, PA), September 8, 1900.

57. Trimble Report, 40.

58. *La Questione Sociale*, September 1, 1900.

59. Trimble Report, 101.

60. Verbale d'interrogazione di Quazza Emma, July 30, 1900, in Archivio Centrale dello Stato (cited hereafter as ACS), Ministero dell'Interno, Atti Speciali 1898–1940 (cited hereafter as Min. Int. AS), busta 1, fascicolo 2, "Reggicidio di Monza."

61. See Trimble Report.

62. During one interrogation, Bresci claimed that he had disarmed Passaglia, while during another he denied being present at the meeting when the shooting occurred. See Galzerano, *Bresci*, 106, 118.

63. *La Questione Sociale*, July 15, 1899.

64. *L'Era Nuova*, July 17, 1915.

65. "Marat's recollections of 'old Paterson' in *L'Adunata dei Refrattari*, October 15, 1932.

66. Fabbri, *Vida y pensamiento de Malatesta*, 110; *Umanità Nova* (Rome), October 27, 1921.

67. *New York World*, August 1, 1900.

68. Galzerano, *Bresci*, 118.

69. Ibid., 94.

70. Ibid., 412.

71. Trimble Report, 48; also Galzerano, *Bresci*, 669.

72. Postal inspector in Pittsburgh to U.S. district attorney in Pittsburgh, December 26, 1900, in U.S. National Archives, Record Group 60, Department of Justice, Year File (1900), File 11717/1900.

73. *La Questione Sociale*, September 1, 1900.

74. Galzerano, *Bresci*, 277.

75. *L'Aurora*, September 8, 1900.

76. Petacco, *L'anarchico che venne dall' America*, 34–36. See "Liste des passagers italiens entré au Havre le 26 Mai 1900 par le paquebot 'Gascogne,'" in ACS, Min. Int. AS, busta 1, fascicolo 2, "Regicidio di Monza."

77. For whatever reason, the names of Laner and Quazza do not appear on the passenger list: "Havre le 26 Mai 1900 par le paquebot 'Gascogne,'" in ACS, Min. Int. AS, busta 1, fascicolo 2, "Reggicidio di Monza."

78. Petacco, *L'anarchico che venne dall'America* 36–37; Gremmo, *Gli anarchici che uccisero Umberto I*, 13–19.

79. Quazza letter of May 28, 1900, to her father, in *Paterson Daily Press*, August 9, 1900.

80. Verbale d'interrogatorio di Quazza Emma, July 30, 1900, in ACS, Min. Int. AS, busta 1, fascicolo 2, "Regicidio di Monza." Also interrogation of Quazza on August 2.

81. Letter of July 12, 1900, to Quazza, quoted in Petacco, *L'anarchico che venne dall'America*, 37.

82. Petacco, *L'anarchico che venne dall'America*, 38–41.

83. *La Questione Sociale*, January 14, 1900; Tremble Report, 56–57.

84. Galzerano, *Bresci*, 348.

85. Ibid., 132–33.

86. Ibid., 347–53; Petacco, *L'anarchico che venne dall'America*, 39–43.

87. Quotations and detailed account in Petacco, *L'anarchico che venne dall'America*, 48–54.

88. Borghi, *Mezzo secolo di anarchia*, 47.

89. Levra, *Il colpo di stato della borghesia*, 399–400; A. William Salomone, *Italy in the Giolittian Era: Italian Democracy in the Making, 1900–1914*, 2nd ed. (Philadelphia: University of Pennsylvania Press, 1960).

90. The report is quoted in Giuliano Turone, "Il processo per il regicidio di Umberto I," in *Il Risorgimento* 1 (1982), 44–45.

91. For material on Quazza, Laner, and Quintavalle, see ACS, Min. Int. AS, 1898–1940, busta 1, fascicolo 2, "Reggicidio di Monza."

92. Turone, "Il processo per il regicidio di Umberto I," 37, 43; Galzerano, *Bresci*, 212, 420–23, 520, 527–29; Gremmo, *Gli anarchici che uccisero Umberto I*, 179–80, 187–91.

93. Police chief of Milan, report of July 30, 1900, quoted in Turone, "Il processo per il regicidio di Umberto I," 44–45. Gremmo (*Gli anarchici*, 133) claims that Colombo was incarcerated for only one month.

94. Galzerano, *Bresci*, 353–56, 374–80; Turone, "Il processo per il regicidio di Umberto I," 40–42; *La Questione Sociale*, October 20, 27, 1890.

95. Galzerano, *Bresci*, 372–89; *Dizionario biografico*, 1: 757–58.

## Chapter 7. U.S. Investigation and Death of the Giustiziere

1. *La Questione Sociale*, July 20, 1900; *New York Tribune*, August 2, 1900.

2. *New York Tribune*, July 31, 1900; *New York Evening Post*, July 30, 1900.

3. *La Questione Sociale*, July 20, 1900;

4. *New York Tribune*, July 31, 1900; *New York Evening Post*, August 2, 1900; *La Questione Sociale*, July 20, 1900.

5. For example, *New York Evening Journal*, August 2, 1900; Ernst Vizetelly, *The Anarchists: Their Faith and Their Record* (New York: John Lane, 1927), 246–47.

6. Ambassador Fava to Acting Secretary of State A. A. Adee, August 8, 1900, U.S. National Archives, Record Group 60, Department of Justice (hereafter cited as DOJ), Year File (1900), File 11717/1900.

7. Report of Captain George W. McClusky, New York Police, Detective Department, August 1900, in DOJ, Year File (1900), File 11717/1900.

8. Italian Ambassador to U.S. Secretary of State, September 19, 1900, in DOJ, Year File (1900), File 11717/1900.

9. Ibid.

10. Giuseppe Galzerano, *Gaetano Bresci: Vita, attentato, processo, carcere e morte dell'anarchico che 'giustizio' Umberto I*, 2nd ed. (Casalvelino Scalo: Galzerano, 2001), 614.

11. Ibid., 614–16.

12. Ibid., 617.

13. Report of attorney James M. Trimble, in Archivio di State di Milano, Procedimento penale contro Bresci ed altri, cartella 2 (hereafter cited as Trimble Report); *Paterson Daily Press*, October 5, 1900.

14. Trimble Report, 40–41.

15. Nunzio Pernicone, *Italian Anarchism, 1864–1892* (Princeton, NJ: Princeton University Press, 1993), 272–73.

16. Trimble Report, 56–60, 90.

17. Ibid., 110.

18. Ibid., 47–48.

19. Ibid., 50–53.

20. Ibid., 37.

21. Italian Ambassador Fava to U.S. District Attorney J. W. Griggs, August 31, 1900, in DOJ, Year File (1900), File 11717/1900.

22. The law firm reports are appended to Fava's letter.

23. Chief of Secret Service Division to secretary of the Treasury, November 2, 1900, in DOJ, Year File (1900), File 11717/1900.

24. See reports throughout DOJ, Year File (1900), File 11717/1900.

25. U.S. district attorney for the Southern District of New York to the Department of State, November 16, 1900, in DOJ, Year File (1900), File 11717/1900.

26. Treasury Department to the U.S. attorney general, February 1, 1901, in DOJ, Year File (1900), File 11717/1900.

27. Acting secretary of the Secret Service Division to the U.S. attorney general, November 22, 1900, in DOJ, Year File (1900), File 11717/1900.

28. Acting postmaster general to the U.S. attorney general, December 1, 1900, in DOJ, Year File (1900), File 11717/1900.

29. Acting secretary of state to the U.S. attorney general, August 29, 1900, with Fava's aide-memoire attached, in DOJ, Year File (1900), File 11717/1900.

30. Translation of the letter dated September 26, 1900, sent by the State Department to the Justice Department, October 1, 1900, in DOJ, Year File (1900), File 11717/1900.

31. Postal inspector, Pittsburgh Office, to district attorney of Pittsburgh, December 26, 1900, in DOJ, Year File (1900), File 11717/1900.

32. Arrigo Petacco, *L'anarchico che venne dall'America* (Milan: Arnoldo Mondadori, 1969), 5 and 143–49; Giovanni Artieri, *Cronaca del regno d'Italia* (Milan: Mondadori, 1977), 1: 598, 708–9, 718–91, 861–65; Galzerano, *Gaetano Bresci*, 875–76, and Gianpietro Berti, *Errico Malatesta e il movimento anarchico italiano e internazionale, 1872–1932* (Milan: Franco Angeli, 2003), 322–23.

33. Galzerano, *Gaetano Bresci*, 794–97; Petacco, *L'anarchico che venne dall'America*, 135–41.

34. Galzerano, *Gaetano Bresci*, 798–803; Petacco, *L'anarchico che venne dall'America*, 140–41.

35. Galzerano, *Gaetano Bresci*, 792–93, 802–5; Petacco, *L'anarchico che venne dall'America*, 136–39.

36. Galzerano, *Gaetano Bresci*, 815–21; Petacco, *L'anarchico che venne dall'Italia*, 153–62.

37. Petacco, *L'anarchico che venne dall'America*, 161.

38. Galzerano, *Gaetano Bresci*, 815–16, 820–21; Petacco, *L'anarchico che venne dall'America*, 160–63; Berti, *Errico Malatesta*, 322–23; Umberto Levra, *Il colpo di stato della borghesia: la crisi politica di fine secolo in Italia, 1896–1900* (Milan: Feltrinelli 1975), 403; Ugoberto Alfassio Grimaldi, *Il re 'buono'* (Milan: Feltrinelli, 1980), 468.

39. Giovanni Giolitti, *Memorie della mia vita* (Milan: Fratelli Treves, 1922), 1: 163.

40. Subprefect's report of June 26, 1899, quoted in report of the prefect of Genoa to the minister of the interior, June 28, 1899, in Archivio Centrale dello Stato (Rome; hereafter cited as ACS), Ministero dell'Interno, Direzione Generale di Pubblica Sicurezza, CPC, busta 286 (Malatesta), fascicolo 31568, sottofascicolo 2.

41. For reports on Malatesta in this period, see, for example, Agent Calvo to Italian ambassador, London, May 9, 15, 23, 1899; November 25, 26, 28, 20, 1900, in ACS, Ministero dell'Interno, DGPS, CPC, busta 286 (Malatesta), fascicolo 31568, sf. 2. For an excellent article about Italy's spy service, see Pietro Di Paola, "The Spies Who Came in from the Heat: The International Surveillance of the Anarchists in London," *European History Quarterly* 37, No. 189 (2007), 189–215.

42. The report is reproduced in its entirety in Artieri, *Cronaca*, 1: 853–56.

43. Ibid., 1: 846.

44. Gaetano Natale, *Giovanni Giolitti e gli italiani* (Milan: Garzanti, 1949), 467–70; Artieri, *Cronaca*, 1:846, 849.

45. Berti, *Errico Malatesta*, 319, 322.

46. See Malatesta's letter of May 18, 1901, to an unknown correspondent in Malatesta's CPC file. The letter has been reproduced numerous times; see Lorenzo Gestri, "Dieci lettere inedite di Cipriani, Malatesta e Merlino," *Movimento Operaio e Socialista* 17, no. 4 (October–December 1971): 329; and Rosaria Bertolucci, ed., *Errico Malatesta epistolario 1873–1932: Lettere edite ed inedite* (Carrara: Centro Studi Sociali, 1984), 76–77.

47. "Virgilio" reports to Italian ambassador in London, October 20, November 4, December 10, 28, 1901.

48. Quoted in Artieri, *Cronaca*, 1: 855.

49. Gaetano Natale, *Giolitti e gli italiani* (Milan: Garzanti, 1949), 470–71.

50. Artieri, *Cronaca*, 1: 848–52; Berti, *Errico Malatesta*, 323.

51. Berti, *Errico Malatesta*, 321–23; Artieri, *Cronaca*, 1: 713, 718–868; Galzerano, *Gaetano Bresci*, 863–76; Petacco, *L'anarchico che venne dall'America*, 143–62.

52. Artieri, *Cronaca*, 1:713, 718–868; Galzerano, *Gaetano Bresci*, 863–76; Petacco, *L'anarchico che venne dall'America*, 144–62; Berti, *Errico Malatesta*, 317–22.

53. For these accounts, see Galzerano, *Gaetano Bresci*, 839–61.

54. *Umberto e Bresci: 1900–29 Luglio-1903, Terzo anniversario della caduta del tiranno d'Italia*, per cura di un gruppo di anarchici di New York [n.d.]. This pamphlet was in Nunzio's possession. It has since been donated to The Tamiment Library and Robert F. Wagner Labor Archives at New York University.

## Conclusion: Terrorists or Giustizieri?

1. Quoted in Raffaele Majetti, *L'anarchia e le leggi che la reprimono in Italia* (Caserta: Domenico Fabiano, 1894), 41.

2. *Discorsi parlamentari di Francesco Crispi* (Rome: Camera dei Deputati, 1915) 3: 808.

3. Ufficio del Proc. Gen. del Re presso La Corte d'Appello di Parma al ministro di grazie e giustizia, March 3, 1898, I Archivio Centrale dello Stato, Ministro Grazie e Giustizia. Direzione Generale Affari Penali, Miscelanea, busco 104, fascicolo 13.

4. Speech of February 28, 1894, in *Discorsi parlamentari di Francesco Crispi* (Rome: Camera dei Deputati, 1915), 3: 687–88.

5. *New York Evening Journal*, August 2, 1900.

6. Daniel Pick, "The Faces of Anarchy: Lombroso and the Politics of Criminal Science in Post-Unification Italy," *History Workshop Journal* (1986): 78.

7. Guglielmo Ferrero, "Gli ultimi attentati anarchici e la loro repressione," *La riforma sociale* 1 (1894): 988–89.

8. Ibid., 990.

9. Ibid., 992–94.

10. *Il Secolo* (Milan), as quoted in Pier Carlo Masini, *Storia degli anarchici italiani nell'epoca degli attentati* (Milan: Rizzoli, 1981), 37.

11. Pietro Gori, *Opere*, vol. 9, *Pagine di vagabondaggio* (Spezia: Binazzi, 1912), 83.

12. Quoted in Giuseppe Galzerano, *Gaetano Bresci: Vita, attentato, processo, carcere e morte dell'anarchico che "giustiziò" Umberto I*, 2nd ed. (Casalvelino Scalo: Giuseppe Galzerano, 2001), 93.

13. *La Révolte* (Paris), March 1891.

14. Quoted in Jean Maitron, *Histoire du mouvement anarchiste en France, 1880–1914* (Paris: Société Universitaire, 1951), 211.

15. "Questioni di tattica (fra anarchici)," *L'Agitazione* (Ancona), February 17, 1897, quoted in Maurizio Antonioli and Pier Carlo Masini, *Il sol dell'avvenire: l'anarchismo in Italia dalle origini alla prima guerra mondiale* (Pisa: Biblioteca Franco Serantini, 1999), 61. The authors' collection of *L'Agitazione* begins with the issue of April 19, 1897.

16. Masini, *Storia degli anarchici italiani nell'epoca degli attentati*, 52–54.

17. *National Catechism* (1866), as reproduced in Sam Dolgoff, ed., *Bakunin on Anarchy* (New York: Vintage, 1971), 100.

18. "Rivoluzione o riforma," *Volontà* (Ancona), September 13, 1913.

19. For comprehensive accounts of anarchist activities from the death of Umberto I to the onset of World War II, see Fabrizio Giulietti, *Storia degli anarchici italiani in età giolittiana* (Milan: Franco Angeli, 2012); Luigi Di Lembo, *Guerra di classe e lotta umana: l'anarchismo in Italia dal Biennio Rosso alla Guerra di Spagna (1919–1939)* (Pisa: Biblioteca Franco Serantini, 2001).

# Index

Acciarito, Pietro, 1, 97, 132; attempted assassination of King Umberto I, 90–91; background of, 92–93, 175, 176; incarceration of, 164–65, 166; investigation and trial, 94–96; motivations behind attempted assassination of Umberto I, 144, 175, 176–82; search for accomplices and "confession," 97–105
Adowa, battle of, 89, 117
*Agitatore, L'* (Neuchatel), 118
*Agitazione, L'* (Ancona), 95, 113, 129–30, 131
Agostinelli, Cesare, 82, 95, 130, 131
Agresti, Antonio, 136–37, 138
Alberici Giannini, Stanislao, 7
Alexander II, Czar, 13, 19, 35, 37–38, 41, 42
Alexander III, Czar, 38, 42
Alfieri, Vittorio, 8
Alfonso XII, King, 13, 26,
Alsin, Juan, 108
Amadio, Angelo, 125, 126
*Amico del Popolo, L'* (Milan), 68
*ammonizione. See* Italian anarchists
*Anarchia, L'* (Naples), 40
anarchists, negative portrayal of, 2, 3–4
Angelelli, Alfredo, 99–105
Angiolillo, Michele, 1, 4, 8, 115, 120, 122, 170; assassination of Canovas, 112; background of, 108–12; motivation behind decision to assassinate Canovas, 144–45, 160, 174–82; trial and execution of, 113–14
Anti-Authoritarian (Anarchist) International: and the Bern Congress (October

1876), 7; and London Congress (July 1881), 35, 55; and Marx, 35
*anti-organizzatori. See* individualist anarchism and individualist anarchists
Antonioli, Maurizio, 4
*Art. 248, L'* (Ancona), 63, 80, 130
Ascaso, Francisco, 46
Ascheri, Tomás, 107–8
*Asino, L'* (Rome), 94, 198n22
association of malefactors or "*associazione di malfattori*." *See* Italian anarchists
*Aurora, L'* (West Hoboken and Yogohany, PA), 140, 144, 145, 146
*Avanti!* (Rome), 94, 118
Avogadro di Quinto, Felice, 132
*Avvenire, L'* (Buenos Aires), 139
*Avvenire Sociale, L'* (Messina), 94, 131

Bakunin, Mikhail, 5, 7, 8, 42; death of, 22; influence on Italian anarchists, 17–20, 21, 56, 119, 174, 180; and insurrections, 22–23, 57; and Marx, 35; and Mazzini, 18–19; and terrorism, 19–20
Banda del Matese. 23–24, 26, 29, 31, 38, 39. *See also* Italian anarchists
Bandi, Giuseppe, 180
Bandiera, Attilio and Emilio, 10
Barbato, Nicola, 87, 110
Baronio, Ninfa, 136
Bava-Beccaris, Fiorenzo, 126, 128
Belelli, Ennio, 168
Beltrani-Scalia, Martino, 86, 98–100

NUNZIO PERNICONE was professor emeritus in the Department of History and Politics at Drexel University. He is the author of *Italian Anarchism, 1864–1892* and *Carlo Tresca: Portrait of a Rebel.* He died in 2013.

FRASER M. OTTANELLI is a professor of history at the University of South Florida. His books include *The Communist Party of the United States from the Depression to World War II* and he is also coeditor of *Letters from the Spanish Civil War: A U.S. Volunteer Writes Home.*

The University of Illinois Press
is a founding member of the
Association of American University Presses.

University of Illinois Press
1325 South Oak Street
Champaign, IL 61820-6903
www.press.uillinois.edu

Printed by Printforce, United Kingdom